"Nutcracker" Nation

JENNIFER FISHER

"NUTCRACKER" NATION

HOW AN OLD WORLD BALLET
BECAME A CHRISTMAS TRADITION
IN THE NEW WORLD

Yale University Press · New Haven and London

Published with assistance from the Louis Stern Memorial Fund.

Designed by Nancy Ovedovitz and set in Scala type by
Tseng Information Systems, Inc. Printed in the United States
of America by R. R. Donnelley & Sons.

The Library of Congress has cataloged the hardcover edition as follows:
Fisher, Jennifer, 1949–
"Nutcracker" nation : how an Old World ballet became a Christmas
tradition in the New World / Jennifer Fisher.
p. cm.
Includes bibliographical references (p.) and index.
ISBN 0-300-09746-8 (cloth : alk. paper)
1. Nutcracker (Choreographic work)—History.
2. Christmas—United States. I. Title.
GV1790.N8F57 2003
792.8'4—dc21   2003005866

A catalogue record for this book is available
from the British Library.

The paper in this book meets the guidelines for permanence and
durability of the Committee on Production Guidelines for
Book Longevity of the Council on Library Resources.
ISBN 0-300-09746-8 (pbk. : alk. paper)

10   9   8   7   6   5   4   3   2

To my mother, Eleanor Thomas, who took me to my first ballet class and all my Nutcracker rehearsals, and who—just as importantly, it turns out—bought me my first ballet book

Contents

Preface

Every Christmas, a world-weary dance critic once wrote, we are all "one more *Nutcracker* closer to death." This quotation, attributed to Richard Buckle, has always been a favorite of mine, because it's funny, it's true, and it masks a deeper meaning, just like *The Nutcracker* itself. Long a synonym for "obligatory whimsy each December" in the dance world, *The Nutcracker* is the ballet we love to hate — love for its classical heritage and Tchaikovsky score; hate because it sometimes seems like an inescapable cliché in a world that craves constant innovation. But by labeling the ballet a signpost on life's journey, Buckle inadvertently placed it in the same category as many other ineluctable and sometimes-feared rituals and rites of passage, the ones that dot everyday life and give it meaning. There are birthday parties, bar and bat mitzvahs, graduations, marriages, funerals, Christmas dinners . . . and, in North America at least, *The Nutcracker*, regular as clockwork, performed anywhere someone has ballet shoes, a Tchaikovsky CD, and a dream. Sometimes the dream is just to survive financially, so traditionally powerful is the ballet's earning potential. But calling attention to the popularity and inevitability of *The Nutcracker* acknowledges the fact that it matters, like other "performances" that mark a certain time of year as special by echoing revered themes and values.

Still, *The Nutcracker* is "just a ballet," isn't it? That too. More specifically, it's a classical ballet that premiered in 1892 at the imperial

Maryinsky Theater of St. Petersburg in Russia, and has undergone untold alterations on its travels since then. Based ever so loosely on a long short story by E. T. A. Hoffmann, *The Nutcracker* has enjoyed limited success in Russia, but it has been taken to heart by North Americans—and altered at will, sometimes resulting in a virtual change of citizenship for the good-natured Nutcracker. Never married to the month of December back home, it's a Christmas-time phenomenon in the United States and Canada—the annual *Nutcracker*, praised for its money-making potential and popularity with audiences and young dancers. Its very availability is what brought *The Nutcracker* into my life, first as a young performer, when I got a taste of the ballet life in my local production, then as a dance scholar who wanted to figure out what the phenomenon of *The Nutcracker* meant to people who put it on and to those who buy tickets.

When I first decided to make *The Nutcracker* the topic of my Ph.D. dissertation—a fairly unprecedented choice—I found myself face to face with the ballet's checkered reputation, its trivialization by major critics, and the assumption that the annual *Nutcracker* was simply a fad that had gotten out of hand because of the public's questionable taste. On the other hand, my conviction that the ballet was in some way a ritual—a meaningful yearly activity for dancers and audiences alike—was strengthened by the general reaction to my project. People who knew the ballet even slightly would get a keen look in their eyes and say things like, "*The Nutcracker* as a ritual, yes, hmmmm, that's true—God knows we do it religiously; explain *that*." "People are fanatical about it," someone else would say. "Why *that* ballet, why so often? How did it latch on to the Christmas season so securely?" Dancers wanted to know why they wore their toes down to the same tunes every year; artistic directors wanted to know why people thought they owned the ballet and were opinionated about its every aspect; parents wanted to know why their children were desperate to progress from mouse to snowflake, from bon-bon to flower soloist. And everyone wanted to know why, when they ostensibly disdained the clichés of *The Nutcracker,* they got tears in their eyes every time miniature angels tripped onstage or the Sugar Plum Fairy leaped into her cavalier's arms to all those wonderfully overwrought crescendos in the grand pas de deux.

Fortunately, there was encouragement from some quarters of the dance scholarship community as well. Sensitive critics had explored sociological implications of *The Nutcracker,* making intelligent guesses about why it appealed to North Americans. Dance anthropologist Cynthia Jean Cohen Bull had pointed out the fact that ballet should be studied in relation to its social, institutional, and cultural contexts, just as one would approach the dance forms of Ghana or Bali. Previously, ballet had been too often considered a "universal" art form, too removed from ethnic or even sociocultural roots to fit in to anthropological studies—with the notable exception of Joann Kealiinohomoku's enlightening but neglected essay "An Anthropologist Looks at Ballet as a Form of Ethnic Dance," which proved a great inspiration to me. I resolved to pioneer the field of "*Nutcracker* ethnography" and, like Bull, who used her personal ballet experiences as a starting point, began by thinking about the ways the ballet had surfaced in my own life. It was then that I remembered a journey I had made a few years before, and the way it reminded me of the travels of ethnographers who had gone much farther afield.

In the early 1990s, when I moved from Toronto to a dusty, sprawling town in Southern California to attend graduate school, I thought of myself as a stranger in a strange land—something like an anthropologist arriving in a remote village for the first time. Although Canada is a lot like the United States, Canadians prize their slim but significant differences from the juggernaut to the south. And, although I had actually lived in the United States before spending my adult years in Toronto, I felt there would be multiple culture shocks ahead. For one thing, I was uneasy about being transplanted from a major urban center to an outpost of Los Angeles, too far into the desert to feature a decent bookstore or café, much less a major dance company like those I was used to following. Also, I hadn't owned a car in Toronto, and now I was in the thick of freeway culture and far too close to what Canadians imagine to be the land of drive-by shootings. All in all, I wasn't looking forward to it.

But an odd thing happened straight off the freeway ramp, as I drove along downtown streets, deserted on a Sunday, on my way to the university. I saw a sign that said "Riverside Ballet Arts," an ambitious title, I thought, for a town in a region well known for never supporting a major ballet company. On a whim, I stopped in front of the studio, not thinking anyone would be there; then, when I found the door open, I started up a long flight of stairs without knowing what I would do when I got to the top. But something made the experience familiar, and not only because this staircase resembled that of so many other second-floor ballet studios. It was because I heard the children's march from *The Nutcracker*, and I saw a fleet of children and adolescents dressed in pink tights and black leotards with numbers safety-pinned onto them. Dance bags were scattered around, as were a clutch of parents, filling out cards or reading books. These were *Nutcracker* auditions, unmistakably—last year's little mice hoping to be party guests, last year's waltzing flowers hoping to be the Arabian soloist.

I stopped to read a schedule, which told when potential party children would be seen, when girls on pointe were to audition, when adult party guests should come (no experience necessary). I looked around and felt pretty much at home. This new territory couldn't be that foreign after all, I thought—they spoke *Nutcracker* here, and I knew all about *The Nutcracker*. That December, I went to see what the local version was like, and eventually I started asking myself exactly why people did these local productions at all and what difference it made in their lives.

It seemed clear what had to be done. Critics and dance historians had already documented much of the history of the ballet, both in Russia and in North America. But in order to expand upon aesthetic categorizations and stereotypes of *The Nutcracker,* I needed to do fieldwork among "my people"—participants in ballet's only yearly ritual performance, including dancers, artistic directors, volunteers, parents, backstage staff, teachers, students, and audience members. My previous experience in the ballet world, as a dancer and critic, would contribute—I was a partial "insider" and had been in the field nearly all my life—as would the many friends, colleagues, and strangers I had involved in *Nutcracker* conversations over the years, and the many rehearsals of various *Nutcrackers* I had attended. With ballet, as with most Western theatrical art forms, a big distinction is usually made between amateur and professional companies, but I suspected that at *Nutcracker* time they had more in common than not. The quality and spirit of each company varies, but everyone involved in the phenomenon is joined together by the Tchaikovsky score, by the holiday theme, and by the ballet's history. I talked to people who had all levels of involvement with the ballet and called them "*Nutcracker* participants," who gather together in "*Nutcracker* communities"—temporary or semipermanent groups that included performers, producers, crews, and audience members.

And so I went forth with notebook and tape recorder in hand, deciding to focus on two ballet companies, one professional and one amateur. They were miles apart—both geographically and where resources were concerned—but I thought they both represented many aspects of the traditional *Nutcracker* movement throughout North America. From my years of living in Toronto, I was familiar with the National Ballet of Canada, which in 1995 had just premiered a new production by artistic director James Kudelka, replacing the 1964 version choreographed by their founding director, Celia Franca. On the amateur front, the fledgling Loudoun Ballet in Leesburg, Virginia, first started doing a *Nutcracker* in 1990, using students, nondancing community members, and a few visiting professionals. Both productions relied heavily on young performers from the companies' related schools, which were organized along the lines of a traditional

ballet conservatory. In each location there was a community of devoted balletgoers, with plenty of attitudes and opinions about the
ever-recurring *Nutcracker.*

People who talked to me about *The Nutcracker* were generally very
open and intrigued by my project, although somewhat puzzled about
why I was hanging around for so long, watching and asking about
so many aspects of their experience. They were used to encounter-
ing two kinds of *Nutcracker* writers—the critic who assessed performances and the "human interest" reporter who wanted to know how
many hours children rehearsed and how much snow actually fell during the first act. I, on the other hand, asked things like, "Does it matter that *The Nutcracker* is ballet?" (yes, usually it did), and, "Would
you come to see it if it were in July?" (well, no, it just wouldn't seem
right). Gradually, people got used to my presence and my questions. I
heard a lot about people's attitudes toward *The Nutcracker* and started
thinking about the number of things that had influenced them.

In answer to a question I am inevitably asked, I've never gotten
tired of studying *The Nutcracker* because at close range it's always fas-
cinating in its infinite variety. Tchaikovsky, it must be said, helps, as
does an appreciation for ballet. Nor am I alone among professionals
in having a high tolerance for *The Nutcracker.* An orchestra conductor once told me that no one is bored in the pit because Tchaikovsky was at the height of his orchestrating powers when he composed
the score, and each player has something engaging to do. Admittedly,
this doesn't prevent musicians from having some occasional fun in
the pit after several weeks of performances—a few claimed they had
switched parts toward the end of a run.

It's true that professional dancers will complain about having to
do endless performances of the same ballet, but, as every aficionado
knows, a *Nutcracker* cast is never really the same from day to day;
it's a living thing, with people constantly moving through the ranks,
children just catching on and infusing the process with edgy enthusiasm, and audiences buoying everyone's spirits on a good day and

challenging the dancers on a particularly silent night. It's Christmas, after all—a time of year that has always provided this ballet considerable niche appeal.

After years of looking into the annual *Nutcracker* phenomenon, I thought about calling this book "Everything I Know About Life I Learned from *The Nutcracker*." But I settled on a less categorical title that still hints at what importance lurks behind candy-striped tutus. We may all be one more *Nutcracker* closer to death each December, but if we're lucky, for a while we may also get a glimpse of what makes the moments till the end worthwhile.

Acknowledgments

My first mentor in the world of *The Nutcracker*, although he certainly didn't know it at the time, was choreographer Fernand Nault, who, between his career with Ballet Theatre (later American Ballet Theatre) in New York and his tenure at Les Grands Ballets Canadiens in his native Montreal, came to set a *Nutcracker* on a group of mostly fledgling dancers at the Louisville Ballet. He probably remembers it as a place where two or three snowflakes couldn't make rehearsal once a week because of orthodontist appointments, but some of us were seriously soaking up the atmosphere every moment. His *Nutcracker* was beautiful, dramatically exciting, and musical (it's still performed in Montreal), setting in motion my relationship with a ballet I would return to as a dance scholar many years later.

Academic advisers and colleagues who offered important help during the researching and writing of the dissertation that preceded this book include dance scholar Selma Odom and ethnomusicologist Beverly Diamond at York University in Toronto, and at the University of California, Riverside, Marguerite Waller (English and Women's Studies) and Zhang Longxi (Comparative Literature), with early contributions from Sally Ness (Anthropology), and Marta Savigliano (Dance). My primary dissertation adviser, Nancy Lee Ruyter, from the dance department at University of California, Irvine, was more valuable than I can say, giving her time and expertise with unstinting rigor and grace. I thank Dean Peter Mileur at UCR for making her involvement possible, and for taking on hooding duty for an "orphan" at my Ph.D. graduation ceremony.

Crucial at early stages of my research were the writings and advice of dance anthropologist Cynthia Jean Cohen Bull (aka Novack), who showed me where the "ballet territory" was in terms of ethnography. As the dissertation turned into a book, dance historian Lynn Garafola was generous with advice and resources. Susan Brenneman, my editor at the *Los Angeles Times*, sparked some key conceptualizing conversation in her usual gold-standard way.

At my two primary research locations, as well as in other situations, participants surrounding *The Nutcracker* gave their time and thoughts generously and with enthusiasm. In Leesburg I was welcomed as an honorary member of the *Nutcracker* community. To Loudoun Ballet artistic director Sheila Hoffmann-Robertson, my friend and collaborator in spirit on this years-long *Nutcracker* project, I owe a great deal. Her observational skills, her generous spirit, her passion for excellence, her compassion for people—and her possession of one of the best memories around—all made my task much easier and more joyful.

In Toronto I'm grateful to National Ballet School director Mavis Staines, who opened her doors to me with characteristic generosity, and I thank many times over Laurel Toto, longtime teacher and supervisor of small performers in the National Ballet of Canada *Nutcracker*. Artistic director James Kudelka and archivist Sharon Vanderlinde helped me understand the ethos of the current production, as well as its history.

Both in Leesburg and in Toronto I'm especially indebted to those willing respondents who made taped monologues for me, using my questions, in my "introspective interviewing" experiment; they were all brilliant. I'm also indebted to Victoria Koenig, artistic director of the Inland Pacific Ballet, near my home in Claremont, California, where I discovered that the *Nutcracker* tradition is carried on in stellar fashion.

Many thanks go to the archivists, photographers, and organizations that helped me discover illustrations for the many lives of *The Nutcracker*. They include: Lawrence Adams and Amy Bowring at Dance Collection *Danse;* Alan Albricht; Heidi Beeler; Bibliothèque National de France; Rosemarie Cerminaro at Simon and Schuster; Disney Publishing Worldwide; Annette Fern at Harvard Theatre Collection; Harry Ransom Humanities Research Center; Anna Simic and Kevin Myers at Inland Pacific Ballet; Axel Koester; Paul Kolnik; Susan Kuklin; Andrew Oxenham; Lydia Pawelak; Herman and Linda Porter; Viji Prakash; David Smith; David Street; Cylla von Tiedemann; Philip Ulanowsky; Tony Vaccaro; Jack Vartoogian; Jennifer Veit at New York City Ballet; Arlene Wagner ("the Nutcracker lady") at the Leavenworth Nutcracker Museum; and the Washington Ballet.

At Yale University Press, my editor, Harry Haskell, provided the kind of conversation, encouragement, and expert advice I thought came only from the shepherding editors of eras gone by. I thank Chris Erikson and Susan Laity for careful and detailed copyediting and proofhandling.

Finally, I thank my friends and family, who have patiently accepted the fact that every conversation can be made to relate to *The Nutcracker*. Support of every variety came from my brother, Ron, my father, Dale, and my friends Catherine and Iris McCall, Phillip Schreibman, and Kristi Magraw. I am also fortunate to have a Los Angeles family, made up of the encyclopedic Anthony Shay and the artist/choreographer/wizard Jamal.

To my mother, Eleanor Thomas, I reserve the last and largest thank you, for thinking it would be a nice idea to expose me to ballet, for always being interested in the details, and for buying me endless *Nutcracker* gifts. Of course, she couldn't have known she would still be buying me *Nutcracker* memorabilia decades after I retired from the corps, but she has rolled with the relevés. Her faith and natural optimism, her example and her support, have made it possible for me to do anything worthwhile that I have managed to do.

"Nutcracker" Nation

A few years ago, as I sat in the audience of my local Nutcracker *and waited for the first act to begin, a young woman in front of me turned to her companions and said, "You know, Tchaikovsky really hated this ballet." Her husband and the couple with them looked at her blankly and said, "Oh," and "No kidding"—clearly not sure what this meant in terms of their own willingness to pay for tickets and dress up to see the ballet on this particular afternoon. I wanted to jump into the conversation and fill in the fine points surrounding reports of Tchaikovsky's disapprobation—he was depressed about a lot of things when he badmouthed the ballet, I wanted to tell them, and it wasn't even a ballet yet, he was just having trouble getting started with the music. I wanted to tell them that Tchaikovsky actually liked the finished score and that he would surely appreciate its status now and the way it keeps sustaining the hundreds of* Nutcrackers *that dominate each Christmas season. I wanted to tell them that the first* Nutcracker, *which was the only one Tchaikovsky knew, back in 1892, was fraught with birthing pains—no one could have completely loved it—but now there were more excellent versions than you could shake a wand at. I wanted to tell them that the production they were about to see, by the Inland Pacific Ballet, was charming, well danced, and did the taped Tchaikovsky proud. But I refrained.*

I refrained not only because I knew that a dance history lecture from a stranger rarely goes over well but because I suspected that these facts wouldn't matter to them anyway. For whatever reasons (and there may have been many), they had decided to come to a Nutcracker *matinee and they were ready to enjoy it. Sure enough, when I talked to them afterward they said they had liked the ballet enormously, without a second thought for the composer's opinion, or indeed for the pronouncements of any* Nutcracker *naysayers—those many critics who object to perceived deficiencies of the ballet, or the fact that it pops up more often* than toast every Christmas. "You know," a fellow critic once said to me disdainfully, "they don't even like The Nutcracker in Russia," as if this were sufficient reason to stop researching the ballet immediately and boycott further performances. But American audiences never seemed to care. The young couples I talked to after the matinee that day loved the music, the costumes, the ballerina, and the striving young dancers. They were pleased to have such a nice way to celebrate the season—and they thought they'd come every year to The Nutcracker and bring their own children, when they had them. After all, it was "culture," it was fun, and it was in their own backyard. The fact that the ballet came from Russia made the whole thing "historical" in some vague way, but that history had little to do with their lives. It occurred to me that for most Americans, the ballet's reputation back in the old country simply didn't matter.

In fact, the whole idea that Tchaikovsky was an original Nut-basher fits into a mythology that is particularly relevant here—that The Nutcracker is an underdog, a newcomer who found a new life. It was then that I started thinking of The Nutcracker as an immigrant. Maybe the ballet was not appreciated in its native land, but once it landed in the egalitarian land of the free, it got another chance.

The Early Years

In the first half of the twentieth century, when waves of immigrants were steadily adding to America's evolving mix of ethnic groups and blended identities, *The Nutcracker* also arrived. Born in 1892, the ballet had a checkered past, but its image was about to change. Technically, the Russian import was just visiting at first, making its initial, truncated appearances in the tours of Russian ballet companies. But eventually *The Nutcracker* would become a kind of immigrant, having its first full-length professional American production in 1944 at the San Francisco Ballet, then finally settling down at the New York City Ballet in 1954. After that, it was everywhere, including back in its homeland—which makes the ballet a peculiar kind of immigrant, one with a split personality. Or perhaps the term should be "multiple personalities," since *The Nutcracker* has never ceased assimilating to new locations in a multitude of ways.

There are so many versions, in fact, that it may seem hard to talk about the ballet as a single entity. The seeker of a definitive version will certainly come up empty. And although bits of Lev Ivanov's original choreography have been handed down in some form, there isn't enough documentation available to reproduce the production that premiered at the Maryinsky Theater in St. Petersburg. But even after so much dispersion and alteration, there are strong ways in which all *Nutcracker*s are related, like far-flung relatives who don't necessarily correspond. A kind of DNA testing for identification purposes would consist of looking for a few basic elements in any given *Nutcracker*. If it has some version of the original ballet libretto, uses Tchaikovsky's score and a ballet vocabulary—or, on rare occasions, another form of concert dance, such as tap or jazz—then it's probably a *Nutcracker*. Aliases can be tricky: *The Southwest Nutcracker* and *The Harlem Nutcracker* are family members that have just settled down elsewhere, but I once went eagerly to see something called *The Notcracker*, and it turned out to be an interloper, a set of satirical sketches that could as easily have been called *Not "A Christmas Carol"* for all it had to do with the ballet. Satirical versions—the black sheep of *The Nutcracker* family—always stray from the pack, but if they refer generously to the original, they are likely to be invited to a family reunion. Because membership in this clan is rarely contested—there seem to be enough revenues to go around—the title, plot, and music have become the ties that bind in the ever-expanding *Nutcracker* family.

What's amazing is how many things *Nutcrackers* have in common —a tree must grow, mice have to fight, snow will fall, and candy ends up dancing. Even when small budgets or plot alterations eliminate one of these must-see events, similar stories unfold. Maybe someone decides that the main character won't be a little girl but a grandmother or a wartime Russian ballerina or an illegal alien (it's happened)—the ballet is still about having a dream, a journey, family ties. In the majority of versions, it all starts with Clara (sometimes Marie or Masha), an optimistic little girl whose parents are having a party on Christmas Eve. A nutcracker doll is always given by Drosselmeier, a mysterious uncle or godfather figure, then fought over, broken, and repaired. Puppet performances take place, as does social dancing for young and old partygoers. After the party there is a midnight scene, which bleeds into fantasy when the Christmas tree magically expands and Clara witnesses a battle between mice and toy soldiers. When the Nutcracker doll, who has come to life, starts losing the fight, Clara saves him by throwing her shoe at the aggressive Mouse King. This selfless act triggers transformations and journeys;

the Nutcracker becomes a prince and leads her into a snow scene, which is evidently on the road to his ancestral kingdom.

The second act takes place when they arrive on the Nutcracker's home turf, the Land of the Sweets, a frothy looking place often peopled by angels as well as edible things. Its inhabitants welcome Clara and the Nutcracker, listen to the tale of how she got there, and present her with a suite of dances from other lands—or at least dances that a ballet choreographer imagines might happen in other lands. Spanish dancers have flair, Chinese are dexterous and delicate, Russians bound like Cossacks, and Arabian dancers slink about regally. Bits of dessert also dance, maybe some candy canes or pink-and-mint petits fours. There are usually a few storyland characters—Mother Ginger and tiny offspring hidden in her plus-size skirt, or perhaps shepherdesses and lambs. Then there is always a waltz for flowers and an impressive pas de deux between the reigning Sugar Plum Fairy and her consort. Many productions end (though the original ballet did not) with Clara leaving her fantasy land and waking up back in her own bed.

Anyone who has seen more than one *Nutcracker* knows that these details vary endlessly, because on this continent *The Nutcracker* thrives on multiple personality syndrome. But when it comes to the ballet's provenance, things get a little more definitive. All *Nutcracker*s, from the ones that feature Mikhail Baryshnikov or Darci Kistler to the ones that star Jason and Kimberly from down the street, trace their roots to the original 1892 production, back in old St. Petersburg. And whether or not the ballet's imperial Russian originators are rolling in their graves, each new incarnation, from professional to amateur to *Nutcracker*s on ice, claims imperial Russian parentage. Even during the Cold War, when my mother was assuring her friends that my love for Russian ballet did not mean I was a Communist, most Americans appreciated *The Nutcracker*'s Russian heritage. Not its actual, detailed history—few balletgoers care exactly what the 1892 production looked like and who starred in it or how the plot has changed since then. But the general idea that the ballet is Russian has always appealed to Americans, providing as it does the assurance of "the real thing." Even today, when North American ballet companies rank among the best in the world, there is still a healthy respect for Russian ballet—especially when it comes to the Tchaikovsky works: *Swan Lake, The Nutcracker,* and *The Sleeping Beauty.*

Among these, *The Nutcracker* has traditionally been the poor cousin, no matter how much money it generates—or perhaps *because* of how much money it generates by appealing to such a large audience. The complaints of cognoscenti have generally been couched in the aesthetic realm—its plot isn't cohesive enough, its appeal is largely decorative and for children, its structure is insufficient to support deep involvement. There is also, to be sure, a kind of class prejudice exercised when it comes to *The Nutcracker,* even in the putatively egalitarian New World. It's a ballet that makes itself at home in every town that has a dancing school—can this be a good thing? The fear is that *The Nutcracker* gets marooned on the level of spectacle, but that characterization ignores the complexity of the phenomenon of annual *Nutcracker*s. The spectacular elements comprise only one level of the ballet's existence in North America; on other levels—that of Christmas celebration, a rite of passage, community solidarity, for instance—the meaning of life for *The Nutcracker* becomes very rich in its adopted home. Like any immigrant might, the ballet started dressing up differently once it found success in North America, but its heart has always been in the right place—or in several right places, as the case may be. *The Nutcracker* is the ballet immigrant who made it big on a lavish scale, and has thus engendered a certain amount of resentment and suspicion. After all, it's the only classical ballet from the Old World which, after a rocky start at home, made North America its primary residence.

When it comes to the ballet's Russian pedigree, you might say that *The Nutcracker* was born into an elite family with great expectations. At its birth, on December 6, 1892, at the Maryinsky Theater in St.

Petersburg, the golden age of Russian ballet was in full swing. The czar, blissfully unaware that the Russian royalty was just two and a half decades from extinction, was still gracing the royal box at ballets and operas and furnishing ample funds for imperial theater budgets. Theater directors, in return, provided ballets that often reflected the splendor and elegance of the czar's world—stories of benevolent royals decked out in jeweled costumes, presiding over sets with elaborate arches and working fountains. The performers constituted another kind of royalty, with ballet stars from all over Europe enjoying extended engagements at the Maryinsky, and Russian artists attracting their own cults of celebrity. Italian ballerinas, with their toes of steel and technical bravura, were very popular at the end of the nineteenth century—the somewhat sturdily built Antonietta Dell'Era would be the first Sugar Plum Fairy. Each ballet's variations and divertissements provided a smaller showcase for homegrown performers. By the end of the nineteenth century, they were developing into some of the finest dancers in the world, having assimilated aspects of ballet development in Paris, Milan, and Copenhagen.

In 1890, a few years before *The Nutcracker*'s premiere, *The Sleeping Beauty* had masterfully combined all the glorious elements of imperial ballet, with its dazzling Tchaikovsky score and choreography by veteran balletmaster Marius Petipa. It set the standard for all subsequent productions, garnering excellent response from the knowledgeable and opinionated St. Petersburg critics and balletomanes. This group was not shy about pouncing on any new work they considered unworthy of "their" imperial theater stage—as they would demonstrate once the next Tchaikovsky ballet emerged. But because *The Nutcracker* started out with same creative team that produced *The Sleeping Beauty*, there was no reason to think it wouldn't have similar success. In hindsight, there were ominous signs—the plot was less conventionally cohesive than many; there were children featured in leading roles, a practice sure to confound the cognoscenti's great love of masterful dancing. And, due to illness, Petipa opted out of

7

the project as rehearsals began, leaving its completion to his less experienced assistant, Lev Ivanov. The handwriting might have been on the wall (there were rumors that Petipa was not all *that* ill), but since most rehearsal periods have their ups and downs, it was surely hard to predict critical reaction.[1]

Subject matter for the new ballet was cleverly chosen from E. T. A. Hoffmann's 1816 short story "The Nutcracker and the Mouse King," which enjoyed great popularity in Russia at the time. As with *The Sleeping Beauty*, the idea to adapt the tale came from Ivan Vsevolozhsky, the sophisticated ex-diplomat who was director of imperial theaters. In the process of writing the libretto, with contributions from Petipa, he made major changes, as anyone who reads Hoffmann immediately realizes. Vsevolozhsky and Petipa, both French speakers, relied on a slightly altered French retelling of Hoffmann written by Alexandre Dumas père.[2] But neither story would have easily fit onto the ballet stage. Engaging in print, the plot was full of time lapses and flashbacks. And so a massive simplification took place, eliminating, for instance, the entire story-within-a-story about one Princess Pirlipat, which today's audiences can see reinstated in Mark Morris's *The Hard Nut*.[3] Also eliminated were any of Hoffmann's images that might have clashed with the elegant ballet style of the era—both the Nutcracker and Marie are cursed into ugliness at different moments, for instance, and morsels of browned fat play a crucial role in the original story's revenge scenarios.

Once the libretto was ready and Tchaikovsky's services engaged, Petipa sent a detailed set of instructions to the composer, outlining what was needed for each scene. I remember, as a young dancer, being shocked to think that the great Tchaikovsky was given a set of descriptions and commands as if it were a grocery list ("The stage is empty. 8 bars of mysterious and tender music"). But back then, ballet composers often wrote music "by the yard," although few produced scores as sophisticated as Tchaikovsky's. He took Petipa's cryptic orders and turned them into rhapsodic passages. From a sentence like,

"The Christmas tree becomes huge. 48 bars of fantastic music with a grandiose crescendo," came a musical passage that sends shivers up the spine and suggests that paradise actually exists somewhere.[4]

However, when the composer first approached *The Nutcracker,* he wasn't exactly thrilled. The story didn't inspire him as *The Sleeping Beauty* had, and, in any event, he was composing an opera at the same time *(Iolanthe)* and making slow progress on both. He was also angry about one of his operas *(The Queen of Spades)* being dropped from the Maryinsky's repertoire, although he had been assured that it had to do with extraneous forces, not the quality of the work. In February of 1891 he had written to his brother that he was "beginning to be reconciled with the subject of the ballet," but within a few months he asked for and received an extension of his original deadline (the ballet and opera were scheduled for the 1891–92 season), and the project was put off until the fall of 1892.[5]

Then, just as he was working on the second act of *The Nutcracker* in France and preparing to leave for a taxing American tour, Tchaikovsky learned of the death of his beloved sister Sasha. "Today, even more than yesterday," he wrote his brother after learning the news, "I feel the absolute impossibility of depicting in music the Sugar-plum Fairy." That summer he wrote to a nephew, "This ballet is far weaker than *The Sleeping Beauty*—no doubt about it." Adding to his worries at the time, middle age was making its presence felt. He wrote to his nephew that his early "sketch" of the ballet took longer than it should have. With a hint of self-deprecating humor that seemed to mask fear, the composer worried that "the old fellow" was "growing less capable of accomplishing anything."[6]

All of which is to say that Tchaikovsky's roiling emotional life may have affected his attitude about *The Nutcracker* early on. Once he did manage to compose, those deeply felt emotions seem to have found their way into parts of the score. While he was still newly in mourning for his sister, for instance, he continued to work on the second act, which might explain why, at the end of what has always been

called a decorative, children's ballet, there is the death-defyingly serious adagio music of the grand pas de deux. Musicologist Roland John
Wiley has suggested that Tchaikovsky actually left a coded message
in the rhythm of the adagio's principal melody, a descending scale
of notes that is repeated "with prayer-like insistence." Because the
phrase bears a close rhythmical resemblance to a line in the Russian
Orthodox funeral service (which translates as "And with the saints
give rest"), Wiley believes it might have been Tchaikovsky's hidden
homage to his sister.[7]

Whatever the trials the composer experienced while working on
The Nutcracker, he undoubtedly experienced some satisfaction with
his score when it was completed. The myth that he hated this wildly
popular music has grown larger than life in North America, where
the disparaging remarks he made while composing it have been
widely quoted (prominently in the Disney film *Fantasia,* when the
narrator assures the audience that Tchaikovsky "detested" his *Nutcracker* score). In reality, once the hard part was over, Tchaikovsky
must have known that he had done something wonderful, even before rehearsals for the ballet began. In the spring of 1892, he conducted a program at the St. Petersburg Musical Society and included
a suite of selections from his upcoming ballet. This *Nutcracker Suite,*
a title often confused with the full-length ballet, was so well received
that five out of its six movements were encored.[8]

When rehearsals for the dancers finally began, Tchaikovsky might
have had a new worry—that a major ingredient in determining the
ballet's success, the choreography, was out of Petipa's hands. There is
evidence that the ailing balletmaster attended some early *Nutcracker*
rehearsals, but the task of composing dances and staging mime
scenes was basically turned over to Ivanov, his assistant. This was
not necessarily a disaster—Ivanov had taken over for Petipa before,
and, in any event, he was working from the veteran balletmaster's
notes, just as Tchaikovsky had. But even though Ivanov would, in a
few years, produce the evocative lakeside scenes in *Swan Lake,* thus

proving he had some lasting balletic poetry within his reach, he was no Tchaikovsky, nor was he as consistently inventive as Petipa. Also, *The Nutcracker* had scenes that required astute staging skills—the busy party scene, the battle—and Ivanov was less organized than Petipa, who often sat at a table working out choreography with paper figures ahead of time. Ivanov often arrived at rehearsal unprepared, sometimes relying on his dancers to suggest ideas.[9]

Ivanov's willingness to let dancers contribute to the process was not unusual; many ballet luminaries routinely inserted their own favorite steps and solos into new ballets. In that way, the instability of *Nutcracker* choreography over the years—even the radical interpretations that now exist—could be considered merely a more extreme kind of "customizing" of a ballet to suit its participants. However, if we believe the few stories that survive from the era, Ivanov's mind wasn't always on his job. At one point in a *Nutcracker* rehearsal, with Tchaikovsky at the piano, Ivanov was apparently so distracted by a sideline conversation about card playing (he loved cards) that he joined in and kept talking about card games even as he returned to directing the dancers. In terms of the North American *Nutcracker* inheritance, Ivanov's sometimes indecisive nature explains how Trepak, the Russian dance in the second act, ended up with a dual personality. Petipa's written instructions called for: "Trepak, for the end of the dance, turning on the floor," referring to the athletic feats of Russian character dance. But evidently Ivanov didn't like the variation he came up with in rehearsal, and when someone suggested a hoop dance instead, the dancer Alexandre Shiryaev choreographed his own solo.[10] Today, Trepak usually follows one of two traditions; it's either an athletic Slavic character dance, featuring one or more males dressed in peasant shirts, ballooning pants, and boots, or a candy cane dance with hoops, a tradition carried on in Balanchine's version.

Bit by bit, the various elements of *The Nutcracker* came together, and it was as ready as it would ever be for its December premiere. The ballet was not, as is commonly imagined, alone onstage the night of its birth; it was actually one of a pair of fraternal twins, the second half of a program that began with the Tchaikovsky opera *Iolanthe*. It's easy to imagine that having two premieres on the same night resulted in reduced stage time for complete run-through rehearsals. But perhaps no amount of polishing would have helped *The Nutcracker* wow the critics completely that night.

For one thing, it was a very long evening. Today it's hard to imagine a concert that doesn't end until after midnight, as was the case this night. But the end of the nineteenth century was a time when, presumably, attention spans were longer, and babysitting was not a problem for the largely aristocratic opera and ballet audiences (who, in any case, felt free to come late and leave early). First came *Iolanthe*, an opera about a blind princess who is awakened through love. It's a darker tale than *The Nutcracker*, and some historians have suggested that Tchaikovsky meant the ballet to provide balance, and not stand alone in all its frivolity. But there's little evidence that Tchaikovsky saw the ballet and opera as two halves of a whole; his contract, for instance, doesn't stipulate their twinning. In the event, they were separated almost at birth—or at least after that season's eleven dual performances. Both went on to live productive lives apart—*The Nutcracker*, of course, becoming the better known of the two. Just after the ballet's premiere, however, you would have been hard-pressed to predict such long-lived, widespread popularity.[11]

The reviews of the first *Nutcracker* are best characterized as mixed, but the negative pronouncements were so categorical that they have always tended to stand out. "First of all, *The Nutcracker* can under no condition be called a ballet," a newspaper critic known as Domino proclaimed. "It does not satisfy even one of the demands made of a ballet." He may have been the first in a long line of critics who have categorized *The Nutcracker* as "mere spectacle" because of its lavish decoration and its unusual structure—all story and little dancing in the first act, then all dancing and no story in the second. "Un-

The decorative balls of fluff on the crowns of Ivanov's snowflakes
in 1892 show up in Balanchine's 1954 *Nutcracker,*
but by then they are only on the dancers' wands.

usual structure" is my term; Domino called *The Nutcracker* "a panto-
mime absurd in conception and execution, which could please only
the most uncultured spectators." It's an assessment not far from that
of some contemporary critics who have called *The Nutcracker* "eye
candy" or "Disney-ized." In 1892, the fear was that the imperial ballet
was edging its way into the territory of the commercial, cabaretlike
theaters that dotted St. Petersburg. Why bother to have an esteemed
ballet academy, why learn classical dance at all, if it were only to perform in such "experiments," said Domino, who was in high dudgeon
that day. More ballets like *The Nutcracker,* he predicted, would mean
"death for the company."[12]

There were some nice things said about the ballet, too. The snow
scene, for instance, was generally a hit. The nearly sixty snowflakes,

The original Fritz and Clara were Vasily Stukolkin and
Stanislava Belinskaya; Russian critics did not find the casting
of children in major roles charming.

all wearing long white tutus dotted with fluff balls and matching
crowns, were pronounced "an elegant allegory of a snowdrift." A few
of the mechanical dolls' dances were praised, as were certain of the
second-act variations. "Tea" was so popular with the audience it had
to be repeated (a common practice for crowd-pleasers at the Maryinsky), whereas the Waltz of the Flowers, costumed in elaborate gold
cloth, was said to work better for the corps than the soloists (lyrical ensemble dances were a great strength for Ivanov). Nevertheless,
even after a certain amount of praise, yet another critic called *The
Nutcracker* "one more step downwards" for the Maryinsky, a ballet
"produced primarily with children for children" with "precisely nothing" to contribute to "the artistic fate of our ballet."[13]

The great number children in the cast was definitely a sticking
point. Imperial conservatory students were customarily seen in small
parts in ballets and operas, but were not considered worthy of much

attention until they matured. They were all right in moderation, acting as somber pages or miniature adults, but childlike behavior in an imperial ballet just wouldn't do. One critic complained: "In the first scene, the entire stage is filled with children, who run about, blow their whistles, hop and jump, are naughty, and interfere with the oldsters dancing. In large amounts this is unbearable."[14] It would take North American audiences, years later, to find any charm in this kind of youthful enthusiasm.

The notices for individual dancers at the premiere varied from critic to critic, as was often the case in fin-de-siècle St. Petersburg, where factions often supported favorites for reasons beyond dancing ability. Dell'Era, for instance, was generally praised for her strong pointe work and masterful technique as the Sugar Plum Fairy, but one critic, who was opposed to the veneration of foreign dancers, called her "corpulent" and "podgy." Nevertheless, Dell'Era reportedly received five curtain calls. The difficulty in knowing the merit of the various performances is illustrated by the reaction to Olga Preobrajenskaya (Preobrajenska), an up-and-coming ballerina who, as the Columbine doll, was called by one critic "completely insipid" and by others "charming" and "enchanting."[15]

There were no split opinions about the battle scene, however; the idea of chaos was evoked—and not in a good way. It probably didn't help that many of the students playing soldiers were not from the ballet school, but were chosen, in some ill-advised scheme, from a military academy. One imagines lines of little boys getting carried away with toy rifles, body-checking any mice who got in their way. In his diary, audience member Alexandre Benois (who later designed for Diaghilev) wrote of the scene: "One cannot understand anything. Disorderly pushing about from corner to corner and running backwards and forwards—quite senseless and amateurish."[16] The lighting was evidently murky, but it's hard to imagine that more illumination would have helped; anyone who has seen various stagings of mice versus soldiers knows how much patience and rehearsal it takes

Antonietta Dell'Era, the original Sugar Plum Fairy
(seen here in another role), was called "corpulent" and "podgy" by
one critic after the 1892 *Nutcracker* premiered.

to corral child battalions. It's possible that the easygoing Ivanov just couldn't whip that scene into shape.

The *Nutcracker* libretto also drew a tremendous amount of fire. Fans of Hoffmann's story thought the ballet failed to capture its mood, and lacked dramatic coherence. The transition from living room to fantasy world was considered too abrupt, for one thing, and no one liked waiting for the "main event," the ballerina, who didn't strut her stuff in the grand pas de deux until nearly midnight on opening night.[17] Over time, critics would continue to bemoan the "lopsided" libretto, and all kinds of adjustments would be made to it, some of which were bound to help. In North America, Clara often wakes up back in her own bedroom at the end, as she does at one point in the Hoffmann story. This has given the fantasy part of the plot a dream rationale, similar to one now well known from *The Wizard of Oz*. But it's possible that North Americans never worried much about the scenario "making sense." Perhaps they never objected to its basic "flight of fancy" premise the way the ballet's original critics did. In the New World, where "rags to riches" myths flourished (and had some roots in fact), the ballet's abrupt transition from middle-class living room to overdressed fantasyland might never have been too troubling.

From today's perspective, it's hard to imagine that the Tchaikovsky score was ever slammed by the critics, but in 1892, a few found it lacking. Ballet music at the time tended to be far less complex in terms of orchestration and rhythm, so it's possible that audiences were overwhelmed by some of the score. After the first performance, Tchaikovsky took his bows with Ivanov and attended an opening night dinner, but unalloyed celebration was brief. On one hand, critics pronounced *The Nutcracker*'s music "astonishingly rich in inspiration," and "from beginning to end beautiful, melodious, original, and characteristic." But on the other, the party scene music was deemed "burdensome," the social dances "heavy and wooden," and the grand pas de deux music "awkward and insipid," "quite simply boring," and "unsuitable for dancing."[18]

Response to *Iolanthe* was also varied, and perhaps even more negative. Although Tchaikovsky wrote, "the abuse does not annoy me in the least," he admitted that in such cases, "the emptiness and futility of all our efforts becomes so evident." Presumably he wasn't cheered by the backhanded compliments for *The Nutcracker*, such as, "It's a pity that so much good music is expended on such nonsense." He might have briefly felt better when, in January, he conducted a program that included *The Nutcracker Suite* in Odessa, and received a laurel wreath and many requests for encores. But within a year, Tchaikovsky was dead, without suspecting the revered place in history his ballets would attain.[19]

After the premiere, the life of *The Nutcracker* in Russia was full of ups and downs. Despite the less-than-glowing reviews, the work appeared on a majority of ballet evenings for the rest of the 1892–93 season, so it may have enjoyed some audience popularity. During that summer, excerpts from the second act were included on programs for the imperial ballet's Krasnoe Selo season, just outside St. Petersburg. After that, the ballet disappeared from time to time, resurfacing as the showcase for a particular ballerina, and, in 1909, in a revival that attempted to recapture the original production, because alterations had already occurred. Throughout the Soviet years, *The Nutcracker* was usually paired with another short work, and sometimes only the second half was performed. Eventually the ballet went through several rechoreographings in its native land, principally a 1919 version by Alexander Gorsky in Moscow, Fedor Lopukhov's 1929 sociopolitical re-envisioning, and two prominent versions performed for many years by the Kirov (Vasily Vainonen's in 1934) and the Bolshoi (Yuri Grigorovich's in 1966).[20]

Since *The Nutcracker* wasn't a virtuoso showpiece for its leads, it wasn't popular with Russian principal dancers, even after the Clara character was combined with the Sugar Plum Fairy in the adult role of Masha (a move first made by Gorsky). Never wedded to the Christmas season, the ballet was often relegated to school performances. According to St. Petersburg dance scholar Elizabeth Souritz, Russian choreographers have spent considerable energy trying to overcome the perceived faults of *The Nutcracker*'s child-centered libretto and to bring the ballet into line with "the psychological depth of the score," whereas in the United States, *The Nutcracker* "answers a different purpose"—mainly as "a favorite Christmas entertainment for children."[21] On the surface, this assessment sounds true enough, but to accept its reductive conclusion is to ignore the cultural dimensions of the North American *Nutcracker* phenomenon—and the concomitant fact that a child-centered libretto may also contain psychological depth. *The Nutcracker* is more meaningful here than Russian observers suspect, so it may be more appropriate to say that the ballet just didn't turn into something *they* found meaningful. Once the ballet coalesced with the Christmas season in North America and was reinforced by notions about the innocence of childhood, rites of passage, and dreams coming true, it grew up on its own—into something that Russians don't recognize.

The Nutcracker first left home in the early part of the twentieth century, like many other imperial theater alumni who set out on adventurous tours to the West. After the 1917 Russian Revolution, many of them stayed abroad to take advantage of more varied artistic opportunities. Perhaps *The Nutcracker* was particularly like George Balanchine, a Maryinsky graduate who went to Paris during the modernist 1920s and then settled in the United States, where he combined his Russian ballet heritage with the different energies he found there. When Balanchine created a *Nutcracker* in New York, his version was inevitably tinged with Russian memories (he had danced in the ballet at the Maryinsky), but he also felt free to depart from tradition. Later, some North Americans would copy his *Nutcracker* choreography, and many more would adopt his free-spirited approach to restaging a classic.

Unlike others in the Russian ballet diaspora, *The Nutcracker* at first traveled incognito, when bits of it were slipped into ballets with other names. There was an early cameo appearance in the 1909 Paris season of Serge Diaghilev's Ballets Russes by way of a solo to the Trepak music in Fokine's *Le Festin*. Then, when Anna Pavlova formed her own troupe, she chose the more lyrical Snowflake Waltz for a ballet called "Snowflakes," which was included on her tours around the world from 1911 to at least 1920. Choreographed by her balletmaster, Ivan Clustine, it might have contained some of Ivanov's ensemble choreography but also had a pas de deux for Pavlova and a partner, perhaps starting the trend for adding a featured couple to *The Nut-*

cracker's snow scene. For her 1926–27 European tour, Pavlova also used the snow scene music for a pas de trois. Meanwhile, Diaghilev's company had continued to play fast and loose with various parts of the *Nutcracker* score. The Sugar Plum Fairy's music was used for a Nijinsky solo, oddly enough, in a two-act version of *Swan Lake* in London in 1911. The same tinkling celesta was interpolated for the Lilac Fairy in *The Sleeping Princess*, the 1921 Ballets Russes version of *The Sleeping Beauty*. Since no one seems to have considered Tchaikovsky scores sacred, the Arabian and Chinese dances, as well as the coda of *The Nutcracker*'s grand pas de deux, also made it into that production.[22]

But the fact that Tchaikovsky had composed music for a ballet with its own story did not go unnoticed for long. As early as 1932, a few Russian expatriots were staging a partial *Nutcracker* for Canadian ballet students in Vancouver, British Columbia. A photograph survives, showing rows of tiny tots in mouse heads, tiny Arabian vests, fluffy skirts, and Russian headdresses. At the center sits Santa Claus, portending the impact of North American Christmas on *The Nutcracker*.[23] That same decade, there were various full-length productions in Europe. In 1934, a *Nutcracker* with significant ties to St. Petersburg took place in London. Staged for the Vic-Wells (later Royal) Ballet, it was based on a choreographic notation score brought to England by Nicholas Sergeyev, the Maryinsky's former chief régisseur. Because the written dance score (in Stepanov notation) isn't a complete record of the ballet, Ivanov's choreography couldn't be reproduced exactly, but Sergeyev provided an intriguing link to the original. His version wasn't revived each year, nor did annual *Nutcracker*s ever become anywhere near as popular in England as they did in North America. Still, parts of the Royal Ballet's *Nutcracker* retain an aura of authenticity for many in the dance world, even though the ballet has undergone countless changes over the years. Because of the wide availability of a video from 1984 (by which time the ballet had been much altered), elements of its choreography, especially the

By 1932 Santa Claus (center) had found his way into a
Nutcracker in Vancouver, British Columbia.

grand pas de deux, show up frequently in productions that claim to
be "after Ivanov."[24]

In the United States, another "after Ivanov" production became
familiar during the 1940s and 1950s, when the Ballet Russe de Monte
Carlo crisscrossed the country with a condensed *Nutcracker*. One of
several Russian troupes that tried to keep the spirit of Diaghilev alive
after his death in 1929, this company was originally based in Europe,
but became increasingly dominated by American dancers as it spent
the World War II years in North America. The Ballet Russe *Nutcracker*,
staged by Alexandra Federova in 1940, made fairly short work of the
plot, opening with a brief party scene, moving to the Snowflake Waltz
(eventually eliminated), and then to the second act divertissements
and grand pas de deux. In shadowy film footage from the era, the Bal-

let Russe sets look simple—a standing candelabra for the party scene, a painted backdrop of snow-peaked mountains for snowflakes—and the variations are lively, looking as if they could please audiences with a broad range of tastes. The showpiece was obviously the grand pas de deux, which was often spectacularly danced by stars of the time, among them Alicia Markova, Alexandra Danilova, Igor Youskevitch, and Frederic Franklin. It must have been impressive for audiences in towns where few high-flown arabesques had been seen before. The production was lauded by at least one notable critic of the time, Edwin Denby, who was clearly charmed by the way the ballet combined classical rigor with the resonant themes of familial anxiety and social harmony. In 1944, he wrote that the tirelessly touring version was a "serene old vehicle" that "still works as a theatre piece," even though it was "cut, patched, and mauled by years of hard wear."[25]

Another event in the 1940s marked the beginning of the end of the peripatetic existence of *The Nutcracker* in North America—the first full-length American production, mounted in 1944 by Willam Christensen for the San Francisco Ballet. Christensen, who had staged *Nutcracker* excerpts, had never seen the complete ballet but was encouraged to stage it by Russians émigrés who had settled in the Bay area. He dutifully sought advice from Balanchine and Danilova when they were passing through San Francisco with the Ballet Russe. Danilova demonstrated some passages she recalled from the Maryinsky *Nutcracker,* whereas Balanchine advised Christensen not to worry about the original but to create his own. That's what Balanchine himself did for his New York City Ballet in 1954, giving the ballet a permanent residence on both coasts. By all accounts, Balanchine had a great affection for *The Nutcracker,* but his choice was also based on the fact that the complete ballet would be new to New Yorkers, who had already seen the full *Sleeping Beauty* and *Swan Lake* presented on tours of London's Sadler's Wells Ballet.[26]

Both the San Francisco Ballet and Balanchine's company were young at midcentury and needed to solidify their reputations by staging full-length classics. No one could have known that *The Nut-cracker* would turn into an annual money-making venture; Christensen did not at first repeat the ballet each December, but caught on by 1950. After the successful 1954 February premiere of Balanchine's production, the ballet was scheduled for a full month the following Christmas.

Neither artistic director was probably paying much attention to a strange bit of *Nutcracker* competition at the time, the animated 1940 Disney film *Fantasia,* which featured its own fairies and dancing flowers—the literal kind. As the cartoon alter ego of *The Nut-cracker, Fantasia* has not been much explored as a dance piece, but its choreography is actually very good. Balanchine isn't on record as a *Fantasia* fan, but he was a man who once made a ballet for circus elephants, and it's easy to imagine him enjoying a Tea danced by mushrooms instead of people. He might even have recognized that the film's lush musicality and inventive movement choices unwittingly did a lot to prepare North Americans for "real" ballet and to nourish the growth of the annual *Nutcracker* movement.

In 1940, the same year the Ballet Russe premiered its *Nutcracker* in towns across the continent, *Fantasia* might have been playing in movie houses right next door. A fantasy of fanciful characters whose adventures unfold to classical music, the movie features a cartoon ballet to the most hummable *Nutcracker* tunes. This *Nutcracker* segment doesn't appear in *Fantasia 2000,* a sequel that does reprise one part of the original ("The Sorcerer's Apprentice," starring Mickey Mouse), but the 1940 *Fantasia* has always been around, first in theaters and eventually on videocassette. In the 1960s and 1970s, when annual *Nutcracker*s started to bloom in North America, *Fantasia* undoubtedly served as a kind of ambassador for the ballet. Perhaps nothing could have made *The Nutcracker* more viewer-friendly for North Americans, who might not have suspected they liked to watch figures floating to symphonic music. In a country relatively new to classical art forms, viewers who watched *Fantasia*'s flowers swirling to Mirle-

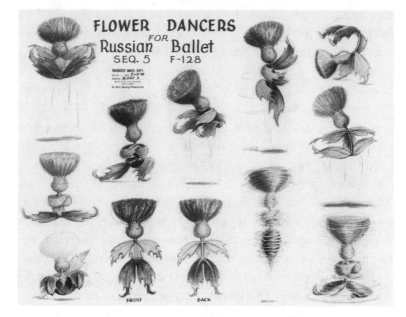

Drawings for the thistles who dance in the Trepak section of the
1940 Disney film *Fantasia* indicate their range of movement
in Russian-style steps. © Disney Enterprises, Inc.

ton flutes or lithe fairies skating rhythmically into arabesques on a
frozen lake were being introduced the aesthetics of ballet.

At first glance, a classical ballet and an animated Disney movie
might not seem to be in the same *Nutcracker* family, but on closer in-
spection, they're like kissing cousins who travel in different circles.
It's clear that some of the *Nutcracker* segment in *Fantasia* owes its
embodied vibrancy to the use of human models, a common method
of Disney animators, so in that way it draws from the dance world
directly. The diminutive fairies fly about in arcs that match musical phrases, stop to balance or skitter on sharply pointed toes, and
take off again to swoop and hover in the air like sylphides. Waving

their wands at intricate spider webs, they leave behind drops of dew that vibrate in time to the notes of a harp. The figures in Trepak attack their choreography differently, bounding into Russian character dance steps with the elegant athleticism of a staged version. Lines of male Trepak "dancers" are thistles (blossoms as heads and stems as limbs) and the women are irises (petals for heads, arms, and skirts). They skip forward with "arms" folded in front of them, do split leaps, and keep the beat with exuberant exactitude before jumping back into a floral arrangement in the last freeze frame.

Human models also seem to have been used for the basic steps of the Chinese Tea variation, which consists of mushrooms scurrying and bowing in swiftly moving lines. The sultry Arabian Coffee variation gets its ambiance from an underwater setting, where fish take over dancing duties, gliding this way and that to the smoky English horn melody. Wispy long tails curve in sweeping ribbons behind them, as bubbles rise and quick ripples of disturbed water enhance the wavering notes of violins and clarinets. At one point the heads of four fish come together and are seen from above, à la Busby Berkeley, their tails making an abstract pattern of curves and angles. The cartoon version of the Arabian soloist is a female fish with seductively blinking, long-lashed eyes, in keeping with the Orientalist fantasy that so many ballet companies make of this variation ("It gives the fathers something to look at," Balanchine reportedly said about his own Coffee vamp). By replacing a "mysterious" Middle Eastern setting with this murky underwater world, Fantasia's Arabian dance avoids the exotic ethnic generalizing that many ballet versions gleefully present and settles for a fishy femme fatale stereotype.

The animated figures in Fantasia come closest to looking like a corps de ballet when an ensemble of fluffy flowers swirls on the surface of a pond to the twinkling Dance of the Flutes. Sometimes rising from the surface, so that their multicolored blossoms look like bell-shaped tutus, the flowers form geometrical patterns, spin, change di-

rection, and drift in a way that brings to mind balletic adjectives —
graceful, buoyant, flowing, floating. In this case, the floating is literal
and the flower corps disappears over a waterfall.

None of this fits into a plot; the narrator at the start warns that
no nutcracker will be seen except in the title. Instead, the structure
resembles the suite form used in a traditional *Nutcracker*'s second
act, with one discrete variation following another. There does seem
to be a theme in *Fantasia*, the shift of seasons, which provides the
"motivation" for the animated figures to stay in motion. The Waltz of
the Flowers, which concludes the *Nutcracker* segment, moves briskly
from one weather change to another — dragonfly fairies bring fall
colors to greenery with a tap of a wand and loose leaves zig-zag rhythmically on a breeze as they drift toward the ground. Fairies hitch a
ride on the feathery tails of migrating seeds, snow falls, and they ice
skate as the waltz rhythm escalates. At the end, a cavalcade of snowflakes cartwheel across the screen in diagonals that run from alternating top corners of the screen. This strategy of shifting focus constantly and matching various shapes and rhythms to the music keeps
the Waltz of the Flowers alive, whereas in ballets with repetitive choreography, it can seem endless.

Bracketing the compulsory whimsy that saturates the film's *Nutcracker* are hints of the opera house, a place probably unknown to
much of *Fantasia*'s audience, both in 1940 and today. Conductor
Leopold Stokowski and a group of orchestra members make a brief
(nonanimated) appearance before and after the *Nutcracker* segment,
warming up and looking austere but lively in color-tinged silhou-
ettes. Stokowski's larger-than-life figure is seen from behind when
he first starts to conduct, as if he's looming sternly between the audience and the show, but soon the screen is full of drifting puffballs
and incandescent fairies in a forest, and the world is cartoon-friendly
again. *Fantasia* seems to say that classical musicians might be as ap-
proachable as the animated characters who move to their music — at
least these players are, their intimidation factor appreciably reduced

by their willingness to play for dancing mushrooms. If many North Americans didn't know what to make of classical music and dance, they understood cartoons. *The Nutcracker* as envisioned by Disney is a literal fairy tale and a romp through idealized nature. It stars plants and invertebrates who dance, all twirling, gliding, and stamping in time to the music. Nothing has to make sense in this alternate *Nutcracker* universe, everything just keeps moving inventively along. It's just a hop, skip, and leap from there to Clara's dream.

To the St. Petersburg critic who thought it was a pity that so much good music in *The Nutcracker* was expended on "such nonsense," *Fantasia* says, no, it isn't. Despite the playfulness of the movie's animated characters, the film takes the music very seriously—not by providing grave subject matter but by creating images that soar and undulate in ways that creatively expand Tchaikovsky's rhythms, melodies, and orchestral effects. Soon after *Fantasia* became popular, ballet producers in the New World started to make *Nutcracker*s for all tastes. Some would still search for cohesiveness of plot and tone, but the "well-made play" mold increasingly did not fit, and audiences didn't seem to worry about that. The juxtapositions that *Fantasia* introduces so baldly—highbrow music for dancing plant life—opened the door to a fanciful world that existed beyond high art envisionings. Not that the annual *Nutcracker* movement turned thereafter exclusively to whimsy and cartoon fun; traditional versions also lean heavily on a sense of nostalgia for an Old World time gone by. And on ballet. The presence of Tchaikovsky and classical ballet saturate most examples of the annual *Nutcracker* trend, and ballet became a symbol of elegant striving in the New World. But there would never be firm rules about how the ballet realm was to be evoked, since North America didn't have the same kind of "aesthetic police" that old St. Petersburg did. Nor would there be a complete capitulation to the demands of spectacle. So *The Nutcracker* happily settled into new classical territory, featuring toddlers beside ballerinas and pointe shoes next to mouse paws, while never forgetting its roots. It would remain connected to an elevated feeling of involvement with a complex art form, but one that incorporates the lighthearted sensibility of *Fantasia*.

Nowhere is the split personality aspect of *The Nutcracker* accepted and even celebrated more than in the ballet's adopted land. While the Russians toiled away to make the plot more serious by eliminating childish things, North Americans gleefully embraced the duality.[27] The problems of *The Nutcracker*, as they were defined at the premiere, were its lack of cohesion and logic, its sugar content, and its emphasis on children. They would remain sticking points with some critics, but after *Fantasia*, which arrived at a seminal stage of the ballet's North American infancy, many of the perceived problems started becoming assets. *The Nutcracker*, something of a "bad seed" in its homeland—a ballet thought to be in constant need of a makeover, often sent to the "children's table" of performing venues, and the recipient of many head shakes and clucking noises over its flawed nature—was about to be adopted and make good elsewhere.

On Christmas night in both 1957 and 1958, Americans could see what was going on at Clara's house while relaxing in their own living rooms when CBS television presented the New York City Ballet in George Balanchine's *Nutcracker*.[28] New Yorkers had already taken the ballet to heart, but these first nationally televised versions were the most intimate encounters to date between the ballet and a wider public. It's hard to believe that Balanchine's elaborate stage production could survive being squeezed into the small screen, not to mention being interrupted by commercials that promised better living through natural gas and Kleenex tissues. But the recordings that survive are engaging, even when compared to later, more polished filmed *Nutcracker*s. On television, you could get a close look at the Stahlbaum family and their friends chatting, exchanging gifts, and eating Christmas candy. Because the party scene feels somewhat cramped on its smallish set, the viewer seems to be sitting along the fourth wall of the drawing room. Then the camera is right in the thick

Balanchine (with eyepatch) as Drosselmeier on the set of CBS
television's live Christmas Day *Nutcracker* broadcast, 1958.

of things when the battle erupts and only a bit farther away when the
snowflakes start swirling. The variations of the second act—spreading into slightly less claustrophobic studio space—seem as much a
command performance for the television audience as for Clara and
her Prince. In the limited studio space, the dancers adjust their steps
admirably, moving up and down with exuberance and side to side
with caution. They all seem so close, so anxious to please, their pre-
sentational personalities bearing down on the camera with singular
avidity.

If *Fantasia* had emphasized *The Nutcracker*'s accessible, fun-loving
aspect, the Christmas night television broadcasts helped establish its
portability and ability to fit in on the home front. To give the TV *Nutcracker*s an added storytime feeling there were narrators—in 1957, an
unseen male even advised the home audience about what to look for,
as in, "Keep your eye on Drosselmeier." By the next year, the atmo-

sphere had gotten more cozy, with actress June Lockhart (who had just become the mother on the network's *Lassie* series) sitting on a couch with a storybook on her lap, reading to Clara, who is dressed in a bathrobe. Once the ballet gets going, Lockhart occasionally clarifies the plot with voice-overs ("So, the Nutcracker destroys the king of the mice," and, "Now, the most magical journey begins") and welcomes viewers back from the four commercial breaks.

Several City Ballet luminaries gave up their Christmas holiday to dance in the 1958 broadcast. During the overture, two of the more glamorous ones are introduced by the fading in of their images—slowly revolving on pointe—over a projected sheet of the musical score. Diana Adams appears, waving her wand, wearing her Sugar Plum Fairy crown and a long tulle skirt; then comes Allegra Kent, dressed in the short chiffon tunic of Dewdrop, the solo Balanchine created for the Waltz of the Flowers. The male stars were saved for later; they were presumably not able to impart the kind of fairylike atmosphere to which a 1950s television audience could immediately relate. Later, Edward Villella athletically attacks the candy cane solo, which Balanchine once danced at the Maryinsky; Deni Lamont flies dexterously into split leaps in Tea; and in the Arabian variation a bare-chested Arthur Mitchell stretches briskly and sensuously, then smokes a hookah, attended by four child attendants dressed as parrots. This last variation seemingly alarmed no one—it was a few years before Americans learned to fear smoking or became familiar with the hookah as marijuana paraphernalia. (In 1964, Balanchine made Arabian a nonsmoking solo for a female dancer.) Balanchine himself takes the role of Drosselmeier, complete with prosthetic pointed nose and glasses blacked out on one side. He often plays into the camera and looks like he's having a lot of fun doing it.

Only a few things go wrong on this live broadcast—during scene changes, some crashes and voices are heard, and once a "special effect" is slightly marred when the camera catches Balanchine putting a small doll behind his back as it supposedly turns into a live-dancer version of the doll. The minimal television technology available at the time must have presented challenges (the now-infamous wavy screen effect is used once when Clara's reality is turning into a dream), but the tree-expanding scene is dealt with cleverly. During the transformation music, the camera is placed behind a hanging tree ornament that turns out to be a balloon. The branches shake as the balloon expands and, in the next shot, Clara finds herself under giant tree limbs, with all the toys grown to human size beside her. At the end of the ballet, a simple split-screen effect is used at the moment when Clara and her Prince normally fly across the back of the stage; they have obviously walked to another set, which allows the residents of Candy Land to fade from sight as Clara and the Prince wave at them in the foreground. Lockhart's voice is heard saying, "From that day on, Godfather Drosselmeier's nephew [the Nutcracker] is Clara's prince and Clara is his princess, and I need not tell you that they lived happily ever after."

The 1993 big-screen version of Balanchine's production is more handsome than the early televised versions and features excellent performances, but because it stays so faithful to the stage, the immediacy of both film and live performance are lost. However, for those who haven't seen Balanchine's *Nutcracker*, some sense of its atmosphere can be gleaned—especially in the party scene, to which the choreographer added a particularly domestic feeling. This is the legacy of Balanchine's version, which set the tone for many that followed. If ballet seemed aloof and restrained to many mid-twentieth-century Americans, a *Nutcracker* that had childlike pleasures and a home-and-hearth feeling brought it down to earth. Even in the vast spaces of the State Theater, the New York City Ballet's home since 1964, Balanchine's Christmas ballet retains some warmth and coziness not always seen in nineteenth-century classics. In many ways he paved the way for the ballet's success in North America by embracing its dual personality. Balanchine's new style of classicism, his rapid transitions and complex, musical maneuverings, are always there,

Balanchine onstage at the State Theater in New York City, directing the bunny who distracts the Mouse King so Marie can fell him with her shoe.

especially in the rhapsodic ensemble dances and the swiftly delicate jumps, turns, and twists of the Sugar Plum Fairy and Dewdrop. But he also embraced the ballet's inner child, years before anyone used that term or thought through its implications for a story ballet.

In an interview about *The Nutcracker*, Balanchine remembered his own excitement at Christmastime in St. Petersburg, back when, as he put it, "No one asked children how they lived, what they thought. Children simply tried to become as much like adults as quickly as possible, and that was all." He philosophized about the value of childhood in a key that was melodious to citizens of a young country, saying that "if an adult is a good person, in his heart he is still a child."[29] Not surprisingly, then, Balanchine didn't bemoan the presence of children in his ballet—for many years, he rehearsed them himself with patience and enthusiasm. When he was first choreographing the ballet in 1954, he "seemed like a child himself," remembers his first Sugar Plum Fairy, Maria Tallchief, so excited was he about making the tree impressive and incorporating the children from the School of American Ballet, which he considered integral to the future of his company.[30] Many of his child dancers would later recall "Mr. B" taking them by the hand and showing them a step or taking as much care with their costumes as those of his favorite ballerinas.

Nor was Balanchine afraid that his choreography would be overshadowed by the ballet's spectacular aspects; it was he who insisted that the Christmas tree be gigantic and three-dimensional, even in the lean early years of the company in the somewhat cramped City Center Theater. As costs for the initial production started to swell, he was asked if he could possibly do the ballet without the tree. For Balanchine, the answer was simple—"No, ballet *is* the tree." Getting into the spirit of American Christmas symbols, he even added reindeer at the end of the ballet to lead the flying sled that carries Marie and her Prince away from the Land of the Sweets. There were no reindeer at the Maryinsky, Balanchine admitted (few people probably suspected how *many* ways he departed from the original), but reindeer were appropriate for "the general mood" of the scene and American audiences responded well to them.[31]

It was altogether a lucky break for the immigrant *Nutcracker* to fall into the hands of Balanchine, a compatriot who seemed to know just how to dress up the ballet to fit into its new home. He was also the equivalent of a sponsor with connections. By 1954 Balanchine had a significant following, and there was no need to decide if *The Nutcracker* was a ballet worthy of annual revivals—Balanchine did it, and for many he could do no wrong. No one would question the "authenticity" factor either, because Balanchine had danced in the ballet at the Maryinsky only a few decades after Ivanov had choreographed it. Although his version was distinctly his own, with only a few traces of Ivanov, Balanchine was simply "the real thing" for Americans, like Russian ballet itself. And of course, the cognoscenti knew he com-

bined tradition with innovation in a noteworthy way.[32] Best of all—
for the immigrant *Nutcracker,* at least—Balanchine was no snob. Although he's best known for his renovations to ballet technique and
his pristine neoclassical masterpieces, he could also be a showman
with a sense of humor, making ballets about saloon girls or patri-
ots who pranced on pointe to Sousa marches. This ability to combine
the "high" art of ballet with popular images comes across in his *Nutcracker,* which is not only full of swift, intricate classical dancing but
also resonates with the joys of family life and souvenirs of childhood.

Although Balanchine made no attempt to change the setting or
characters to suit an American locale, as many choreographers would
later do, he added many domestic details that seem well suited to the
sensibilities of his audience. His children in the party scene strike a
balance between formal manners and rambunctious behavior, bowing and curtseying as well as jockeying for position to look in the
keyhole to the drawing room and playing leapfrog. They love Herr
Drosselmeier, but they also fear him a little—children love a mysterious character, Balanchine said. He remembered his own joy as a child
when adults could do magic tricks, and he tried to make Drosselmeier
a more important character than he had been in St. Petersburg. At
one point during the party scene the children gang together to chant
"magic" at Drosselmeier, insistently requesting that he bring out his
mechanical dancing dolls. At other moments the party offers a few
glimpses of childhood primal scenes—not only the famous party-
rage moment when Marie's brother Fritz breaks the nutcracker, but
earlier, when Fritz eagerly offers his hand to each girl who is choos-
ing a dancing partner and is pitifully ignored. He's rescued by his
mother, but within seconds he demonstrates how he got his reputation by pulling his sister's hair.

Balanchine also added a hint of innocent romance to his *Nutcracker*
by including the character of Drosselmeier's nephew, whom Marie
ends up marrying in the Hoffmann story. The way Marie first meets
the nephew (who will become the Nutcracker Prince) suggests that

Balanchine was influenced by the Hollywood movie convention of the "meet-cute"—the moment when a film's male and female stars lock eyes to show that they're destined for each other. As they're introduced, Marie and Drosselmeier's nephew shake hands in a dreamy, slow-motion way and repeat this gesture throughout the ballet as if to reiterate their magic connection. Since Balanchine's Marie and her Prince look about ten years old, they don't end up married and living "happily ever after." Instead, the young Prince presumably takes Marie safely home in his flying sled. In saying goodbye, the Sugar Plum Fairy seems very motherly as she kisses Marie on the cheek and looks fondly after them like a parent sending her children on a long trip.

There is another scene, earlier in the ballet, that seems to emphasize the home-and-hearth side of Balanchine's *Nutcracker* even more, in a way particularly uncharacteristic of other ballets. It occurs between the time Marie falls asleep in the deserted living room and the moment when the clock strikes midnight and fantasy takes over. In the first part of the interlude, Mrs. Stahlbaum comes looking for her daughter and, having reassured herself all is well, goes to bed; then Drosselmeier comes to repair the nutcracker, which in most productions manages to become a prince without this added intervention. The plot isn't advanced at all by these two fairly leisurely mime scenes, so why did Balanchine invent them instead of moving straight into the more eventful transformation and battle? Whatever his reasons, the effect is to emphasize the ballet's domestic heart. Mrs. Stahlbaum's extended motherly moment establishes a feeling of tranquillity, while Drosselmeier, the godfather with mischievous flair, disrupts that mood, but with a familial link that promises safe passage for Marie. The mime is realistic (in contrast to the nineteenth-century code of other ballets), and the way Marie's mother sweeps across the stage with a candle before her gives the scene a grand kind of serenity, as does the violin solo Balanchine chose to interpolate at this point. It's from *The Sleeping Beauty,* but doesn't seem completely

Behind a scrim Marie sleeps, as her mother (Saskia Beskow)
makes sure she is well covered, in a particularly domestic scene
that Balanchine added to his New York City Ballet production.

out of place because of the theme, which Tchaikovsky had reused for
The Nutcracker transformation music that follows. A lone violin traces
a delicate, yearning melody as Marie's mother makes her long cross,
wondering where her daughter has gone. In the drawing room, she
shakes her head over finding Marie asleep on the couch, with her arm
around her nutcracker doll. Feeling a chill in the room, she makes
sure the windows are securely closed and takes off her shawl to drape
it carefully over her sleeping daughter. She gently strokes Marie's
forehead and glances back, seemingly savoring the tender moment
after a hectic holiday.

Drosselmeier enters after this interpolation, and reinforces the
atmosphere of parental doting—but with a twist. Each dancer has

his own flair in the role, but in the 1958 televised version Balanchine cuts loose with impish mime details few others might have dared to insert. Despite the classical context, he looks for all the world like one of the great physical comedians seen on television at the time, like Sid Caesar and Milton Berle. As he sits beside Clara and takes the nutcracker on his lap, the camera goes in for an extended two-shot, showing Balanchine removing the doll's handkerchief bandage and blowing his nose before returning it to his pocket. He then embarks on a frantic examination of the nutcracker's mouth, managing to close it hard on one hand, after which he wags his finger at the doll, as if his creation had turned on him. As he puts the doll back in Clara's arms and is about to steal away, he lingers (perhaps vamping for time or merely continuing his improvisation). He makes odd little finger shaking gestures at the tree, like waving bye-bye, which is presumably a signal for the tree's upcoming growth spurt. He then hunches his shoulders mischievously before blowing Clara a kiss and leaving the room.

It's hard to overestimate the impact of Balanchine's seal of approval on *The Nutcracker*. Although he wasn't known to all Americans, his work had a certain amount of national recognition. In the decade or so following the two full-length *Nutcracker* broadcasts, the grand pas de deux alone tended to be featured on television at Christmastime, sometimes on network variety shows such as *The Ed Sullivan Show* and *The Bell Telephone Hour*. These outings no doubt solidified the classically rigorous side of *The Nutcracker*'s personality, while its domestic aspects were exploited in multi-page spreads in national magazines. During the 1950s, *Life, McCall's,* and *Look* magazines featured colorful scenes showing City Ballet dancers around the tree, or flying through the air, or even posed at the edge of a layout advertising the latest Christmas toys and fashions.[33] For ballet directors around the nation, the possibility of gaining visibility by fitting into the Christmas season must have seemed attractive.

Although San Francisco can claim the first full-length American

Ballet and advertising pair up in this scene from a four-page color layout
featured in *Look* magazine, December 23, 1958. Drosselmeier and his
nutcracker doll are dressed for the nineteenth century, but the child
models wear the latest "'party pinks,' $9 to $17." The spread includes a
plug for the New York City Ballet's CBS broadcast airing that same week.

Nutcracker, the New York City Ballet's version undoubtedly had the
most influence, both because of its proximity to television network
headquarters, where Christmas programming was chosen, and because of its enormous appeal in an influential dance capital. Choreographers as well as dance lovers made pilgrimages to New York to
see what the master had done, and dancers who left New York carried
aspects of Balanchine's production to various parts of the continent.
In the 1950s and 1960s, before *The Nutcracker* became almost exclusively a Christmastime ballet, City Ballet did it during their summer

season in Saratoga, and on trips to Los Angeles and Chicago, each time incorporating a community of local ballet students in the cast.

It's not that all North American *Nutcracker* choreography started to resemble Balanchine's—many choreographers would put their own stamp on the ballet and many copied other versions, especially those with a putative connection to Ivanov. But Balanchine's incorporation of a familial feeling in his production is something that seems to have significantly imprinted the *Nutcracker* trend. As a godfather figure, he helped the immigrant *Nutcracker* establish a stable home in New York. After that, it was just a matter of time before the ballet found even more routes to becoming a naturalized citizen.[34]

In the early 1990s I was talking to a woman who took ballet classes as a hobby, when she started reminiscing about dancing in her local Nutcracker while growing up. "It was a wonderful time in my life," she said, her head tilting and her gaze wandering into the distance. "There's just something about that ballet." She returned to the present and said more briskly, "Well, Christmas just wouldn't be the same without The Nutcracker." Every December since she stopped dancing, she told me, when she hears the music she has at least one moment of getting "all choked up." It could be embarrassing, she said, like the time she found herself crouching down in the aisles of a gift store, overcome with emotion as the strains of the Waltz of the Flowers came over the sound system. I laughed with her, because I recognized the moment. I remember sitting at a holiday dinner the year after I left the ballet, hearing the grand pas de deux's deathless descending chords playing in the empty living room and wondering if I could explain my tears by saying I was disappointed in the quality of the mashed potatoes.

Evidently you can leave The Nutcracker, *but* The Nutcracker *may never leave you. The ballet's rhythms and a host of associated memories don't disappear, they just get filed away in part of the brain and released in flashbacks filled with sometimes inchoate memories and emotions. Some artistic directors and longtime ballet veterans call these flashbacks "Nutmares," but that's another story. Beneath the anti-Nut rhetoric there are usually soft spots for the iconic seasonal ballet. You don't have to have danced to feel this on some level—just witnessing exquisite performances or watching people strive to do their best can do it. Seeing your daughter or any child trying to embody gracious manners and attempt complicated steps can pluck the heartstrings.*

And, of course, there's the whole Christmas thing. The Nutcracker serves up an idealized Christmas on a platter full of treats that everyone has been promised at one time or other—by our parents or by books and movies and TV specials. Christmas can be a joyful and problematic holiday for nearly everyone: it's not religious enough for some, it's too religious for others; it's lonely for those without family, and it's too full of relatives for those who have had enough of being known by a childhood nickname. There's pressure to spend money, to commune, to be festive, and "the holidays" can become a time of heightened expectations and recurring disappointments. The Nutcracker, however, is simpler. Like Christmas, it always comes around in December, but no one expects quite so much from a ballet, so its gifts can be discovered in a more relaxed manner.

When I watch a good Nutcracker in times of stress, I have an even deeper appreciation for the small oasis of beauty, aspiration, and togetherness that it can momentarily provide. The first dance performance I attended after the attacks of September 11 was a non-Nutcracker Balanchine program, and I thought of what a welcome, stabilizing experience his choreography could be. It reminded me of his core classical values, and how, back in 1954, when he made his Nutcracker, he combined the Old World creatively with shifts in the New World as they came at him.

TWO

Making Friends at Christmastime

Balanchine may have had a strong effect on the fate of the immigrant *Nutcracker,* speeding along the assimilation process, but he did not single-handedly make the ballet a Christmas tradition. That process was helped along by two fortuitous aspects of the *Nutcracker's* multiple-personality syndrome—its ability to make the rarefied ballet world feel more accessible, and, perhaps most important, its connection to Christmas. Nothing breeds success like a happy marriage between a major holiday and an appropriate performance. In the late 1950s and early 1960s, when Clara and the gang started turning up in dozens of locations across the United States and Canada, they found they were welcomed most heartily in December. Although a stray *Nutcracker* will still show up in July from time to time, its scheduling inevitably produces furrowed brows. Didn't they get the memo? Wasn't there enough *Nutcracker* to go around at the appropriate time? It's as if the covenant between New World audiences and *The Nutcracker* depends on this understanding about timing. Out of season, *The Nutcracker* seems like an uninvited guest.

After all, one of the reasons the ballet got to be the welcomed regular visitor that it is—virtually a new family member—is because it dovetailed with existing holiday traditions and attitudes in North America. The ballet's visual impact seemed perfect—festive greenery, gifts, and wintry scenes in the first act, followed by a tinseled fantasy land in the second. Added to that, like icing on a Christmas cake, was its ability to represent ballet itself, at a time when ballet began to be perceived as a serious art form that "gave culture" to upwardly mobile aspirants. In the 1950s and 1960s, many children of postwar prosperity were sent off to ballet classes (at least the girls were) to learn to be graceful, and what could be more alluring than their debuts in a ballet that required children? It was just a matter of time before the character traits of *The Nutcracker* helped it progress from the status of an immigrant to that of a new citizen.

Back in Russia, as Balanchine was fond of pointing out, Christmas was a rather solemn affair, ideally devoted to reverent thoughts about Christ's birth. At least it was never as festive as Orthodox Easter, when "bells pealed joyously throughout the night" to celebrate the Christian belief that Jesus arose from the dead. Because the Russian holiday was not so jolly, Balanchine never got used to his compatriots in New York laughing and gossiping in church at Christmas services.[1] But in North America, Christmas had evolved into a jovial, sometimes secular celebration, all about jingle bells, fattening food, and commercial delights. Even the potentially grave themes of charity and goodwill took on a festive air—just picture the transformed Scrooge, giddy with delight as he gives things away at the end of Dickens's "A Christmas Carol." Like Scrooge, many North American Christmas traditions have roots in England, Germany, or Scandinavia—Christmas cards, caroling, Santa Claus, tree decorating, and elaborate gift-giving. These customs often had pagan or religious precedents, of course, some of which evolved from social custom, and all of which prospered in a climate of aggressively circulated commercial images. Santa Claus, for instance, started out as the Dutch St. Nicholas, but his red-suited image came from the pen of American political cartoonist Thomas Nast in 1863; and Christmas cards grew from the British calling card tradition but didn't become a profitable industry in America until the 1870s.[2]

The Nutcracker found its place among many other secular holiday narratives that became hallmarks of the season, among them *A*

Christmas Carol, Charlie Brown's Christmas, and *It's a Wonderful Life.*
Like the ballet, these performances, in their many incarnations, are
now widely associated with "the spirit of Christmas" without making
reference to the religious aspect of the holiday. Although editorial
writers and religious Christians alike tend to bemoan the loss of
"the real spirit of the season" as if it were a recent phenomenon,
secular celebrations at Christmas have a long, entrenched history.
By the time *The Nutcracker* earned a place in the Christmas performance pantheon, many fights over how this ostensibly religious holiday should be celebrated had been fought. Christmas has always been
a particularly difficult holiday for the Christian Church to dominate.
A primary reason for this, historian Stephen Nissenbaum suggests,
is that in the seventh century the church placed Jesus's birth date
(which could not be historically determined) at a time of year already
dominated by winter solstice revelry and postharvest feasting.[3] These
were wild times, when weapons were brandished, women ravished,
and all sense of decorum lost. Early church officials sought to abolish
all "heathen" practices, but they often fought a losing battle against
the boisterous public celebrations of Christmas.

Nissenbaum traces this "battle for Christmas" in North America
from early settlements to contemporary times, starting with the Puri-
tans' losing struggle to suppress what they thought of as pagan holiday celebration. The warring factions are characterized as advocates
of "Christmas as a domestic idyll" versus those who celebrated "carnival Christmas," which had links to the European carnival tradition
Mikhail Bakhtin has chronicled so thoroughly. In American cities
over the years, Nissenbaum points out, there were fewer and fewer
examples of the pugnacious, disruptive behavior he calls "Christmas
misrule," which included donning disguises, drinking, status rever-
sals, and aggressive begging (though as late as 1843, public Christmas
celebrations in Philadelphia resulted in arrests for drunkenness and
disorderly conduct).[4]

The times were definitely changing—and in a way that would benefit the eventual ascendancy of the annual *Nutcracker*. A significant step toward the domestication of the holiday came in the 1820s, when Clement Clarke Moore's poem "A Visit from St. Nicholas" was published widely in the popular press. This familiar verse about "the night before Christmas," when "children were nestled all snug in their beds" emphasized the Victorian idea that "the only pleasures that qualified as true holiday mirth were those of home and hearth."[5] This theme of domestic bliss, picked up later by Balanchine in his *Nutcracker*, recurred throughout the nineteenth century, notably through articles, illustrations, and advertisements in the popular press. Instead of carousing with alcohol at Christmas, a Victorian writer advised, one must be contented with "coffee and fragrant tea." *Punch* magazine, along with other periodicals in mid-nineteenth-century England, offered coy cartoons on the mistletoe-kissing theme, reflecting one fairly tame way of "acting up" within the social constraints of the times.[6]

Few Christmas historians mention *The Nutcracker*, but Nissenbaum does call the Hoffmann story that inspired the ballet an example of the way carnival customs were tamed. Hoffmann's heroine, he says, is "a proper young girl" who has "an extended fantasy of misrule in which her world turns crazily upside down," offering readers a suggestion of ancient revelries in a safe environment. In other words, the *Nutcracker* story is what he calls "a secure yet exhilarating Christmas treat—a carnival of the mind."[7] In some ways, the annual *Nutcracker* can be seen as a product of the taming of Christmas; that is, the ballet is a public event that celebrates the holiday in an energetic but orderly way. All that's left of more raucous, rebellious holiday customs are safely staged remnants of a "world upside-down," where mice fight with swords and candy dances. While Nissenbaum refers to the experience of *reading* the *Nutcracker* story as "a secure yet exhilarating Christmas treat," *dancing* and *watching* the ballet have become an even more vividly experienced "carnival of the mind." The physical experience of dancing, or the communal and individual thoughts and feelings engendered by attending a performance, seem to offer more scope for the *Nutcracker* tradition to attain meaningfulness in the lives of participants. The coffee and fragrant tea recommended by the Victorians as appropriate Christmas beverages are consumed in a proper fashion in the drawing room scene of *The Nutcracker,* and are transformed into exotic and sensuous—but safe—dances in act two, in effect providing contemporary remnants of both carnival misrule and its taming.

In addition to calming down Christmas misrule, there were other reasons for Victorians and Anglo-Americans to create a warm and cozy, domestic version of Christmas. Anxiety about rapid industrialization and constantly shifting social conditions might have resulted in great longing for an idealized, domestic celebration, the same way the current annual *Nutcracker* boom may benefit from nostalgia for "simpler times." The Christmas iconography of the Victorians was drenched in snowy scenes, horse-drawn carriages, homecomings, and warm fires, harking back to an unspecified, seemingly timeless age of "Merrie Olde England." The writings of Charles Dickens, notably his "A Christmas Carol" (1843), touched imaginations on both sides of the Atlantic and emphasized the importance of generosity, family, and childhood innocence. Like *The Nutcracker,* Dickens's popular Christmas tale makes people nostalgic for "a colorful but stable past" in the face of a fraught present.[8] The people I talked to in *Nutcracker* communities were usually not concerned with exactly *what* time period they were longing for, but many said the quaint customs and happy families of the *Nutcracker* party scene, as well as Clara's safe return to the bosom of her family, are good reminders of "old-fashioned" values that are often lost in the complexity of "modern life."

"*The Nutcracker* is part of the Christmas tradition, like reading 'A Christmas Carol' or going to church," said one thoughtful fourteen-year-old Loudoun Ballet performer, who had grown up performing a variety of *Nutcracker* roles. "The human animal falls into a very orga-

nized form of life," he said. "We repeat *The Nutcracker* not just because one of your kids is in it, but because in this chaotic world that
we live in, *The Nutcracker* is one of the few things that *does* repeat
itself year to year. It represents what a debt we owe to our history and
our ancestors and it brings friends and family back together."

The *Nutcracker* participants I talked to tended to explain the ballet's connection to "old-fashioned family" in two specific ways. First,
its plot emphasizes the warmth of a large family Christmas gathering
and the happy home to which Clara eventually returns; and second,
the performance event brings today's families together, sometimes
onstage and more often in the audience. (Ironically, *Nutcracker* season takes the performers themselves *away* from their families. This
commonly acknowledged fact is always wistfully explained as one of
the sacrifices one has to make so that other families can enjoy the
ballet.)

The Nutcracker's ability to represent an "old-fashioned Christmas"
is aided by the fact that it generally *looks* so old-fashioned—reproduc-
ing stylistic details of the version of a domestic Christmas which became most popular in Anglo-America. Costumes for *The Nutcracker*
usually approximate Victorian style—or, since most producers aren't
costume historians, something vaguely "old-timey." The atmosphere
echoes, in a general or specific way, antiquated images on Christmas
cards and in Christmas department store windows, or even in illustrations or stage versions of Dickens's "A Christmas Carol" (which is
technically set in an earlier time period). There are long dresses with
ruffles and possibly bustles for women, tailcoats and cravats for men,
sailor suits and knickers for boys, ruffled dresses and bows for girls,
and an assortment of hats, capes, muffs, and shawls. Movement style
for the party scene is formal and genteel, with adults adopting a consistently erect or exaggeratedly correct posture, nodding and bending
from the waist in greetings or mimed conversation, avoiding free-
flowing, large gestures, except perhaps to discipline an overanxious
child or to create a comic effect.

According to Sheila Hoffmann-Robertson, artistic director of the Loudoun Ballet, amateur performers in the party scene never have to be told how to move, they "just pick it up." I watched party guests instantly adopt what they thought of as a dignified or prim personality, carefully controlling and confining their movements or emphasizing fussy, small, quick gestures. They often referred to the contrast between the way they might act normally and the way they imagined proper Victorians to have acted. They might well have been influenced by movie and television portrayals of "old-fashioned" Christmases, with children in party dress bristling with anticipation for gifts and groaning tables, while adults look fondly on, embrace one another, and gather round for festive dancing.

The Christmas tree, around which party guests gather in the first scene of *The Nutcracker*, is a prime example of the way nineteenth-century Americans adopted European customs with ancient origins. The tradition of decorating a tree at Yuletide came from Germany, and was established in the United States by the mid- to late nineteenth century, but Christmas greenery had much older origins, having been a fertility symbol for the Romans in pre-Christian times.[9] Christians invented new symbolism, so that trees and wreaths eventually were said to represent everlasting life with Jesus and fresh starts with God. Christmas historian Penne L. Restad colorfully describes reasons that the decorated Christmas tree became popular in the America of the nineteenth century: "Candies, toys, and candles transformed a common tree into an exotic and fanciful vision of delight that lightened the gloom of winter. At the same time, it expressed perfectly the age's romanticism that made nature a metaphor for moral ideals. Its symmetry and perpetual green when all outside was barren reflected beauty, order, and life in God-created nature."[10]

Restad is describing the Christmas tree's appeal for Anglo-Americans of a different era, but she might well be describing the delight of my respondents when they talked about the Christmas-tree-growing scene in *The Nutcracker*, or their reactions to any number of "exotic and fanciful visions of delight" that occur in the ballet. The moment when the tree magically expands was often called an emotional highlight (the music has particularly expansive crescendos). It seems that the "sense of beauty, order, and life in God-created nature" that Restad attributes to the evergreen is amplified in *The Nutcracker* by the use of classical ballet, romantic music, and glittering costumes. Just as the Christmas tree came to represent both sacred and profane holiday rituals in nineteenth-century living rooms, *The Nutcracker* combines celebration and awe in a theatrical context.

The Nutcracker's focus on children, in the audience and on the stage, can easily be related to the evolution of modern Christmas as a children's holiday. It has been said that the Victorians invented childhood, or at least idealized its innocence and made children a focal point of their Christmas celebrations.[11] Before that time, as Nissenbaum puts it, children were "miniature adults who occupied the bottom of the hierarchy within the family, along with the servants." Nissenbaum understands children's rise to prominence during the holidays in the nineteenth century to be a twist on status-reversal rituals of older times. Instead of a charitable focus on the poor — wealthy landowners serving soup to indigents — the household's children became the centers of attention and recipients of lavish gifts.[12] The ambience of the *Nutcracker's* first scene, of course, depends on gift-giving rituals; indeed, the plot depends on Clara's most treasured gift of a nutcracker doll. Most productions show the excitement, and even greediness, of children grabbing Christmas gifts, but the idea of charity also makes its way into some versions, when arriving guests give money to beggars in the street. It's a moment when some choreographers make a gesture, however brief, toward the custom of remembering the less fortunate at Christmas.

As the heroine of a Christmas story, Clara joins other young characters like the child who helps Santa navigate in *Rudolph the Red-Nosed Reindeer* (1939), the boy hero of *Amahl and the Night Visitors* (an opera about the three wise men, composed for television in 1951), and the jaded little girl who rediscovers optimism and magic in the film *Miracle on 34th Street* (1947). Clara represents the innocence and imagination of childhood and a belief in miracles that is presumably rekindled at Christmas. My respondents said again and again that Clara's message is that "dreams can come true." *Nutcracker* advertising campaigns and stories in the popular press reiterate these themes by saying that the ballet appeals to "children of all ages," and by showing photos of child performers and the delighted faces of young audience members.

The ballet's child-friendly aspects made it especially ripe for adoption in a culture that honored and almost fetishized youth. *The Nutcracker* started booming around the 1960s, at the same time the baby boomers were growing up—or, rather, trying *not* to grow up, at least in the traditional way. By the 1980s, many of them were introducing their children to ballet, even as they refused to give up their own high-top sneakers and baseball caps. As a ballet that related to everyone's "inner child," as well as to ex–flower children, *The Nutcracker* was in the right place at the right time.

With its joyful Yuletide atmosphere and its emphasis on youthful delights, *The Nutcracker* quickly became part of the modern North American Christmas, as if it had always been there. In that way, it's an "invented tradition," a category that includes events like the modern Olympic ceremonies, bat mitzvahs, and Kwanza. Historians coined the term invented tradition to refer to any relatively new custom that re-creates some version of the past—preferably an impressively picturesque version—and gains importance with every repetition. One theory is that invented traditions come about as an adaptive strategy for changing times, when old rituals lose resonance.[13] In the case of *The Nutcracker,* its transformation into an annual event in North America occurred over the second half of the twentieth century, a time when attendance at conventional church services declined and family members were increasingly living too far apart to celebrate Christmas in traditional ways. With new immigrants continuing to pour into Canada and the United States, the ballet also gave newcomers and non-Christians an instant community and a secular ceremony of sorts, something special to do during a holiday that dominates the North American landscape.

When *The Nutcracker* became coupled with Christmas, it took on the character of a hopeful suitor, someone who was accidentally wearing just the right clothes and talking about just the right things to get on the good side of his "date"—the theatergoing public. But it wasn't enough just to show up at the right time, looking good. It also helped that *The Nutcracker* looked good in the right way, and with its impeccable ballet vocabulary, it tended to appear pretty substantial. To find out what my respondents thought about ballet itself as an art form, I asked, "Does it make a difference that *The Nutcracker* is ballet?" The answer was always yes, although not everyone could immediately say why it mattered. So I would ask them, "What if the story were told with tap dancing or hip-hop?" Then responses got more detailed and a collective portrait of ballet's appeal began to emerge.

For both ballet insiders and relative outsiders, ballet was said to be an important art form, one that was illustrious, formal, complex, beautiful, and demanding—sometimes brutally so—but rewarding. Because of ballet's power to move people, as well as its dignity and history, the art form seemed appropriate for a meaningful Christmas celebration. Many people said the score—"that amazing Tchaikovsky music"—helped make *The Nutcracker* august enough to repeat every year. The idea that ballet was a "pretty" thing to watch also came up frequently, but few people stopped with this assessment. They seemed well acquainted with the rigors of ballet, and aware of how much hard work was involved in mastering it on an elite level. Then again, it was presumed that almost anyone could get a foot in the ballet door at *Nutcracker* time, and even those studying it part-time participated in the great project of ballet as an art form. The dual personality of *The Nutcracker* surfaced again and again—it was elite but accessible, serious but fun, decorative but meaningful.

These attitudes about ballet weren't gleaned from studio classes and opera house performances alone, and I became curious about how ballet images circulate in ways that *Nutcracker* audiences might encounter them. Today, perhaps more than in any other era, you don't have attend the ballet to know something about it—or at least to believe you know something about it. All you have to do is read newspapers and magazines and watch films and television, or talk to people who do. *Nutcracker* participants may know a lot about ballet or very little, but generally they have been drawn to it because ballet seems like an important endeavor on some level—or occasionally because they are encouraged or coerced by someone who thinks it is. I see members of the *Nutcracker* communities I encountered as occupying positions along a continuum, from slight ballet acquaintance-ship to expertise. Many of them, especially the women, had taken ballet classes, but that wasn't always a primary way people formed attitudes and opinions about the art form in general. I started making lists of the places where ballet images circulate in everyday life—on television, on stationery and posters, in ads and movies. It seemed to me that *The Nutcracker* both benefits and suffers from the dissemination of popular ballet images and that audiences bring with them many notions of what to expect and what benefits might accrue from their *Nutcracker* habit.

In the late 1990s, I saw a television commercial that typified some of the most common stereotypes of ballet. Created to sell a popular pain reliever, the ad was a mini-narrative about a husband and wife who are scheduled to go to the ballet but have to cancel their plans because the wife has a headache. It's easy to imagine they are on their way to the once-a-year *Nutcracker,* especially because the husband doesn't look like someone who is often talked into going to the ballet. At first he is seen alone, ostensibly lamenting (to his wife in another room) their inability to make the performance. In fact, he is happily settling in for an evening before the television, which is blaring some kind of sporting event. Then his wife appears behind him, announcing that her headache has gone due to the pain reliever the commercial is selling, so they can go to the ballet after all. The next scene shows the unhappy husband dressed in a suit, his wife adjusting his tie. "You're going to *love* the ballet," his wife says. He replies miserably, "Bring along the Tylenol."

This commercial so neatly sums up negative associations with ballet that it inspired an indignant editorial from the editor of *Dance Magazine*. His main concern seemed to be the commercial's inference that ballet gives men headaches, but the notion that ballet is from Venus and men prefer sports is only one of the messages here. There's also a hint of ballet's association with class consciousness, in that the husband has to change from his sweatsuit to a suit and tie, in which he is clearly uncomfortable. His fear that the performance will give him a headache could also be related to a belief that ballet is a closed system which only those with specialized knowledge can understand. Or perhaps the gender gap *is* the main issue, because he presumes ballet is a graceful, delicate display unsuitable for men. The long-suffering wife can be seen as a culturally superior person or a nag, depending on your point of view. In my conversations at various *Nutcracker* locations, I found that even among fans, there were those who had ambivalent attitudes toward the world of ballet, and they were not always clear-cut along gender lines. But *The Nutcracker* was somehow different. It wasn't "snooty" like some ballets could be, yet it benefited from the rarefied elegance so often associated with the art form.

To figure out why the *Nutcracker* settled into North America so easily and why all kinds of people keep coming, it helps to look more closely at the landscape in terms of ballet images in general. "Classical ballet has a stable technique and is more or less familiar to everyone," dance theorist Francis Sparshott has said, with the Western philosopher's certainty of not being contradicted. "As with other arts, readers may in fact not know what one is talking about, but they will not feel that they have a right to their ignorance."[14] With his tongue only partly in his cheek, Sparshott describes a situation I encountered often during my research—that many people know enough about ballet to apologize for not knowing more. With ballet's specialized vocabulary and sometimes arcane plots, it's not surprising that many people think it takes a specialist to understand it. As Carol, the receptionist on *The Bob Newhart Show,* once said while turning down free tickets to *Swan Lake,* "I'm sorry, I just don't know enough about ballet to appreciate it." She is apologetic, polite, almost remorseful.

Sparshott's statement that ballet is more or less familiar to everyone is true, if he means most everyone in Europe, the United States, and Canada. Even people who say they know nothing about it can usually come up with the fact that fluffy skirts, pointed toes, and swans are involved. What Sparshott does not address is *why* ballet is more or less familiar to everyone, and what *version* of ballet makes its way into the popular imagination. And, importantly, why someone might feel intimidated by ballet enough to think they do not have "a right to their ignorance." It surely has something to do with what cultural theorist Evan Alderson has called ballet's "aristocratic subcode."[15] Given ballet's courtly European past and its regal postures, it's not surprising to find it often linked with aristocratic pursuits and attitudes. You can see the way ballet often trades on its prestigious profile in a behind-the-scenes documentary of London's Royal Opera House (home of the Royal Ballet), shown on PBS in the mid-1990s. In one scene, the resident fund-raiser responds to suggestions that the Opera House's elitism factor should be eliminated. "Hang on," she protests, "that's one of my biggest selling points." A corporate donor confirms, "We like it because it is elitist, that's why people like to come here." This donor thinks the Opera House could make its performances more accessible—but not *too* accessible, he says, because "part of what makes this place special is that the audience is special."

Although ballet in Europe has also had a life in low-prestige venues, such as music halls and amateur ballet studios, it developed, for the most part, in royal courts, imperial theaters, and other palaces of "high" culture. It's this perception of ballet that *The Nutcracker* often counters by popping up so regularly in school auditoriums. At the same time, it has benefited from the perceived exclusive quality of ballet, conferring on its participants the gloss of something "high class." There are plenty of aspects of ballet that seem to put up boundaries, many of them an inheritance from its Old World past. Typically, the opera houses of Western Europe and Russia are old and majestic, with classical architecture, chandeliers, and decorating schemes replete with gold and plush velvet. In the United States and Canada, arts complexes such as New York's Lincoln Center and Washington, D.C.'s Kennedy Center are more modern in style but still retain a regal atmosphere. And if the imposing character of the venues and high ticket prices are not enough to deter many people from entering, there is also an implied dress code and even a code of behavior — using a hushed tone of voice, for instance, or standing to let someone pass you in an row of seats. Other theater protocols may confuse newcomers; you need to know where to check coats, where to get programs, when to clap, when to stand, and when to return to your seat after intermission.

As with any specialized artistic activity, those who are intimidated by balletgoing may feel they lack what Pierre Bourdieu calls "aesthetic competence." This is a more specific designation Bourdieu gives to the general concept of "cultural competence," the ability to understand, interpret, and react correctly to circumstances and events in a given cultural setting. For North Americans, ballet has acquired "cultural capital" by virtue of its link with European royalty and its associations with museumlike venues. Bourdieu notes that works of art acquire meaning and value by virtue of their being exhibited in "a place which is both consecrated and consecrating."[16] Accordingly, no matter how many times *The Nutcracker* shows up at your local high school auditorium or dancing school, it retains an association with the swank milieu of ballet.

Another facet of ballet's aristocratic subcode is the notion that doing ballet can confer a sense of regality by association. In the case of the late Princess Diana of England, many biographical articles and films linked her childhood ballet classes and her ability to assume a royal role. A 1991 British documentary shows Diana chatting with dancers of a ballet company to which she lent royal patronage. The narrator says that "childhood lessons fostered the dream of becoming a dancer herself," but that Diana realized eventually she had grown too tall. It is pointed out that Diana continued lessons at Buckingham Palace for a while after she became a princess, and although she eventually replaced this exercise with swimming, she maintained "the figure and stature of a dancer."

When it comes to being a professional dancer, money and privilege are not necessarily a part of the scenario. Talented ballet students without funds are often able to win scholarships, although getting to a point where talent is noticed and supported may pose a challenge (pointe shoes, to mention only one expense, can cost from fifty to eighty dollars a pair, and many are needed each month or even each week). Cheap or free classes are frequently offered in community centers or through outreach programs, but ballet still tends to retain its associations with privilege. It's not surprising when you consider the kind of royal markers found in ballet, both in its noble, sometimes archaic postures and in the prince and princess characters of fairy tale plots. For my *Nutcracker* respondents, this sense of the regal seemed clearly understood as a theatrical kind of aristocratic air, not a literal class distinction—in ostensibly egalitarian North America, one only plays at being a queen. But people did sometimes refer to ballet as a "classy" thing to do. As anthropologist Sherry B. Ortner has noted, "American natives almost never speak of themselves or their society in class terms," but they often make distinctions by displacing the category of class into other discourses—such as those of ethnicity, race, gender, and money.[17] Ballet is surely one of the sites of displacement. Dance anthropologist Cynthia Jean Cohen Bull said that as she grew up in a white, lower-middle-class, midwestern town, she knew that ballet was treated with more respect than other kinds of dance, and was performed for "a white audience of social status." For her family, she said, "ballet was a means of giving 'culture' to granddaughters of immigrants."[18]

Another feature of ballet's tony profile is its association with the qualities of smoothness and effortless grace. So strong is this association that the word "ballet" is often used to describe any complex physical activity done without a hint of awkwardness. The docking of two space vehicles is called "a space ballet"; the changing of the guards looks like "a military ballet." Sports commentators are constantly comparing the smooth power moves of athletes to dance, as if conferring upon jocks the ultimate compliment—that they are strong and efficient in getting the basketball into the hoop or the puck into the net, but they do it with such grace that it's an aesthetic delight.

This association of ballet with controlled and graceful coordination also comes in handy in the world of advertising, which relies so strongly on immediate public recognition of symbolic references. Ballet images are used to promote various new technologies, with photos of ballet dancers in midflight representing "the smoothest performance yet," and to emphasize the smooth performance of cars in television ads. One car commercial in the late 1990s interspersed scenes of a ballet pas de deux, full of expertly coordinated spins and lifts, with shots of a car hugging a winding mountain road. The slogan was: "Some people just seem to have all the moves." Another commercial, for a sport utility vehicle, emphasized both the elegance and the power of the product by showing the two sides of ballet—grace and power—in a very literal and comic way. First, a ballerina in a tutu is shown floating across the screen in a classical enchaînement; then she suddenly stops in front of a concrete block and performs a karate move with her head—cracking the block in half. In the next shot, the vehicle in question locomotes serenely over a road, then crashes through a cement wall. This idea that ballet is deceptively graceful and raw power lies beneath the surface often arises in *Nutcracker*-goers' interpretations of the floating female dancer — she's sweet, but watch out.

The use of ballet dancing as a symbol for controlled elegance in contrast to awkwardness is played out in countless comedies on North American television. An episode of the 1990s situation comedy *Ellen* had a scene in which the bumbling Ellen tries out a ballet class and ends up looking a lot like Lucille Ball making a fool of herself in the old *I Love Lucy*. At the barre, Ellen is confronted with silent, statuesque dancers who make all of the usual ballet moves, while she seems unable to stop rambling inanely and gets her flexed foot caught in nearby venetian blinds.

On the other hand, a few animated television series seem to concentrate on ballet's transformative power, perhaps because it's easy to make a cartoon character into an excellent dancer quickly. A normally sluggish character might suddenly impress bystanders with balletic finesse, as is the case when Bart Simpson escapes a jeering crowd by doing a newly learned grand jeté across a ditch. In doing so, Bart follows in the animated footsteps of Fred Flintstone, who once used pirouettes to win a bowling tournament.

In descriptions of real people, ballet is sometimes used as a shorthand explanation for a person's elegant carriage and confident bearing. A 1997 newspaper article about Chelsea Clinton, daughter of then-president Bill Clinton, was subtitled "Goodbye to Gawky," noting that "the ballet training has paid off." After years of covering each role in the local *Nutcracker* the first daughter performed, the press made the association between ballet and the confidence she displayed in public after an awkward adolescence. In fact, the youngest Clinton had always looked self-possessed on stage, so it's likely that age and experience were more relevant than ballet training. There is actually a ballet-world cliché that dancers are klutzes offstage, but many of the *Nutcracker* participants I spoke to talked about the way ballet helped dancers develop physical confidence and a graceful way of

Chelsea Clinton, center, taking class at the Washington Ballet School during the mid-1990s. The press attributed her evolution into a composed young public figure in part to her ballet training.

moving. Parents were more likely than dancers themselves to note the physical changes they saw, commenting on the way ballet helped previously awkward or shy children develop spatial awareness, self-confidence, poise, grace, and dignity. Like Chelsea Clinton, many of them may have grown out of gawkishness for other reasons, but the connection between ballet and princesslike behavior is strong in many imaginations.

For a lot of people involved in traditional *Nutcrackers*, the idea of ballet as a "high" art is important. Few devotees I spoke to, for instance, had as strong an interest in other kinds of dance. Modern dance, some conceded, was a worthy art form—even tap dancing and the "show dancing" they saw in musicals had some appeal—but they tended to prefer pointe shoes, tutus, and classical lines. In general, ballet represented for them "good taste," as this quality is described by cultural theorist Bennett M. Berger. In certain dominant-class European circles, Berger says, you have good taste if you can distinguish "the coarse from the fine, the facile from the difficult, the mendacious from the disinterested, the common from the rare, the indulgent from the restrained, the banal from the distinguished, and so on through the polarities used by the dominant classes to stigmatize the taste and style of those lower in the order of domination and to dignify the 'purity' of their own."[19]

Such a definition goes a long way to explain why the arts sometimes engender suspicion and resentment among North Americans —attitudes apparent in the pejorative term "culture vulture." Lincoln Kirstein, cofounder of the New York City Ballet, who would undoubtedly qualify as a vulture of culture, once complained: "In America, where skills at speculative ball-games are fixed at a premium past any other human capacity, dancing to good music on a stage has an effete smell."[20] That questionable smell is definitely in the air in scenes from movies and television shows where discussions of who has good taste and who doesn't are the basis of comedy and dramatic conflict. In popular movies like *Flashdance, Billy Elliot,* and *Save the Last Dance,* ballet becomes a primary player in the battle between "high" and "low" culture, often defined in terms of upper class versus working class—or, more likely, "hoity-toity" people and "regular" guys. Ballet might retain a degree of respect and the ability to instill a kind of awe in these shows, but the plot often depends on the discovery that beneath every icy ballet facade there are real human beings who are "just folks." The theme that runs underneath each narrative is somewhat utopian and definitely egalitarian in an American popular culture mode—that in a perfect world, the high and the low and everything in between can happily coexist.

One of the earliest still-popular Hollywood movies to prominently feature the high art–low art divide is the 1937 Fred Astaire-Ginger Rogers musical *Shall We Dance*. The plot uses the common romantic narrative device of "meeting cute," meaning that the two stars who will eventually fall in love experience a lot of friction to get the flame started. In this case the enmity between Fred and Ginger is based on assumptions about the differences between an elite dance form, ballet, and the popular style of musical comedy. In the roots of this vintage plot there are ballet stereotypes and bipolar conflicts that continue to circulate in the realm of today's *Nutcracker*.

In *Shall We Dance*, Astaire and Edward Everett Horton play characters who inhabit the realm of high art: Astaire is Petrov, a great Russian ballet dancer who was actually born Pete Peters—a character probably inspired by the number of British and American dancers who changed their names in the early part of the century in order to seem like "the real thing." Horton is his manager, Jeffrey Baird, an impresario type first seen attending rehearsal in a tuxedo and top hat, looking like a bumbling version of Diaghilev. Baird is established in the first scene as a comic class-conscious defender of "true art," when he demands attention by blustering importantly, "Look here, I don't want to be bourgeois and remind you that I'm the owner of this company but [where is Petrov?]" When he discovers his ballet star working on tap dancing steps in a back room "just for fun," he is horrified, exclaiming, "The great Petrov doesn't dance for fun! I forbid that, that's not art!" All this supercilious posturing is countered by Petrov, who despite his ballet star status shows himself to be a "regular" guy by saying, "Oh, Jeff, I wish I could combine the technique of the ballet with the warmth and passion of this other mood." Baird replies, "After fifteen years of the hardest work, you want to dwindle into a shimmy dancer!"

Petrov himself is called upon to act out the worst stereotypes of a ballet dancer when he overhears the woman he has a crush on, musical-comedy actress Linda Keene (Rogers), calling him, sight unseen, "a simpering toe dancer." In order to exaggerate what she's ex-

pecting and play a joke on her, Petrov adopts a lugubrious Russian accent and a snobbish air. Flying into Keene's living room, he performs
sweeping gestures and fussy dance steps, halting dramatically before
her with a formal bow and heel clicks—always the code gesture for
"European dandy" in American movies. In a subsequent duet, which
he and Keene are forced to improvise when someone brings them
together in public, Petrov begins dancing in his role of a ballet snob,
dashing out in front of his partner as if she weren't there.

It's interesting to see the body language Astaire chooses in order
to play a ballet dancer who is trying to play a more exaggerated ballet dancer. His debonair style as a tap dancer is already balletic—
precise, light, and elegant. So, to show an obvious difference between his regular-guy elegance and his effete-ballet-dancer elegance,
he resorts to exaggerated bowing and fussy gestures. But he under-
cuts his own pseudoseriousness by adding a shrug at the end of a
series of melodramatic gestures. His show-dancing style does not
really change when he's supposed to be doing ballet; he uses no turn-
out, and he arranges his limbs in jazzy angles, without the extended,
lifted, or rounded look of ballet. The orchestra provides dramatic
clashing chords and he is very light on his feet, but neither of these
things is particularly unusual in a romantic Astaire solo. The serious
work of making him look like a snob is accomplished by his relationship to Rogers, with whom he is out of sync. Providing the contrasting mood, Rogers stares at him skeptically, then counters his
sweeping, silent movements by establishing a tap rhythm with small,
downward-directed steps. He soon falls in with her, matching her
step for step. With her no-nonsense attitude, she has given the flighty
ballet dancer a focus and brought him, literally, down to earth.

On the level of body language and cultural clues, it's ironic that
Astaire is supposed to be the snob in this movie, since he is immediately established as a casual guy with no pretensions (he chuckles
self-deprecatingly, and he puts taps on his ballet shoes), whereas
Rogers, who plays a hoofer—a queen of popular entertainment—is

the one who trails chiffon, mink, and maids. The tradition of aloof women who at first spurn male advances dictates the Linda Keene character's body language and manner. She ignores Petrov, purses her lips, and raises her eyebrows as she lowers her lids—literally looking down her nose at him. In the end, it's not really ballet that gets identified with the elitist label, because Petrov does not really inhabit that rarefied world. He is, we are told, a great ballet dancer, but he's off the pedestal in no time. Behind every great ballet-dancing Petrov, the film suggests, there's a tap-dancing guy as regular as Pete Peters. It's a fine precedent for the message of *The Nutcracker,* that inside the elite world of the classical arts, there is always a fun-loving ballet to give it an egalitarian heart.

But the whole idea of *The Nutcracker* being accessible and even providing an entry-level job in ballet is ignored in popular dramas that depend on the "high-low" contrast for dramatic angst. In the 1980s movie melodrama *Flashdance,* a ballet company becomes the main character's escape route from a part-time job dancing in a strip club. Young, beautiful Alex is a tough individualist who is not intimidated by the heavy equipment in the steel factory where she works as a welder, nor by the rowdy customers in the bar where she performs at night. She rides her bicycle fearlessly through the mean streets of Pittsburgh in the middle of the night and lives alone in a converted warehouse. But what really scares her is "moving up" in the world. Able to wield heavy equipment and fend off aggressive males, she is terrified of asking for an application form at the local ballet company. If only she were auditioning for her friendly local *Nutcracker* instead.

But no, Alex is forced to ride her bike downtown to the ballet company offices, where life is serene, elegant, and closed to the unprivileged and inexperienced. She enters an imposing building full of Greek columns, statuary, and dancers who look like they are warming up in an updated Degas painting. No one is sprawled out, taping toes and drinking diet cola, as they would be at a real ballet company; they are all cool and composed. In line to ask for an application to audition, the untutored Alex compares her look—construction boots, army jacket, and unruly hair—with the rest of the women, who appear to be whispering about her. They wear tight buns and placid faces; one has pointe shoes on; another stands in first position in tennis shoes and leg warmers; another wears glasses (a sign that she's an intellectual?); and yet another wears high heels (which Alex's stripper colleagues would also wear, but in this scene one assumes they represent sophisticated attire). A prim-faced receptionist increases the intimidation factor as she hands out application forms with a phrase that sums up the difference between a pop dancer like Alex and a classically trained dancer: "Be sure to list *all* your years of dance education," she intones, "starting with the most recent place you've studied, and the number of years with each institution."

Alex flees the building, but she eventually works up the courage to audition, largely because of the influence of an Old World friend, an elderly Russian woman who has always taken her to the ballet. In the audition scene, the worlds of high and pop culture miraculously merge. At first, the panel of five judges sits stuffily behind a table at the end of a long room that looks like a library, but as Alex goes through an energetic and creative aerobic dance routine, they start to thaw, tapping their feet and nodding to the beat. It's the same "snobs are won over and get down" scene played out in other popular dance films such as *Fame, Breakin'* and *Center Stage*. Once again, the elitist ballet world turns out to have a heart big enough to welcome even an untrained steel worker, just because she has enthusiasm and raw talent.

On the other hand, broad comedies and dramas on American television have rarely been concerned with seeing two sides of the ballet world. For comic purposes, ballet has been used in situation comedies as a symbol of class difference and pretentiousness. In one episode of the long-running sitcom *Cheers,* the snobbish, well-bred barmaid Diane decided that her true calling was ballet. She determined, Zelda-like, to become the ballerina she had never been, returning to classes taught by a formidable-sounding balletmistress called Madame Likova. Since Diane's scholarly and artistic preferences were constantly pitted against the cruder preoccupations of the bar regulars, her sudden ballet obsession fit in well with the pattern. She was able to float into the bar in a pastel leotard and chiffon skirt after ballet class, holding her swanlike neck and her head especially erect, and using the bar railing as a warm-up barre as she spoke of her lofty goals. The humor came from the contrast between her unrealistic ambitions (she is ungainly and in her thirties) and her inability to fit in to the graceful profession she covets. As her barroom cronies watch a videotape of her clumsy attempts, she says in an earnest, faraway voice, "Ever since I was a child I wanted to dance so badly." Her friend Norm can barely suppress his laughter and says, "Well, you got your wish." Diane's dream is dashed when she's faced with her lack of expertise in the presence of professional dancers.

More often, female characters in situation comedies do not try to reenact their long-lost ballerina ambitions—they just recall them wistfully in conversation, so that ballet becomes the symbol for the unreachable dream of any female character. In the single-woman/workplace comedies *The Mary Tyler Moore Show* and *Caroline in the City*, the main characters reveal their true childhood ambitions in episodes that emphasize the idea that everyone makes compromises in life. In each case, the main character gets a faraway look in her eye and reluctantly admits that she "always wanted to be . . . a ballerina." She then takes a bit of ribbing from friends who are surprised at her revelation, and she looks a little embarrassed. In the end, both Mary and Caroline decide that their current respective professions are far more suitable. This theme of how remote and inappropriate the ballet dream is for adult women who have left it far behind can also be seen on a late 1990s cover of the *New Yorker* magazine. The primary figure in the color sketch is a ballerina onstage, flying into an wide arabesque with her arms stretched skyward, her eyes closed, an ecstatic smile on her face. Just below her, in the darkened audience, a plump middle-aged woman in pearls is imitating the dancer's pose from the waist up, as the mouths of her astonished companions fall open in horror. The message is clear: many are called, few can answer. But the dream sometimes persists, these images say, no matter how unrealistic it was.

For women who want to recapture the dream in real life, the local *Nutcracker* is often on the agenda. I heard a story about one socialite ballet mother who hadn't had a ballet lesson for decades but wanted to be the Sugar Plum Fairy when she found out there would be a *Nutcracker* in her small town. She badgered the local dance teacher for pointe lessons, hoping to brush up in the few weeks before the auditions. It was discretely suggested that she might audition for one of the parents in the party scene, which she happily did once she saw the sixteen-year-old whiz-kids who were trying out for Sugar Plum. *The Nutcracker,* many artistic directors have said to me with a sigh, is a place where pipe dreams are chased after, as well as a place where serious students can pursue realistic ambitions.

Younger *Nutcracker* participants have often been inspired by the ballerina dreams explored in dance fiction written for children and adolescents. One of the major themes is professional ambition, explored in novels about young women who have talent, drive, and a deep-seated love of dance. Sociologist Angela McRobbie believes that such stories, with their active, energetic, motivated heroines, provide "fantasies of achievement" that suggest escape routes to young women whose futures might otherwise seem limited. Using examples from the Noel Streatfeild classic *Ballet Shoes,* as well as *Fame* and *Flashdance,* McRobbie proposes that "dance operates as a metaphor for an external reality which is unconstrained by the limits and expectations of gender identity and which successfully and relatively painlessly transports its subjects from a passive to a more active psychic position." [21]

McRobbie's contention that dance can be "a participative myth . . . a way of taking one's destiny into one's own hands" is very much in line with my own relationship to ballet narratives and one I heard echoed in my *Nutcracker* interviews.[22] As many young women did, I imagined that being a snowflake in *The Nutcracker* was only the first step to a career as the Sugar Plum Fairy. I read a lot of ballet fiction and devoured biographies of ballerinas such as Anna Pavlova, Tamara Karsavina, and Margot Fonteyn. In all of these books there were active, impressive, independent women who traveled, were revered, and made their mark in the world. One of the best books of ballet fiction, featuring young prototypes of this kind of woman, is *Ballet Shoes,* written in 1937 and adapted for television in the 1970s. Set in prewar London, this story is about three orphans, one of whom, Posy, is a budding ballerina. All three girls train at a theatrical academy and get acting jobs to help support their impoverished guardian. Focused and self-confident almost (but not quite) to the point of arrogance, ten-year-old Posy sneaks off to audition for a famous balletmaster who is on tour in London, and she arranges to continue her studies at his school in Czechoslovakia. Her story having been written in the years before the annual *Nutcracker* tradition took off, Posy bypassed the snowflake route to stardom, but I didn't see that as a disadvantage.

A ballet heroine who studies as assiduously as Posy, but who is much more thoughtful and well-rounded, is Drina, about whose adventures Jean Estoril wrote a series of novels (first published in the 1950s and 1960s, reprinted in the 1980s). Also based in London, Drina studies at a professional academy but often travels to see relatives in different countries and ends up unexpectedly getting the chance to dance there—hence the titles of some books in the series: *Drina Dances in Italy, Drina Dances in Switzerland,* and so forth. Her world revolves around ballet, but she is not cloistered. On the contrary, Drina's connection to dance helps her understand and adapt to a wider world. When she has to spend time in a strange boarding school, where the girls only talk about clothes and boys, and have no idea "what it meant to be dedicated to an art," she survives by involving the students in a ballet she choreographs. She finds her "balance" in hard times by returning to the barre, and she even learns about political oppression by reading the published diary of a young ballet dancer she knows, who has escaped from a Soviet bloc country.

While Drina dreams of a ballet career realistically—she attends a professional school—the protagonists of several current ballet stories are headed in the opposite direction. These are the girls for whom ballet is the impossible dream, one they would never pursue except that their parents insist they take classes. Typical of this new breed of ballet stories is *Baseball Ballerina*, a small book designed for readers in grades one to three. Written in the first person and heavily illustrated, it's about a girl who is afraid her baseball teammates will discover she takes ballet and think she's "a wimp." Her mother, who wants her to "do more girl things," makes her wear pink and attend the classes of an "old and very strict" ballet teacher. In the end, the girl discovers that her energy is welcomed by the teacher, that teamwork is as important in ballet as in baseball, and that her friends appreciate her finesse onstage as much as in the outfield—especially when she makes a great catch after someone's crown flies off during her recital. The heroine is not converted at the story's end—she is still dreaming of baseball—but she has come to tolerate ballet because it proves useful, fun, and less stigmatizing than she feared.

A series of small books called *No Way Ballet*, about three relatively uncoordinated ten-year-olds, also features a girl who would rather be playing sports but is forced into ballet lessons. Her compatriots are a TV addict and an aspiring artist—also balletphobic. They live in fear that school friends will see them in tutus and they cut class a lot, but gradually they gain a respect for ballet (as all young people in these dance-friendly books do) because of their enthusiastic teacher. Struggling along in six different installments, falling over or crashing into fellow dance students, they occasionally even find rewards in performing—they get to show off, impress people, and have fun. Basically "caper" novels for kids, the *No Way Ballet* series uses ballet as an arena where one can work out conflicts, face challenges, and learn to live through troubled times. Because of ballet class, the girls learn that it's fun to be creative ("Express your own inner swan," they are told); that they can live through making mistakes (you just get back up from that fall); and that it feels good to work hard and help others (they help their teacher save the studio). In an idealized way, they represent a huge number of young women who have a brush with ballet classes but probably won't stay with dance long. They dance well enough to impress school friends; they have a brief fling with choreography and impress everyone; and they go to a Lincoln Center performance at which *they* are impressed by a ballerina who seems to dance the way they feel. With the ballet studio as a backdrop for their adventures, they—like the baseball ballerina and *Nutcracker* participants from shore to shore—can be seen as part of the American trend to "regularize" the world of ballet, to bring "high" art closer to their own realm.

Ballet Stories, a 1997 collection of short stories and book excerpts, also contains many spunky nonballerina types whose dreams are not the conventional ones of ballet fiction. In "Grace," for instance, the title character is a self-possessed young woman who describes herself as "a born loser in a leotard." Knowing her mother has forced her into classes because of unfulfilled childhood ambitions, Grace tricks her mother into coming to the studio on the night when adult classes are held. Soon the ballet dream has been transferred to the right person, and the daughter becomes the proud observer of her mother's progress. The realization that you can't dictate another person's dream is a theme that also appears in Streatfeild's *Dancing Shoes,* a follow-up to *Ballet Shoes.* In this novel about two orphaned sisters, one pushes the other to fulfill their mother's wish that she study classical ballet because she is talented, but comes to accept the fact that her sister's ambitions lie elsewhere.

Not surprisingly, *The Nutcracker* often appears in ballet stories and novels. Along with *Swan Lake,* it often becomes a primary symbol for the ballet world. The *No Way Ballet* crew gets into trouble at Lincoln Center while on a *Nutcracker* field trip, and one of their balletomane mothers is always humming music from the ballet. In the *Drina* books, as in so many others, the aspiring ballerina literally dreams of dancing the role of Clara. Two of the tales in *Ballet Stories* are representative of the most common ways *Nutcracker* is used in ballet fiction: either as a competitive arena for aspiring dancers (in Susan Clement Farrar's "Samantha and Lizinka") or the background for the "ballet capers" of young dance students, as in Jahnna N. Malcolm's "Rehearsal Revenge." In the latter story, several rambunctious troublemakers, who are happily cast as mice in *The Nutcracker,* play a fairly vicious practical joke on their arrogant, ballet-obsessed rivals ("the bunheads"), who dance the Waltz of the Flowers. Again, ballet is brought down to earth, this time literally, by soap flakes that coat the snobbish dancers' shoes.

Snowflakes that have been replaced by soap flakes also figure in Nancy Drew's *Nutcracker Ballet Mystery,* which takes place in an atmosphere familiar to hundreds of *Nutcracker*-goers in small towns — except that someone is trying to sabotage the production with a series of mysterious accidents and thefts. Nancy's bravery and expert sleuthing are prominent, of course, along with the theme of good triumphing over evil, and at times the story mimics the plot of *The Nutcracker.* Nancy herself was more of the klutz type back in her childhood dancing days, we're told, having nearly knocked over the Christmas tree in the party scene. But as an amateur detective offstage, she goes through many of the same experiences Clara has. She basks in the familiar embrace of friends and family during the holiday season; then, while she's snooping around trying to find out who's causing all the mishaps, the nutcracker doll falls and breaks, nearly hitting her. After that, she's chased by the story's villain, although it's Madame Dugrand, the school's director, who eventually takes down the culprit — a seemingly mild-mannered costume assistant who turns out to be a failed rival from Madame's past. By the end, Nancy is admir-

NANCY
DREW®

THE NUTCRACKER
BALLET MYSTERY
CAROLYN KEENE

110

THE SPOTLIGHT'S ON NANCY
WHEN SABOTAGE
THREATENS TO SPOIL A
HOLIDAY SPECTACLE!

Some *Nutcracker*s have more serious production difficulties than others.
In the fictional town of River Heights, the ballet's survival depends on the
derring-do of a former child dancer who finds sleuthing more to her taste.

ing the beautiful dancing from the audience, just as Clara does from her throne on the stage, both having proved themselves heroines. "Another successful *Nutcracker* performance," whispers her friend, "thanks to Nancy Drew!"

In accounts of real people, *The Nutcracker* is often seen as a vehicle for launching young dancers into the orbit of professional ballet. Each year, photographs of Claras or Marias and Fritzes appear in newspapers from coast to coast, and many articles describe the heady atmosphere of rehearsals for the ballet. The challenges and rewards of life backstage are also the subject of a popular coffee table book called *A Very Young Dancer,* by photographer Jill Krementz. It's about Stephanie, a ten-year-old School of American Ballet student who played Clara in the New York City Ballet's *Nutcracker* in 1977. A brief text, told in the voice of Stephanie (presumably written by Krementz from interviews) accompanies photographs of classes, rehearsals, and performance. The narrative emphasizes Stephanie's joy when she is cast, her dedication during rehearsal, her awe of senior ballerinas, and finally, her return to the classroom, where she still has to keep her stomach in.

The theme that emerges in Stephanie's story is common in popular press accounts of young *Nutcracker* dancers—that if you work hard and undergo a few trials, you can reap the rewards of your endeavors. It is, perhaps, the theme that attracts, haunts, or inspires adult women who dreamed of a ballet career. This is also a message reinforced by *The Nutcracker*'s story, in which Clara and the Nutcracker Prince must triumph over adversity in order to reach the idyllic Kingdom of the Sweets for their reward. These two interlocking narratives—Clara's triumph and the child dancer's success—may contribute to *The Nutcracker*'s enduring popularity in that they have in an inchoate but powerful effect on many people who participate in the ballet. For some, the exhilaration of performance may be left behind and quickly forgotten; for others, the experience makes a lasting impression. A group of ex-Claras who were interviewed as adults in

1984 talked about having been scared or intimidated at times during the process, but overall they had happy memories. Zina Bethune, who was one of Balanchine's first Maries before eventually becoming an actress, said that while she danced the role, she experienced "a kind of high in which everything works in harmony. I guess you could say that such a moment has become my frame of reference for everything else in life."[23]

Abandoning the ballet dream is a sometimes painful theme in real lives as well as fictional ones. On the other hand, the literal pain of dancing is something that some women don't mind leaving behind. In the ballet episode of *The Mary Tyler Moore Show*, there's a poignant scene that show's Mary's depression over her failure to become a ballerina. As she's turning out the lights in her living room, she retrieves her pointe shoes from a wicker trunk to the tune of the familiar Mirleton Flutes variation from the second act of *The Nutcracker*. Looking dejected and wistful, she almost decides to throw the shoes away and give up the ghost of that dream for good. Instead, she puts the satin slippers on one more time, rises to her toes in one swift, hopeful movement—and immediately grimaces with pain. The tinkling music stops abruptly as she lets out a groan. The spell broken, she takes off the shoes and energetically tosses them across the room into a wastepaper basket. You get the idea that Mary will happily go back to work at the television station the next day.

This scene not only provides the requisite laughs and happy ending characteristic of sitcoms, but it reflects, to some degree, what a general audience was increasingly finding out during the 1970s and 1980s—that ballet is an art form requiring painful sacrifices. This had already been suggested by *The Red Shoes*, the 1947 film in which Moira Shearer played a young ballerina who must choose between her demanding career and her (equally demanding) husband. But that was an emotional dilemma, not one involving torn tendons. Biographies and autobiographies of dancers have always contained hints of how difficult the life is, but until recently the hard work of ballet was rarely detailed graphically. Instead, books about ballerinas like Anna Pavlova, Tamara Karsavina, Alicia Markova, and Margot Fonteyn tended to emphasize the pristine, privileged image of the ballerina, instead of the grueling, sweaty procedures necessary to attain such exalted heights. In more recent books, films, and periodicals, the terms of a ballerina's sacrifice have been expanded upon and more strictly delineated. It's unlikely that today's *Nutcracker* audiences don't know how tough ballet dancers have to be.

Perhaps the most notorious book about ballet hard times is *Dancing on My Grave*, written in the 1970s by Gelsey Kirkland, a talented but ill-fated dancer who trained at the School of American Ballet and danced for the New York City Ballet and American Ballet Theatre. Her florid, tell-all autobiography, with its stories of drug addiction, botched plastic surgery, and self-starvation, garnered interest beyond the ballet community. Even for *Nutcracker* respondents who hadn't read the book, Kirkland retained an air of scandal as they watched Baryshnikov partner her in the ubiquitous ABT *Nutcracker* video. Not surprisingly, some *Nutcracker* parents remembered the 1986 Kirkland segment on CBS's *60 Minutes*, which was filled with tabloidlike simplifications and focused on the darkest experiences and allegations in her book. Kirkland accused George Balanchine of encouraging dancers to abuse their bodies in order to reach new ideal forms, citing her own plastic surgery and eating disorders as a direct reaction to his demands. She indicted the institutional ballet community for neglect, saying that they knew of her drug abuse but failed to help her as long as she kept dancing. Her point of view was reiterated by the *60 Minutes* narration, which said that there was "an ugly truth behind the beauty of the ballet world, that dancers are conditioned to be passive and silent, even about the brutal truth in the ballet studio."

An antidote to Kirkland's point of view could be found within a few years in the autobiography of Suzanne Farrell, who was Balanchine's favored muse during the time of Kirkland's tenure with the New York City Ballet. In Farrell's book, her physical and emotional trials—and they were many and spectacular—all lead to success, and she appears to have no regrets. In other words, having been introduced to the grim hazards of the ballet world by Kirkland's biased tale, readers could compare them to the very different reactions of Farrell, so that either outlook, or a combination of both, could be believed or adopted. In some ways, Farrell's book returns to the narrative of success so common to ballerina biographies of the past, but she discusses the rigors and hazards of the profession more frankly than did earlier ballerinas.

"Behind the scenes" information can also be found in several other books about the ballet world, such as *Winter Season,* New York City Ballet dancer Toni Bentley's diarylike memoir of the trials and tribulations of a frustrated corps member; Joan Brady's *The Unmaking of a Dancer: An Unconventional Life,* in which she struggles with fluctuating self-esteem as it relates to her painful on-again, off-again love affair with ballet; and *Falling from Grace: My Early Years in Ballet,* Scottish journalist Una Flett's memoir of her short ballet career in Europe, in which she concludes: "Enslave the body in certain ways of obedience, and mind and spirit will follow suit."[24] In these accounts, there is a genuine love of ballet and appreciation for its rewards, familiar to the reader of ballet success stories, but because these authors deal with failure in one way or another, they also emphasize the negative aspects of their training and ballet company experiences. Their books can be seen as cautionary tales, especially to parents who might already fear for their child's future in the austere, demanding ballet world.

Ballet's grittier side surfaces in other ways too. Documentaries about ballet in the last few decades have almost always featured shots of dancers' physical travails: strained, sometimes terrified faces stare out at the camera in *The Children of Theatre Street,* a popular documentary about life at the school of the Kirov Ballet; sweat pours off dancers' bodies in almost any cinematic ballet biography; principle dancers fall to the ground with exhaustion frequently in *Backstage at the Kirov;* and a close-up lingers on Paris Opera star Sylvie Guillem bandaging her battered toes in the video *Sylvie Guillem at Work.* This graphic emphasis on the physical toll ballet takes replaces more demure images—of the slightly winded ballerina in pink gauze whose makeup is never disturbed, or the immaculate Apollonian prince—with a dancer dressed in sweat-soaked, torn spandex, doubled over in pain.

Although it has never been a secret that ballet is physically difficult, there are now more opportunities to see representations of specific hardships. A popular dance poster, which first came out in the 1970s, shows the feet of a ballet dancer, not in shiny, new pink satin, but in a dirty, torn-to-shreds pair of shoes worn with tattered tights and leg-warmers. This image and others that feature the realistic grime of backstage ballet now appear on greeting cards, T-shirts, and dance bags. Newspaper and magazine articles about dancers with eating disorders have also become more common in the last few decades, as have stories that mention the aftereffects of a ballet career—among them knee reconstruction, bunion surgery, and hip replacement. *Nutcracker* parents and dancers have also become familiar with ballet hazards and correctives through periodicals such as *Dance Magazine* and *Pointe,* which regularly carry advice columns for dancers and feature articles with diet and exercise advice. In recent years, a number of ballet-oriented Web sites, such as balletalert.com, have further increased access to experts, and featured chat rooms where ballet experiences are shared.

It would be hard for anyone involved in a *Nutcracker* to be ignorant of the realities that lie beneath the unruffled surface of ballet. The demands made on *Nutcracker* dancers vary, depending on the level of professionalism and many other factors. Many amateur dancers work hard and feel the pressures and rewards as much as the pros, and some professionals get to relax just a little in familiar choreography at such a festive time of year. For some people I interviewed, the extreme effort involved in learning ballet was a good thing—students pursued excellence at all levels, their work ethic was strengthened, the rewards appreciated. There was also the occasional acknowledgment of ballet as a villain, as a form that excluded anyone who didn't fit into its white, thin world. I've seen *Nutcracker* rehearsal directors whose cruel comments would knock the Christmas cheer out of any performer. But more often—not surprisingly, given the realm I was researching—I've seen and heard about the special atmosphere surrounding *The Nutcracker,* as it cashes in on the holiday spirit and provides a bodily connection to striving and celebration. More than any other time of the year, the disparate ballet communities all over North America have a lot in common during *Nutcracker* season. They all have visions of Christmas and ballet dancing in their heads.

One afternoon, when I was trying to teach some dance history to aspiring teenage ballet dancers in a summer intensive program—not an easy feat, considering the fact that they would rather have been working on their fouettés—I asked them to pretend they were the artistic directors of the fictional "American Ballet Company." Their job was to program a season of strictly American dance, exploring the themes and subject matter of their native land. Because these zealous students knew every available ballet video by heart and had seen many touring companies, they had a lot of ideas and went to work discussing them in a group. In ten minutes their spokesperson was ready to propose their uniquely American season. As I suspected, they weren't much interested in anything but ballet, so no one mentioned "smell the campfire" modernist pioneer pieces like Martha Graham's Appalachian Spring *or Eugene Loring's* Billy the Kid. *But they were well versed in Balanchine, so they decided on a mixed program featuring his patriotically kitschy* Stars and Stripes, *the frontier-town-in-pointe-shoes* Western Symphony, *and* Square Dance. *One of them had recently seen Agnes de Mille's* Rodeo, *and they thought they might also do* Billboards, *a collection of ballets to rock music by Prince. "We wouldn't do any of the classical ballets like* Sleeping Beauty *or* Giselle," *the spokesperson said, "because there are plenty of European and Russian companies to do that. We would stick to what was American." Then she consulted her list and announced smartly that they would, of course, do* The Nutcracker *at Christmas. But that's a Russian ballet, I pointed out. "Well," she said, cocking her head, "not really. I mean,* technically *it's a Russian ballet, but it's, like, more here now. And it's changed and everything, so it's kinda more of an American ballet now."*

She shrugged, and everyone nodded, ready to go on to the next topic. Of course, they got no argument from me—I knew The Nutcracker *had switched nationalities, and not only that, but it now often switched*

ethnicities, locales, sexual preferences, and aesthetic sensibilities. But I didn't realize how widely this was accepted, especially in a discussion about ballets representing America. This group—dozens of adolescent girls and the usual sprinkling of boys—simply accepted the defection of The Nutcracker. They took the annual tradition for granted, either because they knew the ballet was firmly ensconced in the hearts of American audiences and in the budgets of ballet companies, or just because it had always been there, like Christmas. Their perceptions were, no doubt, affected by seeing the Joffrey version, which takes place in "an American city," the program says, and Mark Morris's rec-room adaptation, The Hard Nut, a fun-filled romp drenched in American baby-boomer irony and nostalgia.

At home these students were probably still working their way up the casting ladder in local Nutcrackers of a traditional variety, hoping to pass the Sugar Plum test before auditioning for a big-show version in a big city. It was like talking to minor league baseball players who were working on their game and knew they'd be running around the same diamond when they got to the majors. They knew that, like baseball, The Nutcracker had become a national pastime.

Fitting In

At the Clinton White House, back in 1994, *The Nutcracker* was chosen as the official Christmas decorating theme, and suddenly effigies of the Nutcracker Prince, Clara, and the Sugar Plum Fairy were hanging off trees and mantles all over the building. There was even a needlepoint Christmas stocking on which two nutcracker soldiers were pictured guarding the Capitol, thus accomplishing the difficult feat of linking Christmas cheer to national defense. This wasn't the first time a nutcracker had been drafted to serve as a symbol of U.S. patriotism. The German nutcracker carving industry long ago recognized the American market by offering figurines carved in the image of U.S. presidents, Uncle Sam, and Civil War soldiers. But this was the first time the ballet named for a nutcracker had taken up residence, symbolically at least, in the White House.[1]

It was a moment the immigrant *Nutcracker* had been preparing for its whole life in the New World—all those children and soldiers marching across stages all over the country, all that hobnobbing with the common people to get their support. Finally it was being recognized as a national icon. If the immigrant *Nutcracker* had been gradually earning naturalized citizenship, this was official notification. The reason for its visibility in the nation's capital in the mid-1990s wasn't hard to figure out. In the time-honored tradition of getting to the top because you know the right people, *The Nutcracker* ended up in the White House because of personal connections—the Clintons had a child in the ballet. Not that anyone would have complained about undue influence; by then, so many Americans were involved in *The Nutcracker*, the ballet could have easily won an election on its own merits.

The Clintons' experience was much like that of any other *Nutcracker* family, except that Chelsea had her progress through the corps de ballet ranks tracked by CNN and flashed on the national news every Christmas. It's hard to know whether or not this TV exposure piqued more interest in *The Nutcracker* than usual, but the presidential emphasis on the ballet was new—and fortunately occurred in the years before Clinton's image as a family man was tarnished. The first daughter appeared in the Washington Ballet's production for several seasons, playing the "Favorite Aunt" in the party scene, or one of the court ladies who welcome Clara to the Land of the Sweets. Her parents dutifully came to see her each year, the president sometimes stealing in to see a second performance, standing at the back of the house so as not to draw attention away from the stage. In the official White House booklet describing the *Nutcracker* decorations, a warm personal message from Bill and Hillary made the link between the ballet and nationhood by noting that *The Nutcracker* had inspired American artisans all over the country to create holiday ornaments and trimmings that all Americans could enjoy. It rather sealed the deal on what might be termed "patriotic seasonal family togetherness."

This was not, of course, a sudden elevation to citizenship; the hearts and minds of Americans were won over a period of years, during which various versions were threaded into the fabric of many communities. *The Nutcracker* was a bit like a franchise operation, except that no one was technically in charge, so it never fell into the comfortable but bland consistency that results from licensing agreements. *The Nutcracker* just seemed to sprout up all over, in some ways like any ballet that travels; plots and steps from the classics have always been stolen or borrowed and reworked by itinerant choreographers and dancers. But the kinds of changes *The Nutcracker* underwent over the years resulted not only in adaptation but in virtual adoption, and the ballet often started to look like its new parents. Hulas were added in Hawaii, cowboys in Arizona, hockey players in Winnipeg, Cajun food in Louisiana. Many productions tried to recreate elements of the original *Nutcracker,* or at least stick with traditional stagings, but often the process involved the intertwining strategies of nationalization and localization. For *The Nutcracker,* fitting in to its new home was a many splendored thing.

Clara, it turns out, might have moved from Germany to Georgia, and she might be a jazz dancer, or a student of *ballet folklórico* or *bharata natyam,* a classical dance form from southern India. She could be your neighbor's six-year-old or a teenager you recognize, or she could be played by a ballerina from Beijing who joins the resident ballet company and tries to figure out why *The Nutcracker* is such a big deal in North America. Clara has also been envisioned as an older woman remembering her youth; and, of course, she is often called Marie, as in the original story and the Balanchine version, or Masha, or maybe Claire or Marcy or just plain Mary, if she's trying to seem less foreign than usual. No one formula has guaranteed financial or critical success, but renovations and adaptations seem to keep the ballet alive. Never very secure about its identity back in Russia, *The Nutcracker* has always been a good sport abroad, especially when it came to the satiric nutty-*Nuts* and naughty *Nutcracker*s that were a byproduct of the ballet's establishment as an iconic yearly tradition. Making Clara an illegal alien or a cross-dresser, or having the Sugar Plum Fairy and her Prince duke it out in a boxing ring are merely alternate ways of having the ballet reflect a particular community. From sea to shining sea, the obliging *Nutcracker* gradually became a ballet on which desires, identities, and agendas are projected.

Among traditional productions, an early example of *Nutcracker* relocation occurred in Ohio in 1974, when the Cincinnati Ballet took advantage of the ballet's German setting by soliciting the support of descendants of German immigrants who had settled in Cincinnati. It was found that one could easily imagine the Stahlbaum family in the Ohio Valley instead of the old country, and the production (which has since been renovated) featured set details taken from local landmarks. Several prominent local businesses owned by families of German descent were happy to provide funds for a respected, family-oriented holiday ballet, eventually establishing an endowment earmarked especially for *Nutcracker* performances. Until recently, the indebted Cincinnati Ballet called their production *The Frisch's Nutcracker*, after a restaurant chain owned by the Maier family. (The Frisch's people relinquished this name, reputedly because some unsavory double entendres about cracking nuts became popular, and the title is now a slightly less proprietary "*The Nutcracker*, sponsored by Frisch's.")[2]

In other cities, different European immigrant groups have sometimes been substituted. Scots have proved popular in the party scene, from an amateur version in St. John's, Newfoundland, where kilts and Scottish country dancing dot the scene, to a production in Alma, Michigan—a town nicknamed "Scotland, U.S.A."—which is set in the Edinburgh of 1905. In the latter case, Clara is part of the MacMillan clan, her brother Fritz is rechristened Jamie, and bagpipes are added without shifting the essentials of the plot.

When localizing liberties are taken, the name of the ballet sometimes changes, a strategy that works as a bonding agent for many audiences and ballet companies. "People want to feel as if their version belongs to them," is a refrain heard round the *Nutcracker* realm. The obliging ballet has seemingly never met a relocation scheme it wouldn't try. Cajun country? It calls for a *Bayou Nutcracker*. The Baton Rouge Ballet Theatre set its version in antebellum Louisiana and was lauded for preserving local heritage.[3] And for those who have no patience with Old World nostalgia, there are at least two *Urban Nutcracker*s, one set in contemporary Cleveland, with a character called

The Alma College Dance Company's *Nutcracker,* in Alma, Michigan,
begins at Clara MacMillan's house in the Edinburgh of 1905.

"Drosselmorgan," who is a Web master; and one that takes place in
the Atlanta of the 1940s, featuring soldiers dressed as civil rights
champion Marcus Garvey to provide a little black history reinforce-
ment. The New York–based Dances Patrelle places its *Yorkville Nutcracker* in turn-of-the-century New York, using local landmarks like
Central Park, Gracie Mansion, and the Bronx Botanical Gardens, as
well as some historical characters (Theodore Roosevelt takes a night
off from running the police board to attend a Christmas Eve party
at Gracie Mansion). Coyotes and rattlesnakes show up in the Tucson
Regional Ballet's *Southwest Nutcracker,* set in 1880s Arizona. Farther
west, the proximity of the film industry inspired the Santa Barbara–
based State Street Ballet to do *The Hollywood Nutcracker,* in which
first-act party guests have just finished shooting a movie and are attending a Christmas Eve wrap party at the producer's house. In this

one, Clara wants to be a movie star and idolizes a femme fatale Sugar Plum character.

Often, a dance company adopts a specialized movement vocabulary to match its theme, or at least to provide some unique gestural detail for ballet steps. Not always, though—the Hartford Ballet adopted the name *American Nutcracker* in 1997 without altering the choreography of its previous production. It became "American" mainly through renaming strategies and new costume and set designs, all of which came about in conjunction with a substantial grant from the council of the Mashantucket Pequot Tribal Nation, also located in Connecticut. The setting was switched to America's Gold Rush era, and the Stahlbaum family replaced with a collection of disparate historical figures. They all showed up in northern California at Kings Canyon National Park, where the giant sequoia named "General Grant" served as a Christmas tree.[4]

At the time of *The American Nutcracker*'s premiere, a Hartford Ballet press release called *The Nutcracker* "our national ballet," and launched into a number of explanations regarding the new version's particular form of patriotism. The San Francisco setting, for instance, was said to be an homage to the city where the first full-length American *Nutcracker* was staged, while Hartford still had a presence through the party-scene appearance by Mark Twain, who, in real life, lived in Hartford as an adult. In a slightly strained nod to multiculturalism, the second act dances were called homages to Chinese, Russian, and Spanish influences on the American West. And to acknowledge the ballet's Native American sponsors, Coffee, the Arabian dance, was renamed Eagle Spirit Dance. In fact, it was nothing like a Native American dance—it was a classical pas de deux done in fringed unitards, following the nineteenth-century ballet tradition of adding a few customizing details to conventional costumes. From my viewing of the production's second act (excerpted for a Tchaikovsky program at the Hollywood Bowl in September 1999), *The American Nutcracker* had about as much perspective on cultural diversity as did the imperialist Ivanov original. (Which might have made it "American" in a way not at all intended.)[5]

Elsewhere, *The Nutcracker*'s reputation as "one of the gang" has survived without renaming strategies. The original plot touches on themes that are close to the hearts of North Americans. First, you have an idealized family Christmas, complete with spats that get resolved and plenty of food, drink, and gifts, followed by the battle, where right triumphs over might. With creeping mice and upright, uniformed soldiers, the battle can also represent the victory of a certain kind of culture over a certain kind of nature. And then there's the journey to a new frontier—Clara striking out on her own, a pioneer who finds streets paved with gold, or in her case, snow or marzipan. Because she is brave enough to defend the Prince against his enemies in the first act, Clara gets VIP treatment from the citizens of the Land of the Sweets. But as good as things are over the rainbow, Clara returns to the bosom of her family in many North American versions, because, as Dorothy found out in *The Wizard of Oz,* there's no place like home.

North of the border, Canadianizing of *The Nutcracker* has been a little slower to take off, although in a Toronto gift shop in the late 1990s I did find a tiny wooden nutcracker wearing the formal dress of the Canadian Mounted Police. The first prominent Canadian *Nutcracker* nationalizing occurred in 1998, when the Royal Winnipeg Ballet premiered a version set in pre–World War I Winnipeg. Not surprisingly, street hockey is played by children before the party, and skirmishes in the battle scene include Mounties defending the Parliament buildings from a mouse takeover. The production replaced American choreographer John Neumeier's 1971 version, which used to run in December but didn't have a holiday theme, Neumeier having replaced the Christmas Eve party with a birthday party for Clara.

A few years earlier, James Kudelka's 1995 reenvisioning for the National Ballet of Canada shifted the ballet's location to nine-

The fortunes of nutcracker carvers have been boosted by the ballet's popularity in North America. Here, a member of the Canadian Mounted Police stands ready to open a walnut.

teenth-century Russia, but critics often made a connection to Canada nonetheless. Kudelka's party scene takes place, improbably but picturesquely, in a barn in the Russian countryside, and features snowball fights and folk-dance-inspired steps that could be seen as bringing the ballet closer to the snowy, casual celebrations of a Canadian Christmas. An advertising feature for Kudelka's *Nutcracker* in the Toronto *Globe and Mail* the year it premiered might have set the tone for such a link by suggesting that the choreographer's rural Ontario childhood inspired his *Nutcracker*'s wintry festivities. Kudelka also expanded the role of Fritz (Misha in his production) by having him

Snowball fights and upwardly mobile peasants in the National Ballet
of Canada's Russian-themed party scene (Victoria Bertram and
Rex Harrington, front) provide a change of mood from an earlier version,
which took place in a proper Victorian parlor.

take the journey with his sister, leading some to call his version an
"equal opportunity" or "politically correct" *Nutcracker.*

Because the hero of Kudelka's version is Peter, a stable boy who
is elevated to Prince status in the second act, there's a certain New
World sense of upward mobility built in as well. Gone are the "ex-
cesses of fin de siècle Germany and the fussy, repressed notions of
stuffy Victorian England," one dance reviewer noted.[6] For Canadians, this reference to stern nineteenth-century England might easily
have evoked Canada's colonial past, which in turn could have made
Toronto balletgoers think about the previous National Ballet *Nutcracker.* It was choreographed in 1964 by National Ballet founder
Celia Franca, who came to Toronto directly from the Royal Ballet,
and it had come to seem a bit stuffy and formal for contemporary
audiences. There was much talk about how Kudelka's *Nutcracker* was

more "naturalistic," a term I interpreted to mean more energetic and less fussy. Though the choreography is still precise and balletic, there are more steps from folk dance worked into various scenes. But even before the more Victorian version was abandoned in favor of one by a native son, a newspaper columnist had found a way to relate the National Ballet's *Nutcracker* to its locality, noting that the ballet's student dancers "increasingly reflect Canada's ethnic diversity."[7]

In the United States, some of the most creative customizing spins on the traditional *Nutcracker* have come from African Americans, who have often found themselves outside the overwhelmingly white world of classical ballet. In Washington, D.C., the Sugar Plum Fairy happily became the Brown Sugar Fairy in a version staged for many years by the Capitol Ballet Guild and the Jones-Haywood School. And an amateur group in Southern California sets its *Chocolate Nutcracker* in 1940s Harlem and has "Claire" traveling in her dream to Brazil and West Africa. Unlike *Creole Giselle*, another classical ballet transplanted to an African-American setting, these *Nutcrackers*, along with other urban adaptations, often switch from ballet to jazz, tap, and hip-hop. The purpose isn't to get close to the original — the holy grail for many ballet companies — but to bring the original closer to them. With an adroit choreographer, the immigrant *Nutcracker* has adapted well to a universe where it don't mean a thing if it ain't got that swing.

Jazz was a key inspiration for Donald Byrd's 1996 *Harlem Nutcracker*, born of Byrd's affection for Russian ballets and, he's often said, his desire to do something his grandmother would love. More specifically, he wanted to provide a *Nutcracker* that would bring the tradition closer to the lives of black people and might also give struggling African-American dance troupes the solid Christmastime revenues that so many ballet companies enjoy. Starting with the jazzy "Nutcracker Suite" arrangement by Duke Ellington and Billy Strayhorn, composer David Berger came up with a two-act score, and Byrd peppered the plot with characters, locations, and values he considered central to the concerns of African Americans. In the party scene, guests are no longer Victorian ladies and gentlemen who do country dancing, marches, or minuets, but contemporary Latino neighbors dancing salsa, adolescents who do hip-hop, and visiting carolers who sing gospel.

Emphasizing the African-American reverence for age that Byrd recalls from his youth, he makes Clara a beloved grandmother who welcomes her grown children and their families to her Harlem mansion on Christmas Eve. Recently widowed, Clara sighs over a nutcracker doll that her husband had given her in their youth, during the height of the Harlem Renaissance, while her family swirls around her, bickering as much as celebrating. At the moment in traditional productions when little Clara sneaks back into the living room at midnight after the party and falls asleep, this senior Clara has a heart attack and keels over. A character in black robe and hood hovers nearby, looking suspiciously like Death (the skeleton mask gives him away). The snow scene and journey to the Land of the Sweets then have a new rationale—Clara's life is flashing before her eyes. The second act occurs in "Club Sweets," a swank, swinging nightclub where dancing girls have champagne bottles tucked into their tutus and Sugar Rum Cherry gets her moves from Fosse, not Ivanov.

But Byrd's fantasy flashback is not all fun and frivolity. Toward the end of Clara's dream, there is a series of vignettes representing various African-American struggles—a confusing series of mimed scenes that perhaps are appreciated more for their efforts to acknowledge history than for their effectiveness onstage. More interesting is Byrd's character of Death, probably the least expected guest at any *Nutcracker* party. It's always hard for me to convince anyone who hasn't seen *The Harlem Nutcracker* how well the version works after they find out about Death beckoning to Clara on Christmas Eve. But Byrd manages to tie it all together with a holiday bow at the end. Clara returns from her trip into the past—that is, she regains consciousness and seems normal, but only briefly. When she sees that her family is getting along without her on Christmas morning, and

In Donald Byrd's *Harlem Nutcracker,* Clara (Eleanor McCoy) is a
grandmother who sees her deceased husband (Gus Solomons, Jr.)
in a vision when her memories are stirred by the
nutcracker doll he gave her years before.

that Death has returned for her, Clara decides she's lived a good life
and is ready to go with him. At that moment, she discovers that the
figure under the black robes is her late husband. She happily lets him
escort her up a staircase, in a new-age apotheosis that takes full advantage of Tchaikovsky's thundering, swelling last chords.[8] The concept
of *The Nutcracker* as a sweetly unrealistic fantasy hasn't been elimi-

The Harlem Nutcracker's adult Clara travels through this jazzy snow scene
before arriving at "Club Sweets," which re-creates a hotspot
of the Harlem Renaissance.

nated, just shifted into another realm. In traditional versions, Clara
dreams of an elegant adulthood and a gallant prince, hoping that life
will turn out that way; in Byrd's *Harlem Nutcracker*, Clara has already
enjoyed a long life with her prince. Her Christmas fantasy becomes
an ascendance into heaven with him.

Knowing how deeply African-American-based rhythms and movement styles are woven into American culture, Byrd felt sure his *Nutcracker* would have wide appeal. He kept family and fantasy at the core
of his ballet and added bits of swing, cool, and attitude at every turn.
The annual *Nutcracker* tradition hasn't previously been a prominent
one in African-American communities, Byrd often said in preperfor-
mance talks and press interviews, and he wanted to bring some of its
themes into that realm. He talked a lot about *The Nutcracker*'s ability
to project themes of family togetherness, something that had dimin-
ished when tightly knit African-American communities dispersed as

a side effect of increased integration in the 1960s and beyond. According to Byrd, and my own observations in the mid- to late 1990s, a large number of African Americans seemed to be taking his *Harlem Nutcracker* to heart—as did many others—although the cost of touring and an apparent reluctance on the part of presenters has precluded its presence in many cities.[9]

When it comes to discovering new ethnic facets of *The Nutcracker,* a considerably larger leap was taken by dancer-choreographer Vigi Prakash, a teacher of classical Indian dance in Southern California. Her bharata natyam *Nutcracker,* staged for a few years in the mid-1990s, perhaps represents the steepest challenge to fitting in that the ballet has faced, crossing over a frontier where no *Nutcracker* had dared go before. The idea of adapting the ballet came to Prakash because her daughter's schoolmates made *The Nutcracker* sound so exciting and important every Christmas, while few of them knew anything about the stories or technique of bharata natyam. Starting with the utopian belief that "music and dance transcend cultural, language and ethnic barriers" (as she stated in her program notes), Prakash seemed to find herself marooned along some of these borders in her first attempt to "Indianize" *The Nutcracker.* In some ways, the obliging *Nutcracker* adapted well to new customs—Clara still looks thrilled about getting a nutcracker when she's wearing a sari, and party guests evoke a spirit of communal celebration doing Indian folk dances in front of the Christmas tree in her living room. The Nutcracker Prince turns into a Krishna-like warrior in the battle and tiny snowflakes try to embody the exacting postures of bharata natyam the same way ballet students work to complete pirouettes.[10]

But something was missing. For one thing, Prakash eliminated the Victorian nostalgia that permeates so many North American Christmas traditions. But even more than that, it seemed that Prakash didn't recognize the *Nutcracker*'s dual nature and hadn't suspected the intensity that can underpin the ostensibly lightweight goings-on. For that, most everyone counts on Tchaikovsky's evocative music,

The Mouse King, in the guise of a Hindu warrior (Kanti Charugondala),
threatens Clara (Uma Kadekodi) and her smiling Nutcracker
(Mythili Prakash) in Viji Prakash's bharata natyam
version of *The Nutcracker*.

which Prakash had to eliminate because it was rhythmically unsuitable for bharata natyam. Relying on a programmatic, commissioned
score, Prakash's *Nutcracker* skimmed the cuteness off the top of the
tradition and seemed to lack a point of view with cumulative impact.
Without Tchaikovsky to tease out the complex moods traditional *Nutcracker*s can sustain, Prakash was left with the story as the main ingredient. She followed it dutifully, adding details from her own dance
experience; the Sugar Plum Fairy uses Indian mudras, for instance,
to tell Clara that "In this land, there is no anger, there is no jealousy.
. . . we are all happy, happy, happy!" This is, in essence, one aspect

of the Sugar Plum Fairy, but it isn't usually spelled out in mime. Instead, her benign countenance can deepen into layered radiance once
she dances to the complex, bittersweet music Tchaikovsky designed
for her.

Not compelled to stick with the original second-act "national"
dances, Prakash included a hula, a belly dance, and a Japanese dance
—the latter accompanied by, of all things, the Disney tune "It's a
Small World After All." This, more than anything, defined the tone
of Prakash's Americanizing impulse, which also led her to replace
old-fashioned candy canes and petits fours with Hershey's Kisses
and chocolate chip cookies. Although Prakash's experiment was fas-
cinating for the way both Indian and popular culture references were
woven into the mix, it seemed to miss the mark. Nowhere was there
a sense of home and hearth that so many American *Nutcracker*s have
perfected, nowhere the soaring ambition and catharsis that Tchaikovsky brings even to amateur versions. Prakash herself was disappointed in the result and stopped staging her *Nutcracker* after a few
years in order to rethink. Used to turning to literary sources for dance
(bharata natyam is based on stories from ancient Indian texts), she
decided she'd like to incorporate more of the original Hoffmann tale
into any future bharata natyam *Nutcracker,* because it captured her
imagination more than the streamlined ballet libretto. Without Victorian nostalgia, Tchaikovsky, ballet, or satire, I wanted to tell her,
she wouldn't really have a *Nutcracker,* but I refrained, knowing that
the annual *Nutcracker* movement thrives on contemporary swerves.
There's no reason a resonant Indian classical variant can't be created
eventually.

When I first saw a highlight tape of the second act "national" dances
in the bharata natyam *Nutcracker,* I assumed that Prakash had added
hula, belly dance, and a Japanese dance because there were schools
teaching those forms in her area. It seemed a wonderful way of working a *Nutcracker* into a local community, by acknowledging its cultural makeup and inviting practitioners of other dance forms to be-

come part of it. But it turned out Prakash chose ethnic dances based solely on what appealed to her, just as Petipa did in planning the original and Ivanov did in the execution. Thus Prakash's students of Indian classical dance waved their arms as they imagined hula dancers might do, and took tiny, imprecise steps while twittering fans as "Japanese" dancers. Their intention was to create fanciful "foreign" dances the way a young girl like Clara might imagine them, and it's possible that their stumbling goodwill was received in that spirit. Indeed, it's possible that all of the many versions of *Nutcracker*'s fanciful second act dances are recognized as quaint imaginings. However, in traditional productions, ballet's close connections with the colonializing West has often made these dances more problematic.

The idea of creating "ethnic" dances from the imagination, based on outsider impressions of "foreign" dancing, enjoyed great popularity in nineteenth-century European and American ballet. However, some of the *Nutcracker*'s second-act dances have understandably taken a little heat in today's climate of increased cultural understanding and sensitivity to issues of appropriation and exoticization. The Spanish (Chocolate) and Russian (Trepak) dances aren't usually a problem, probably because they don't depart much from established traditions within their respective countries. Spanish, with its arching backs, mobile shoulders, and head tossing, takes its flair from flamenco and *escuela bolera*, a folk form merged with ballet. The character traits that come through in Spanish variations are usually nobility, pride, and a nimble ferocity—nothing that clashes with moods created in many Spanish dance forms. And when Trepak isn't a candy cane dance, it looks a lot like Russian or Ukrainian theatricalized folk dance—so much so that a few traditional *Nutcracker*s have imported performers from folk companies who bring down the house with athletic kicks, jumps, and spins. Highlighting this rambunctious, daring aspect of Slavic temperament rarely draws accusations of negative stereotyping.

But there are times when *The Nutcracker*'s Old World point of view wears thin, especially when it comes to the Arabian (Coffee) and Chinese (Tea) dances. They are often so broadly drawn and lean so consistently on stereotypes, I call them "choreo-cartoons," which range in tone from innocuously cute to irresponsible and denigrating. These days there are all kinds of "Arabian" vamps slinking along in ballooning chiffon pants with jeweled belly buttons; there's even a popular scenario that presents a boorish male who treats his female companion like a servant. In amateur *Nutcrackers*, many of these Arabian pretenders are teenage dancers who love trying to be an Egyptian Marilyn Monroe on pointe. Then there are perky "Chinese" dances, often a coveted variation in amateur versions, in which young ballerinas get to exercise their newly won pointe shoes (the vibrantly accented, sprightly music encourages a lot of basic, stabbing toe work).

The defining dance vocabulary of most *Nutcracker* Chinese dances includes popping up on pointe with an index finger held aloft to each side, a position widely entrenched nowadays as *the* balletic emblem of "Chineseness." One young Tea dancer in an amateur *Nutcracker* told me she loved her variation because she liked spreading the word about other cultures, a naive but not unusual reaction from dancers who don't know that the "we're number one" hand position doesn't occur in any kind of Chinese dance. It's hard to determine the origins of this gesture; Soviet-era dance historian Yury Slonimsky simply places it in the tradition of "chinoiserie," an eighteenth-century aesthetic movement built on "the European idea of what oriental things were like, or ought to be like."[11] It's possible that the raised single digits are meant to represent chopsticks (there *is* a traditional Mongolian folk dance in which chopsticks are held to each side). If Ivanov was influenced, as Slonimsky suggests, by "graceful statuettes" of Chinese people "thrusting out their arms with pointing index fingers," he wasn't the first—an engraving of a Chinese character who appeared in a 1735 ballet in Paris shows a woman in the wide skirts of French formal wear of the period wearing a pointed hat and holding two tiny fingers aloft.[12]

The evolution of an imaginary Chinese dance: (clockwise from top) the common single-digit hand gesture could have been inspired by a Mongolian chopstick dance (above), or imitations of it in Orientalist ballets like *Les Indes Galantes,* first performed in Paris in 1735. Elizabeth Hahn performs in the Chinese dance at the Inland Pacific Ballet, and Tea gets the fungus treatment when mushrooms do it in Walt Disney's *Fantasia* (© Disney Enterprises, Inc.)

It's hard to speak about *The Nutcracker*'s frothy international imaginings in general terms, because the adaptations vary so greatly, but there are similarities among many traditional versions. And, contrary to critiques that the second-act national dances distort their respective ethnic forms beyond recognition, some Tea and Coffee dances are at least marginally related to the country to which they refer, at least in terms of aesthetics and a few movement motifs. Many times, being "Chinese" means that female dancers hop lightly on pointe and

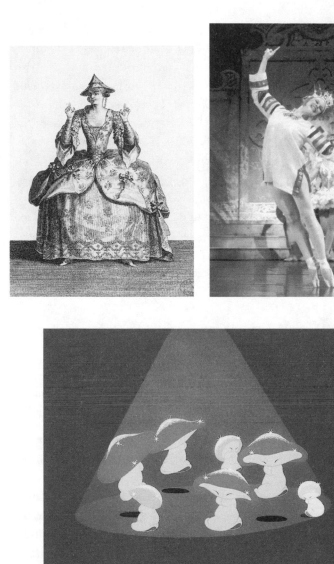

take small, skimming steps that evoke the delicacy of female style in both Chinese classical and folk dancing. Male Tea dancers (and sometimes their female counterparts) often combine dexterous beats with high leaps and acrobatics in a way that is not unlike the movements of the Monkey King character in Chinese opera. Many versions of Tea suggest the grace and smoothness of classical Chinese dance or the jaunty side-to-side movements of Chinese folk dance.

On the downside, there is a certain fawning silliness regularly built into Tea, with much head wagging and vacuous popping out of boxes. In one of the least appealing versions I've seen, on a videotape of the 1985 Royal Ballet *Nutcracker,* four dancers carry umbrellas or fans and flop forward or from side to side like rag dolls. Their exaggerated bows and deep knee-bends are clownlike, whereas the equally unethnographic Chinese duets seen in Russian versions at least keep up a sharp, light energy not antithetical to the Chinese movement aesthetic.

Watching *Fantasia,* I have always puzzled over the animated mushrooms that "dance" to Tea music, tilting and scurrying around in circular patterns—are they insulting caricatures? The rhythmic bowing might pass for a fairly innocuous spin on Asian custom, and the rapid, tiny steps might have been inspired by female characters in traditional Chinese dance forms. More likely, the animators were taken with the resemblance between a mushroom cap and an Asian straw hat, and then adapted steps from a traditional *Nutcracker*—probably the 1940 Ballet Russe version (Ballet Russe dancers served as the models for some characters in *Fantasia*). These jaunty mushrooms might not be an egregious racial insult—everyone gets the animal and vegetable treatment in Disney's world. But the way two gills on each mushroom's underside become exaggerated almond eyes perhaps reflects the cultural insensitivity of another age. More to the point, Chinese Americans at the time *Fantasia* came out (1940) might well have winced at the portrayal, which dovetailed with prevailing stereotypes that revolved around subservience.

After showing the *Fantasia* Chinese dance in several university classes where students were taught to be on the lookout for racist portrayals, I've found that most of them veer right from watching the segment critically to cooing over the littlest mushroom, who has trouble keeping up—it's one of Disney's cuddly characters meant to represent the inner toddler in everyone. By having this one tiny mushroom trailing the others, *Fantasia's* Tea accidentally prefigures the appeal of small dancers that would become a *Nutcracker* hallmark in the ballet's new land. But this surface-level innocence, also seen in stage versions, often diverts attention from the way ballet can diminutize an ethnic group. Not every *Nutcracker* Chinese dance is offensive— far from it—but neither are they all to be defended with the dismissive assumption that any critique is the result of misplaced political correctness.[13]

When concerns are expressed, who is to decide how Tea can be adjusted? One artistic director asked me if I thought that having the dancers back off the stage (they scoot while bowing in her version) was reinforcing a subservient Chinese stereotype. We both considered the European court custom of backing away from royalty and decided that it showed deference in several cultures. But I don't think we discussed the fact the Spanish dancers in the same *Nutcracker* production turned their backs flippantly to queen-for-a-day Clara as they left the stage, even though Spaniards might have been more subservient in their own royal courts. When it comes to stereotyping, there is no doubt that the *Nutcracker* Chinese dancers are generally locked into a relentlessly perky, sometimes subservient personality. Because it's one of the few representations of Chinese dance that many Americans ever see, the potential for understanding anything about actual Chinese people is eclipsed in ballet's hegemonic wake.

When I saw a *Nutcracker* presented by the Guangzhou Classical Ballet, from Southern China, in the late 1990s, I wondered what they thought about performing a Western ballet version of a Chinese dance. According to David Wilcox, the American choreographer who staged their *Nutcracker,* the dancers just shrugged their shoulders while learning an athletic, nonsimpering version of the "Chinese" dance, as if to say, "The Americans think this is Chinese? Okay, I guess." They knew about the healthy American market for annual *Nutcracker*s, and they were hoping to gain acceptance with a successful tour of a national favorite. At least the mostly Chinese cast got to play all the different roles in the ballet that time, unlike Asian or black dancers in North America, who have sometimes been cast only in the "exotic" variations.

It's unclear to me why most ballet companies overlook the possibility of experimenting with guest performers who do actual Chinese dance, as a way of recognizing the fact that world views shift, and cultural exchange is an exciting frontier that the ever-protean *Nutcracker* might enjoy exploring. It's true that a certain unity of style is sought in evening-length story ballets, but *The Nutcracker* has already departed from that formula in so many ways, it might as well take a swerve in the direction of a more authentic ethnic hybridity. Because there are many Chinese dance forms that might work with Tchaikovsky's Tea music, I've always wanted to see a ribbon dance or a Beijing Opera Monkey King solo inserted into *The Nutcracker*'s second act—let Clara *really* encounter novelty and beauty beyond her ordinary world.

A few years ago, by accident, I ran across the most interesting version of the *Nutcracker* Chinese variation I had ever seen. It was on a 1994 videotape of the Australian Ballet's radically altered *Nutcracker,* by Graeme Murphy. Here, Clara is a Russian ballerina who emigrates to Australia (the nationalizing impulse has become a far-flung one), and her journey halfway around the world sets up the Chinese dance perfectly. The choreography is of little interest elsewhere, but the concept for Tea, mercifully, takes the variation out of the nineteenth century in an intriguing way. It begins in silence, with corps de ballet members moving through tai chi patterns, dressed in dark blue work pants and jackets with mandarin collars. They stare straight ahead, breathing into their steady, slow rhythm. Just as you're wondering how Tchaikovsky's perky flutes are going to fit in to this scene, the music starts and Clara arrives in a rickshaw, the driver's feet keeping time with the beat. Having left her ship during an Asian stopover on her way to Australia, she pauses to walk through the group, dressed in a flowered frock and wide-brimmed hat, puzzling over this new "dance." In an instant, the scene becomes a symbolic colonial encounter, and Tchaikovsky's fantasy of exotic "Chineseness" seems to represent the thoughts that Clara has in her head about "Orientals." Confronted with the presence of Chinese people moving calmly in a meditational exercise, Clara wanders among them, looking fascinated. It seems to be her first meeting with another way of thinking and moving—with what is, in fact, cultural difference in motion. As the music percolates to its climax, Clara realizes she has to continue on her own journey and the last, high-pitched musical accent punctuates the encounter enigmatically.

This unusual Tea works only because of the plot changes in the Australian Ballet's *Nutcracker*—changes that take focus away from classical dancing more than many ballet companies would like. And the way it's choreographed and filmed, the Chinese characters are still conceived through the eyes of the West, looking a bit more mysterious than real tai chi practitioners (the dancers' movements are somewhat mechanical and contained, and they freeze dramatically at the end). Still, this experiment seems like a beacon for those who need encouragement to go beyond the narrow casting of many Chinese dances.

Balletgoers whose ethnicity has never resulted in experiences with stereotyping and systematic discrimination rarely pay attention to the pernicious potential of some *Nutcracker* characterizations. Partisans can be defensive and dismissive when complaints arise, ignoring the fact that some choreographies feature obsequious "Chinese" dancers in pointed hats bumping into each other and bobbing their heads inanely. The most popular defense is historical precedent. In other words, Russian imperialists thought up these monolithic portrayals of "somewhere far away," so it's okay to uphold the tradition. But not every tradition deserves veneration, and Ivanov's original choreography—if that's going to be the revered precedent—is impossible to recapture accurately. In any event, wanting to be tied to the stunted multiculturalism of nineteenth-century choreographers is a questionable goal.

When it comes to the Arabian dance, a particularly relevant discourse is that of Edward Said's Orientalism, in which Western colonialists are seen to have systematically projected a monolithic, unchanging identity onto "exotic others." In the *Nutcracker*'s translation of this idea, Coffee often features bare-chested, strutting men in gold turbans and women in jeweled bras and flimsy chiffon pantaloons. They tend to enact fantasies of "the mysterious Middle East" that owe more to Hollywood than to Egypt or Iraq. Tchaikovsky's Coffee music is actually based on a Georgian lullaby, but the choreography is inevitably sensuous, lending itself to female soloists who stretch into sultry extensions and backbends, while they are manipulated by male attendants. Although sensuality is found in dance of the Middle East, the exposed skin, male-female intimacy, and suggestive poses in many *Nutcracker* "Arabians," are miles away from any dance sensibility found in that part of the world.[14]

In 1964, when Balanchine changed his Arabian from one featuring a half-naked male dancer smoking a hookah to a slinky bare-midriff dance for a woman, he was well within societal norms, which countenanced the objectification of the female body, not the male. In keeping with his preference for swift tempi, his Coffee dancer glides quickly in arcs around the stage, striking provocative poses and punctuating them with *tings* from finger cymbals. However, her businesslike pace and almost-kitsch flippancy seem to keep sex-object fantasies at bay. Even the stately Orientalist fantasies in other *Nutcrackers* can look like benign homages to an imaginary "other" when they fall into categories I call the "ethno-fantasy" (drawing aspects of

The "classically exotic" kind of Arabian dance, with
Eric Shah and Samantha Mason of the Inland Pacific Ballet.

costumes and techniques from Eastern dance forms) or the "classically exotic Arabian" (incorporating unusual angles and pacing but
retaining esteemed aspects of ballet technique). There are pejorative
versions (the harem stereotypes of Rudolf Nureyev's Arabian, for instance), but I've seen many more that qualify as interesting ballet–
Middle East hybrids. They don't aspire to ethnographic authenticity;
they seem content to imagine that dancers from "afar" have the same
qualities that are revered here "at home."

While most traditional *Nutcracker* producers seem unconcerned about potential ethnic insults, alternative *Nutcracker*s often work in opposition to stereotypes by lampooning them. In his *Harlem Nutcracker*, Donald Byrd tweaks the one-note "sensual Middle East" Arabian dance by making it an overblown body-building fantasy. He toys with objectifying the male body by having a nearly nude sultan figure at the center, but makes him a comical narcissist who can't get his harem to do his bidding. In *The Hard Nut*, Mark Morris also takes a satirical stab at Coffee, this time creating a drag fantasy worthy of a B-movie desert oasis—a sort of "Morris of Arabia," in which he swans around in chiffon and makes Bette Davis eyes at everyone. And lest the viewer think that only non-European clichés can be tweaked, Morris includes in his second act a "French" dance (using the Mirleton Flutes music) that hits you over the head with the way Americans have traditionally stereotyped the French. Snooty and stylish, one character carries a hatbox, one a baguette, and one a whip. Morris brings surface-level ethnic judgments out of the closet and parades them in a comical corrective to years of unsophisticated *Nutcracker* ethnocentrism.

Experimental and satiric *Nutcracker*s tend to highlight members of communities that have traditionally been excluded in ballet land, often bringing to the mix the rhythms of merengue, reggae, swing, breakdancing, or martial arts. Off-center *Nutcracker*s have featured people in wheelchairs dancing, a piñata dance replacing Mother Ginger, and a Caribbean carnival taking over where waltzing flowers usually reign. Socially reflective *Nutcracker*s have made Clara a divorcée on the make and the Stahlbaums a dysfunctional lot in need of family counseling. The battle scene, naturally enough, has been portrayed as gang warfare on occasion, or it has vanished altogether when special envoys successfully negotiate a peace agreement between mice and soldiers. Feminist versions have worked Barbie and Ken critiques into the scenario and given the Sugar Plum Fairy combat boots. One politically charged *Nutcracker* made Drosselmeier a gay skateboarder whose lover had just died of AIDS—this in the San

The San Francisco Lesbian/Gay Freedom Band invites everyone to rent
a tutu or bring a tiara to join in the *Dance-Along Nutcracker*.

Francisco–based Dance Brigade's *Revolutionary Nutcracker Sweetie*,
once called "a two-act treatise on what ails America and the world."
For several years in the 1980s and 1990s, this version featured dances
for the latest animals and plants on the endangered species list and
put the faces of political bullies on the many heads of the evil Mouse
King.[15]

If *The Nutcracker* has become "the people's ballet" in so many re-
spects, the "dance-along *Nutcracker*," a tradition that exists in more
than one locale, must be the end product of Americans' intimacy with
the ballet. Inviting ticket holders into the performance was a logical
next step, following in the wake of the "sing-along" Handel's *Messiah*
tradition. One notable "dance-along" is given by the San Francisco

Lesbian/Gay Freedom Band as part of their mandate to connect gay and straight communities through musical events. (San Francisco seems to be a hotbed of transgressive *Nutcrackers*.) Enthusiasts of all stripes show up in matching tutus and tiaras and can rent wands and wings from a concession stand on site.[16]

Unconventional *Nutcrackers* have a special appeal to irreverent baby boomers and the generations that followed them, but *The Nutcracker* didn't make it to the White House on its reputation for being cheeky, or even because of its putative multiculturalism. The core of the annual *Nutcracker* movement is still the traditional ballet version, which has its own myriad ways of nestling into different locations, even without offering a specific ethnic or geographical spin. Conventional *Nutcrackers* of all stripes manage to attach themselves to different communities by multiple threads. Some versions attract attention with cameo appearances by local celebrities unrelated to the ballet world, often to raise money for a favorite charity. A popular radio host might make a toast at the Stahlbaum party, politicians might learn how to roll out the cannon during the battle scene, or athletes from local teams might be persuaded to don tin soldier outfits and gang up on the Mouse King. At a San Diego Ballet charity benefit in the 1990s, legendary tapper Fayard Nicholas played Clara's grandfather. Nicholas, who had always loved *The Nutcracker,* brought his own dance floor to the party in the first act and didn't change his way of moving—"I figured I was Clara's *tap-dancing* grandfather," he said.

The presence of unusual guest stars emphasizes the fact that *The Nutcracker* makes friends in high places, but the center of attention is more often the children recruited locally. They guarantee that a sizable number of friends and relatives will have a personal stake in the ballet each year. In all but the best-funded ballet companies, there are also nonprofessional adults—often nondancing adults—who take the roles of parents, grandparents, and maids in the party scene. Whole

Because his grandniece Lauren Porter played Clara with the San Diego Ballet, the legendary Fayard Nicholas, of the Nicholas Brothers, became a tap-dancing grandfather in the party scene for one gala *Nutcracker* in the early 1990s. (Porter went on to dance with Alonzo King's Lines Ballet.)

families end up getting involved, either onstage or in the phalanx of volunteers backstage. And in the audience, individuals, friends, and families make yearly attendance a holiday tradition.

Without this strong level of audience involvement and volunteer support, *The Nutcracker* doesn't thrive. In other words, it takes a village to make a *Nutcracker*. In the Loudoun Ballet production I researched in Leesburg, Virginia, the idea of the whole community pitching in is something I heard in almost any description of the event. It's even enacted at the start of their performances, when party guests travel down the aisles of the theater before mounting stairs to the stage. The performers' literal "coming out of" the community is considered by locals to be one of the more attractive, unique features of their production. (The Mouse King used to come through the audience as well, but too many children took the "evil among us" aspect seriously and became hysterical.) During the production process, pitching in comes from all sides, and often the professional skills of volunteers determine their *Nutcracker* contributions. In Leesburg, a local artist came every year to touch up Victorian detail painted on the sets, which were a collection of movable flats designed by a local architect. The set was built, repaired, and moved by volunteers with some carpentry expertise (or anyone who could hold a hammer). A seamstress and various people who could sew made costumes, and a company board member who had a barn and a truck stored them. When the lights inside the mouse masks started failing one year, a ballet father who was an electrical engineer repaired the wires. In the lobby during performances, a local doctor was on call for ankle injuries while she staffed the flower table, and a retired CIA agent and army veteran was affectionately known as "the general" because of the way he took charge of the unruly little boys who played soldiers (he ran a tight ship, and the quick change from the party to the battle scene ran like a well-oiled military maneuver).When there were any personality conflicts of great note—and they are sometimes as frequent as pliés, as any *Nutcracker* veteran knows—there was even advice on tap from a few cast members who were professionals working in the mental health care and juvenile justice systems.

Audience outreach was considered an integral part of the Loudoun Ballet's *Nutcracker,* a perfect way to combine the spirit of the season with audience building. For their two weekends of performances, a few hundred free tickets were sent to organizations involving people who might not ordinarily come to the ballet—local old-age homes, women's shelters, organizations for people with disabilities and youth at risk. Hometown scout troops took turns serving as ushers, and a different local music group performed Christmas carols before each performance. The two-table ballet boutique in the lobby carried some crafts made locally, and nearby stood a homemade display of photos and text about the ballet's history. For a while, volunteer bakers tried to match intermission snacks to the *Nutcracker* theme—gingerbread and candy canes—but rich chocolate chip cookies, bought cheaply in bulk, won out. The coffee urn was strategically labeled "Arabian Coffee," although it was actually the finest Colombian from the local Starbucks. Following the great American entrepreneurial tradition, the ballet company received discounts on snacks as well as lumber and other materials for the production in exchange for advertising in the program.

All the participants, from the six-year-olds to the oldest volunteers, tended to call the Loudoun *Nutcracker* "a big family" at one time or another. "It's one big dysfunctional family," they joked on days when a fight over who got the blue costume broke out, or when no one could convince one teenager not to use her newly acquired lexicon of dirty words in front of the tots in party attire. But most of the time, it was clear that everyone was working on their happy, "spirit of Christmas" attitudes, and the rhetoric of *Nutcracker* togetherness ran high. People perked up when I wanted to know about their personal *Nutcracker* experiences, an attitude I encountered in Toronto as well, although it took longer to get through the red tape of a professional company there. In fact, no matter where I talked to people involved in the *Nutcracker* phenomenon, I found a heartening amount of enthusiasm for discussing its ramifications.

Many of the people I talked to in both locations couldn't believe their luck at meeting someone as interested in the details as they were. No one tired of enumerating all the wonderful aspects of *The Nutcracker*—parents said their children bloomed after using hard-won skills in performance, that they learned what cooperative effort can achieve, and that the discipline of ballet and performance strengthened character. Children talked about dreams coming true (for Clara and themselves), how all the hard work paid off, and how they liked meeting different people in the audience, as if all of this were as exciting as playing video games or watching TV. The parents of one adolescent girl who was learning-disabled said ballet was the only activity in which she was mainstreamed, and every year the artistic director managed to find (or invent) a role she could fit into.

In Leesburg, volunteers and audience members beamed with pride over what "the community" had accomplished. After a while, I also heard the gossip and complaints about who worked the hardest, who took the credit, and who made the most trouble. There was the time when an offended volunteer quit and refused to return the company mailing and reservations list (actually, this happened twice), and the year a mother withdrew her son because of a casting dispute ("He's not Fritz? Forget it"). Then came the afternoon when three teenage performers were caught drinking wine in the parking lot between performances, putting in jeopardy the company's rental of the high school auditorium, where there was a zero-tolerance policy regarding drugs and alcohol. What I found when I followed some of these behind-the-scenes dramas through to a resolution was that the perceived ideals of *The Nutcracker* were often evoked in order to aid reintegration of disgruntled participants. "The most important thing is that we are able to enjoy this *Nutcracker* as a community," the artistic director told a particularly unhappy crew member one day. "Isn't there some way we can negotiate this difference of opinion and get

The "happy family" aspect of *The Nutcracker* is reflected here in the party
scene of the Loudoun Ballet's production, presided over by
Susan and Frank Shumaker (center).

on with it?" Well, yes, it was decided, why jeopardize the happiness
of a community at Christmas because of a backstage spat? *Nutcracker*
life went on.

In dressing room pep talks before each performance, the Loudoun
Ballet artistic director rekindled flagging spirits by reminding the
cast about their responsibility to the audience. "This may be the tenth
time you've done it and maybe you're tired, but this could be their
first *Nutcracker*," she told them, "and it could be the highlight of their
Christmas, our gift to the community." This avowed spirit of community and Christmas generosity spilled over into welcoming me,
someone who sat with a notebook watching everything, and tape-
recording everyone as they spoke about their lives in relation to *The
Nutcracker*. I heard about the many ways people negotiated their in-

volvement and rationalized the amount of time they donated with no monetary reward—everything from, "It's art; it's just beautiful, I have fun," to, "It's giving back to the community," or, "Kids learn so much from the discipline, it's educational," and, "It celebrates the season, the family, and the community."

I also found out why many volunteers got addicted to the tradition, why they often swore off *The Nutcracker* in January but were ready to plunge in again by sign-up time the next fall. The dancers, of course, had their next roles picked out and worked hard all year to merit a promotion to another level; they were addicted to progress. The adolescent girls were also thinking of which boys they knew who could be drafted to be their partners in the party scene, and adults secretly harbored ambitions of finally getting to wear one of the satin party dresses. Little mice grew into Claras, and Claras became Sugar Plums; bon bons and Claras alike became appreciative audience members, still thinking of themselves as "part of the family." One adolescent boy who started as Fritz became an teenage party guest and then ran lights and served as a butler in the party scene before he finally grew into the Drosselmeier costume. Some performers and backstage volunteers didn't have family living close by (or family they were talking to), and they found the Christmas camaraderie of *The Nutcracker* a cheerful substitute at holiday time. Those who were already members of close families liked getting to know people they might otherwise never have met.

Some *Nutcracker*s sponsor a "Sugar Plum Fair" or "Tea with Clara," and backstage tours to increase community interest at Christmas. To encourage interaction between performers and audience members, the Loudoun Ballet has an autograph signing session after all matinees (a blank page is labeled for the purpose in the program), and a flower table in the lobby sells bouquets that can be given to performers. It was in these postperformance autograph sessions that a particularly warm sense of communal togetherness could be seen. On one particular afternoon, I stood at the back of the auditorium

Lead flower soloist Meredith Piper of the Loudoun Ballet signs
autographs at the edge of the stage after a matinee. Making performers
accessible to audience members is an effective strategy for
recruitment and the fostering of community goodwill.

watching the performers, still in costume, swinging their legs at the
edge of the stage and writing "May all your Christmas dreams come
true," and "Come dance with us, you can be a snowflake too!" on
proffered programs. Parents were taking photographs in front of the
tree for next year's Christmas card, strangers were examining costumes close up, and small audience members were looking at every
performer with big eyes.

When I wandered around in the crowd, I overheard formerly mute,
worried young dancers fielding compliments securely; I met a former
Sugar Plum who was now in medical school and could barely keep
tears out of her eyes when she talked about missing *The Nutcracker.*
I heard about a teenage reporter from a high school newspaper who
said breathlessly, after completing her interviews, "I didn't realize
how much work was involved!" I talked to a high school teacher who
used *The Nutcracker* as part of a unit on American culture ("It's about
Christmas and being polite and having an adventure," she told stu-

The author (second from right) as a snowflake in Fernand Nault's
Nutcracker, set on the Louisville Ballet in 1963.

dents). I heard one young performer declaring, "Our *Nutcracker* is
much better than the Baryshnikov one," and more than one adult saying, "I didn't realize we had such a quality show in our own neigh-
borhood."

It made sense to find this familial spirit thriving in a *Nutcracker*
that depended on community involvement, but as I moved on to
do research in Toronto at the National Ballet of Canada, I wondered
what the attitudes would be like there.[17] When *Nutcracker* season rolls
around in professional companies, I knew, eyes tend to roll, toes are
taped twice, and veteran dancers claim they only *just* got the leftover
snow out of the bottom of their dance bags. This is the real world,
where you can't drop out if you have too much homework, and where
you may never be home for the holidays because the rest of the world
needs to celebrate with a ballet. Could a strong sense of seasonal soli-

darity arise in this climate? The short answer is yes, but I had to dig just a bit to get beyond the knee-jerk *Nut*-bashing that always goes on in the professional ballet world.

Unlike the amateur production in Leesburg, which was less than a decade old, the National Ballet *Nutcracker* had played annually since 1964, and even though a new version had revived the tradition in 1995, the annual-grind feeling was still strong. There were other differences between a professional and amateur *Nutcracker*, of course; the scope and quality of the National Ballet's production put it in a different league than that of a community-based ballet. Although many amateur ballets operate under strict rules and regulations, the stakes are higher with a company like the National Ballet of Canada, with its unions, contract negotiations, well-defined hierarchy, and, of course, its big budget and roster of some of the best-trained dancers in the world. Also, Toronto is a city of about two and a half million people, compared to the relatively rural Leesburg location (Leesburg is within commuting distance of Washington, D.C., but still feels a lot like a small town). In the ballet world, these differences make for a quantum leap, but in the *Nutcracker* world, it's only steps from one Land of the Sweets to another. Dancers in both locations strive for perfection and promotion, children imitate adults, and there is a sense of ordeal and celebration at the same time. Although *Nutcracker* productions and conditions vary, at Christmastime the worlds of professional and amateur ballet have more in common than not.

Like the serious dancers in Leesburg (where the training standard is high), the professionals in Toronto said that in *The Nutcracker,* they hope for good casting, and that they treasure certain moments for their sublime merging of music and dance. Professionals have more reason to complain about the downside of the season, because they do more performances, and a long run of the same ballet often results in fatigue, strain, and increased injury, but these problems show up in amateur companies as well. Professionals are more likely to crave choreographic innovation and so appreciate *Nutcracker* overhauls and new challenges, but in both settings there are performers who embrace familiar moments in their productions, especially when the music seems to enhance a particular movement and sets off memories and emotions. Amateurs are often just getting to know these pleasures; *Nutcracker* veterans can be more cynical. The annual *Nutcracker* may also throw into high relief a dancer's lack of progress in a company. But I found that many longtime National Ballet members had a real soft spot for a ballet they had grown up with; on the other hand, there was little special feeling for it when it came to a few dancers who had trained in places far from annual *Nutcracker* turf. A corps member from Beijing shrugged and said the ballet was like any other to her, but she said this quietly, looking around as if she didn't want to offend her friends who had a stronger attachment to it.

Already members of a closely knit company, National Ballet dancers said the family feeling backstage swells during the holidays. One principal dancer found that the spirit was similar to that of an amateur *Nutcracker* company where she guested each year, but she thought National Ballet dancers were much more like a close family than a community-based company could ever be, even though amateurs get close to one another while pulling together to put on a show. During the National's *Nutcracker* season, dancers decorate dressing rooms, shop together on breaks, bake for each other, and exchange gifts. When student dancers arrive, the adults joke about being invaded by short people (watching their language becomes a priority), but many enjoy the interaction with young dancers, happily passing along performing tips and remembering how they looked up to their idols at that age. Toward the end of the run, those who would have preferred root canal to hearing the Snowflake Waltz one more time said their spirits were often lifted by hearing kids in the house and knowing what a momentous event the show was for them. One principal dancer said that while she might not look forward to another *Nutcracker* on her way to the theater, she brightened up when she passed kids in their best clothes, lining up to get in. Because audiences' enthusiasm isn't usually in doubt and "customer satisfaction" tends to be high, some professionals are heartened by the idea that ballet is connecting to a wider than usual audience.

As in any ballet company, younger company members in the National look forward to *Nutcracker* time as a chance to prove themselves, often stepping into new roles on short notice or showing that they are troopers and quick learners by switching sides in the flower corps when someone falls out with flu. Because there are so many roles and so many performances, dancers are often generous about sharing the spotlight—letting the person with whom they alternate a solo do the role on a day that relatives are there, for example. That makes *Nutcracker* season less competitive than other times of the year. The presence of children in major roles adds another element of egalitarianism to the usual professional hierarchy—"It means not all the focus is on principal dancers," said one corps member. Several company members make guest Sugar Plum and Prince appearances in amateur companies, good-naturedly noticing that they are not always the stars of the show when audience members have relatives onstage. Laughing at the fact that her end-of-show bouquet was taken from her quickly and put back in the fridge for the next night, one guest Sugar Plum said, "We just do our little part like everybody else, and we all worked together to make it work. It's refreshing." At *Nutcracker* time, she said, conditions can be trying with amateur companies (makeshift dressing rooms, a taped score, dancers of variable quality), but at heart, she liked the idea of *The Nutcracker* as "a kind of standard that we can all share." A new National Ballet corps member had actually had the experience of dancing in the Loudoun Ballet *Nutcracker,* having been a teenage Sugar Plum before studying in Toronto. She searched her brain for differences in the experiences; certainly the world of big ballet had at first been intimidating. But she found that her level of striving, her friendships, and the holiday spirit of *Nutcracker* season were similar in both locations.

It isn't that all semblance of the pressure-ridden world of professional ballet disappears at the National Ballet during *Nutcracker* season—not at all; the stakes are still high. One corps member noted that yes, they were close like a family, but when it came to casting and nurturing, "there are always the special children and the ones that are a little less special." One of the years I was researching in Toronto, there were tense contract negotiations going on, but, in general, when Christmas rolls around, there is a slightly different atmosphere backstage, as if an old, benign relative has returned—and professionals can think of compensations for putting up with your relatives. When their familiar *Nutcracker* got a makeover in 1995, the new challenges were appreciated, but most everyone concurred that even in their older version, which had been poking along for too many years, there were rhapsodic moments. The old Waltz of the Flowers, for instance, was "corny" in a way, but wonderful, one long-time company member told me. Maybe it was too easy to dance—but no, he said, reconsidering; it was never that easy, it's just that the familiarity allowed him to "get lost in the music" without being distracted by technical details. It wasn't a production in which you proved your brilliance with something surprising or virtuosic, several company members said, but it had its charms.

The "pitch-in" mentality is naturally not the same with a professional company, but at *Nutcracker* time, that didn't seem to prevent regular National Ballet volunteers and audience members from feeling particularly close to their "home" ballet company, and doing their part to help—at least when it came to atmosphere. If participants in the Leesburg *Nutcracker* tend to feel like a big family and the National Ballet members like a tightly knit family, many people who surround the Toronto *Nutcracker* tend to see themselves a little more like extended family or even distant relations. They may not know anyone in the cast, but they feel like they are being invited to a reunion of sorts. "When you've been attending performances for years and years," I was told by a longtime National Ballet subscriber, "you feel like part of the *Nutcracker* family even when you don't know any-one onstage."

The exception to this attitude was found in a clutch of Toronto balletomanes who sniffed at regular *Nutcracker* attendance and said they only go to see a particular dancer try a new role. Perhaps they take a friend to see the show, but the kind of friend who wants to go was likened to a church member who only shows up at Christmas and Easter. Unlike balletomanes in Leesburg, for whom *The Nutcracker* represents the strongest classical tradition locally, Toronto cognoscenti often described it as a ballet "more for the general public," or for "people looking for something easily accessible." Interestingly, I never encountered this attitude among New Yorkers who regularly go to see New York City Ballet's *Nutcracker;* I talked to several longtime ballet supporters there, both dance critics and "civilians" who paid homage to the Christmas ballet each year. That might be due, at least in part, to the quality of Balanchine's version and the strength of his reputation, compared to the very ordinary Franca *Nutcracker* that ran for years in Toronto. Or it might be a fundamental difference between New York and Toronto balletomanes.

Despite the age and creakiness of the National Ballet's old version, feelings of ownership and loyalty among some ballet subscribers ran high when the new Kudelka *Nutcracker* premiered. The old version only needed new sets and costumes, some complained; there was no need to toss everything out. Others embraced the new, praising the lavish sets and special effects, inspired by—press reports all proclaimed—the company's desire to compete with lavish musicals that were taking away business. Much of the choreography looked so frantic and complex, it seemed as if Kudelka were saying, "My *Nutcracker* will *not* be easy." (It was not his first choice when it came to putting his stamp on a classic, but somebody had to do it.) Some subscribers wrote letters of complaint about what they missed in the old show— "the good old cardboard sets and the brightly-colored costumes said

Christmas for me better than any other play or movie," wrote one dejected audience member. Where was the charm in all the new special effects and fancy choreography? another asked. With characters altered, it was like losing "dear old friends."[18]

One loyal subscriber had less trouble adjusting because she'd already gone through the greatest *Nutcracker* shock of her life when she lived in Winnipeg and went to see the John Neumeier version. She got through the disappointment of finding out Clara was now having a birthday, not a Christmas party, but when the snow-scene music started and there were no snowflakes, it was just too much. "I remember actually sitting in the balcony with tears of frustration in my eyes," she told me, "because they had taken something that I treasured very much and they had tampered with it." Although the jury is still out on Kudelka's tampering (the choreography is too busy for many), letters of complaint dwindled. The consensus was that Kudelka's revisions had left enough of the story line and themes of the ballet intact, so that *Nutcracker* lovers, as one of them put it, didn't feel "as if we had the rug pulled out from under us."

Watching the many ways in which the Leesburg and Toronto residents took their *Nutcracker*s to heart, I realized that at some point in the life of the ambitious immigrant *Nutcracker*—sometime during the rise to prominence after the mid-1960s and throughout the prosperous 1980s—North Americans had escalated the process of assimilation by taking charge of the ballet. No longer was *The Nutcracker* seen as a Russian creation that visited the New World in completed form; it was the template for a ballet. As an immigrant, it had a strong character and warm heart, but it was ready to transmogrify and put down roots wherever it might roam. Companies like the Loudoun Ballet embraced the ballet as a communal event, something that represented their talents, Christmas spirit, and ideals. And in a professional company like the National Ballet of Canada, *The Nutcracker* provided a familiar and familial yearly touchstone, a ballet easily embraced.

Given the wealth of changes *The Nutcracker* undergoes, a less-versatile ballet might have had a strong enough identity crisis to fracture its stability long ago. Yet the annual *Nutcracker* phenomenon continues to grow. There have been hints in annual reports and arts surveys that the movement has peaked and high revenues are no longer a sure thing, but given the power of the ballet to reinvent itself, its demise hardly seems imminent. So many people think they own a piece of it, *The Nutcracker* still ably serves various purposes. The ballet's secret could be its diversity, and, conversely, the fact that participants tend to imagine themselves as some branch of one big *Nutcracker* family. Because the ballet retains an overarching identity, it brings to mind historian Benedict Anderson's concept an "imagined community," within which individuals believe themselves to exist in some kind of communion with one another, even though they may never know the others or know if their beliefs really coincide. Anderson's discussion revolves around national identity and the way a feeling of "unisonance" comes over a crowd or an individual when, for instance, a national anthem is struck up.[19] For the imagined community of *The Nutcracker*, Tchaikovsky's overture can trigger the same response—that moment when, an audience member in Leesburg told me, "you feel so emotional about being part of it all."

Where there are feelings of membership and ownership, there are inevitably in-groups, out-groups, and internecine warfare. But there is also a kind of pride and excitement that arises from the perceived solidarity of the moment. *The Nutcracker* can provide a kind of communal focus that calls up visions of the mythic Dickens Christmas, or stories of tightly knit villages in less complicated times, wherever they are presumed to have existed. In this way, all over the country, *Nutcracker*s serve as temporary communities that foster social connectedness on a limited scale. When *The Nutcracker* works, a longtime Loudoun Ballet board member and performer said, "it comes close to that old community feeling of, 'We've got a barn, let's put on a show'—it's the *ideal* of a community." Although this community is imagined on a different scale in Toronto, audiences members there also sometimes feel like they're a part of the whole endeavor of celebrating Christmas, family, and noble ideals with a ballet.

Although the ballet world, even on the amateur level, is far from egalitarian, this seems to be one way *The Nutcracker* is imagined by its participants—as a welcoming utopian community. This vision is supported by the idea that anyone can pursue the ideal forms inherent in ballet technique and be affected by the potentially transformational music of Tchaikovsky, while at the same time celebrating the themes of home, hearth, and adventure. And when people feel shut out of the ballet world, with all its particular history and stringent requirements, they can take *The Nutcracker* into their own domains, tweak it, dress it up differently, and bring it closer to home. In each incarnation of a *Nutcracker* that grows from a particular community, choreographers and dancers make the ballet move—and make it moving—in new ways. The annual *Nutcracker* is a recently invented tradition, nestled into an imagined community, but it's no less resonant than many older traditions, which all had to have been invented at some time.[20] Its ability to fit in is all part of its unexpected journey. While North Americans dutifully learned to mount classical ballets that tell tales of a peasant girl in the Rhineland or a swan who falls in love, they eventually used *The Nutcracker* to tell a story about themselves.

When I danced in The Nutcracker as a teenager in the 1960s, I considered the Sugar Plum Fairy a role model. Perhaps surprisingly, she has always stood me in good stead. Never did I judge her sugary or frilly, and I was amazed that outsiders to the dance world thought of ballet as a lightweight proposition. I thought of myself as a serious dancer, one aspiring to physical mastery of a complex technique, devastatingly effective acting skills, and a career I thought might reveal the meaning of life. I expected no less. Growing up in a medium-sized American suburb, I took ballet classes from the age of five, admiring my teachers and the ballerinas I read about. It seemed to me that these women were not only talented, they were also independent, noble, inspired, and completely glamorous. I imagined that the ballet world was a place where you could travel, gain admiration, and make a statement. That still seemed possible to me when I switched from ballet to acting after high school and later became a writer. But eventually I found my way back to ballet, mostly because of the power I perceived it to have for me. This time I was watching dance and writing about it, and I still found that ballet was my metaphor for achievement and transcendence. Imagine my confusion when I found out, through the feminist critiques that started to emerge in the seventies, that there was only one defining metaphor of ballet—the one in which women lose, because ballet asked for impossible things from them and was a pernicious taskmaster.

If I had grown up defining life in terms of ballet, these critiques suggested, I had fallen victim to the beauty myth, the coopting of women into passive roles. Evidently, dancing in The Nutcracker as a teenager had not been as innocent and productive an experience as it seemed. According to the ideologues, the surface attractions of ballet can trick you into being recruited into the army of the status quo—often confused with the corps de ballet in Swan Lake or, worse, a beauty pageant. In many ways, this is a beguiling discourse. I was especially taken by Ann Daly's clearly written structural, semiotic analysis of the Balanchine ballerina, *in which she is seen to be manipulated, supported, and confined by her male partner. What brilliant connections Daly made, I thought, as she analyzed the choreography and explained the way it could echo socio-cultural norms and myths about women. I could see that ballerinas on their toes appeared unstable at times, that they are led, spun, lifted, and touched by men in ways they never dared try in return. What were the consequences of being preoccupied by the most stereotypically, conventionally feminine job in the world? To me, wanting to be a "princess" in the ballet world was not the unliberated fantasy of a deluded, oppressed woman—it was a job description. I had not grown into a woman who waited for my prince. What did it all mean?*

It wasn't long before I was made aware of just what the messages I had taken from ballet were. Asked to talk about my favorite book for a national public radio show in Canada, I thought about what book had had the greatest influence on my life. Regretfully, I passed over favorite novels that would have made me seem complex and erudite (I loved Virginia Woolf and Margaret Drabble), and instead, I chose the florid biography of Anna Pavlova my mother had given me as a child. I suddenly realized that—along with ballet classes and performance—this book had been a major inspiration and blueprint for the choices I made in my life. That's not to say that there weren't other influences, but I saw in images of Pavlova, and ballet in general, ways of being that made life seem full of possibilities. When I read about ballerinas as I grew up, I formed ideas about what was possible in life. Around me, women were mostly wives, mothers, and teachers, but I saw that one could reject normative expectations and instead travel the world prominently as an artist. I internalized the idea that dedication, rigor, and sacrifice led to achieving lofty goals. Later I would understand that I had found what anthropologist John L. Caughey calls a "piece of culture"—a portion of cultural knowledge that inspires a person to do something in particular.

When I danced in The Nutcracker, *learning about rehearsal protocols, the demands of the theater, and performance rewards, I was already participating in the important life I imagined for myself.*

What I learned from ballet was that order was always available, at least in the classroom, and it was often quite rewarding, even—or especially—later, in the turbulent late sixties and early seventies, when I was high on the heady fumes of iconoclasm. In terms of rebellion and carving out a spot for oneself, Pavlova seemed brave and steadfast. From all reports she was a tempestuous, demanding person when it came to her art. She wasn't bad at self-promotion, either. And Pavlova's husband, Victor Dandré, came off as something of an equal partner—or perhaps, as her manager, he was more at her service than not. At any rate, I understood that women could achieve great things if they worked hard enough. I could live fast and die young, or I could stretch it out, if I didn't, like Pavlova, refuse a lung operation at age fifty, a choice she made because she would not have been able to dance again. (I was dedicated, but not crazy.)

Stories about imperial ballerinas and many other dancers revealed women with steely strength and maximum resolve, images that resonated with my feelings about ballet class. Learning to dance the princess was not to be the princess—all dancers understood that. The audience could understand, too, and they could take away whatever messages they wanted from a ballet performance. I later interviewed a woman who reiterated that point for me. She had never taken a ballet class, but even without that physical experience, she knew ballerinas weren't passive creatures. When she saw a woman on pointe, she didn't think of the moments when a male partner was stabilizing or spinning her. What she thought of was how strong you had to be to stand on that little pointe, and how glorious it was if, even for an instant, a ballerina was able to balance there herself.

Looking back, it's easy to understand ballet's appeal in terms of my European-American background and upwardly mobile aspirations. I was pleased to align myself with an elite art form that had such obvious ties to the cosmopolitan, regal place I imagined Europe to be. But ballet also seemed like an efficient, American activity. Something about the technique seemed to organize the body succinctly and efficiently, armoring it against the world. I could image myself as a sleek, well-oiled machine in the service of art — a machine with a soul, something I didn't find incongruous at the time. As well, I was drawn to the rhythms, themes, and variations of Western classical music — violins that soared romantically, lush orchestrations that overwhelmed. The Nutcracker was a good place to start. It was classical but familiar, and it began in the living room of a girl not unlike myself.

Another of ballet's appeals was that when you practiced it seriously — as I did even in an amateur context — you escaped a lot of adolescent angst by organizing activities around it. Never mind that adults thought being in The Nutcracker was cute and harmless, the kind of thing a girl should be seen to do. To me it was a seditious activity, removing me from the prescribed rituals of high school socialization, from curfews and the domestic tasks a daughter was expected to perform. As well, it kept me from having to consider part-time jobs as a cashier or fry cook, as my conscientious friends did. Even in high school, I had a purposeful (although not lucrative) career, and it gave me a way of negotiating what I considered the minefields of dutiful daughterhood in a provincial suburb.

The way I first participated in the world of ballet performance is a familiar one to nearly all aspiring American dancers and their parents. There were yearly dancing-school recitals, but that was kid stuff. Anyone in ballet knew that The Nutcracker was the rite of passage on the way to a career. In my hometown, the Louisville Ballet, like hundreds of other small companies, had a yearly, full-length Nutcracker. There was even an orchestra and a choreographer imported from the Mecca of ballet, New York City. As with the Leesburg production I later researched, there were terrifyingly important auditions, in the form of a ballet class during which you wore a number pinned to your chest. And there was a hierarchy of roles to be had, from the lowly reindeer who pulled Clara's sleigh and mice who wore clumsy masks up to snowflakes, then flowers, and, if you were good, featured solo parts.

The first year I was accepted into the company, I thought I had reached the pinnacle of achievement; I was in my version of heaven. But after a week, there was a rude awakening; I was "laid off," because the supply of snowflakes was suddenly found to have exceeded demand. It was devastating — Pavlova had never been unceremoniously dropped from a corps de ballet job, I was sure. It was a bad sign. But I stayed at the barre another year and then was asked to join the snowflake corps again, this time with enough experience to make the cut when stray snowflakes fell to the wayside. Later, as an adult, watching the proactive parents who fought like tigers behind the scenes to prevent their children from experiencing any kind of disappointment (casting children in amateur Nutcrackers today is an artistic director's nightmare), it occurred to me that my parents could have reasonably complained about the disorganized casting decisions that resulted in my yearlong banishment. But in the long run, it worked out. The experience allowed me to practice the art of rationalizing any kind of failure ("they just haven't seen me at my best yet"), a skill that came in handy later in life. And I learned that persistence paid off.

Once an official member of the ballet company, I traveled from the suburbs into a world of shabby downtown rehearsal halls (a loaned gymnasium, a faded former ballroom) for long rehearsals, where we'd watch the few imported guest stars and the local whiz kids, whose styles, in leotards and leg warmers, we tried to copy. Our director at the time, Fernand Nault, had been with American Ballet Theatre in New York since the 1940s (when it was just called Ballet Theatre) and would soon find a home with Les Grands Ballets Canadiens in his native Montreal. His French accent assured us that we were in an exotic world, and his constantly inventive choreography thrilled us. On breaks we would dash out to local dives for Cokes and greasy hamburgers, taking in the gritty street life we never got to see in our pristine suburban housing developments. At last, near Christmas, we had a weekend of four performances in the closest thing Louisville had to an opera house—a large downtown theater where touring productions of My Fair Lady played.

When I talked to young women in the Leesburg production and told them about the parts I used to dance, their eyes lit up, and we were suddenly speaking the same language. They were not surprised—as my young nondancing cousin had been—to think that a fairly sedentary, grown woman was once a lithe ballet dancer; the Leesburg dancers are surrounded by middle-aged former Sugar Plums, and they understand what progression through the Nutcracker ranks and retirement look like. They were interested to know that in my production, "Snow" was done in soft shoes and I had to work my way up to "Flowers," on pointe— the opposite of their casting. They were, by and large, an incredibly articulate group and very ambitious about dancing and other pursuits. I was reminded of how at that age, my Nutcracker experience had set me in motion in public, in literal and metaphoric ways that would echo throughout the years that followed. Some of the preadolescent ballet dancers told me they either wanted to be a ballerina or maybe a veterinarian; or maybe if they didn't dance they would teach, or possibly coach soccer. It's easy to have dreams at that stage in life, I thought, but having started life with the pleasures and rigors of ballet, they were well equipped to reach other goals in the future. Early on, they might be *discovering, as I did, something about beauty, dedication, sacrifice, and reward. Ballet training and experience not only kept me going but led me to an understanding of the way life works. Not everyone discovers this through ballet, but as I talked to more and more people, I found a greater variety of stories than is often envisioned when the topic is* The Nutcracker.

Experiences and Relationships

Although the Nutcracker himself is an easygoing, everyman kind of icon, willing to be part of any professional or amateur community, he has also embraced the celebrity status that has been thrust upon him in the New World. The spin-off products and personal appearances alone keep his image fresh and friendly—he'll appear on a sweater, guard the door to a bar, hold your keys, hang from your ears, or even, if he's feeling sturdy enough, crack the proverbial nut. But in a society that thrives on digging beneath the glossy surface of celebrity, you have to start to wonder after a while—what's the Nutcracker really like? I quickly found out that few people I interviewed about *The Nutcracker* could contribute to a psychological profile of the Nutcracker himself, although they do know some things about him. They said he was stalwart, taciturn, and very neat, for instance, and he tends to wear a brightly colored nineteenth-century military jacket with brass buttons. His tall black hat mashes a shock of white hair, and his curling mustache frames a square, strange mouth made of very large teeth. People often take home a nutcracker replica to remember the ballet, or perhaps a carved action figure of the Nutcracker Prince flying through the air with one leg outstretched and his sword picturesquely brandished. Onstage, his motivations and transitions are fairly transparent. Basically, he's an ambitious, functional toy who, through the pure love of a child, or the magic of a magician (or both), changes from a wooden doll to a tin soldier to a handsome prince. Most observations about the eponymous hero could be summed up in a short phrase, such as, "He's a good guy who has some hard times and comes out on top." In terms of Nutcracker profiling, that's about as deep as these still waters lie.

A background check adds one interesting wrinkle to the assessment of the Nutcracker as the epitome of a stalwart soldier: it turns out he didn't start life as a patriot. In the early eighteenth century, nutcracker carving emerged as a spare-time activity among German miners in the eastern region of Erzgebirge, as a way of lampooning figures of authority. These miners undoubtedly enjoyed the idea that little replicas of soldiers, politicians, policemen, and professors could be put to work cracking the shells of walnuts with their teeth. In the ballet, however, the Nutcracker has usually lost any semblance of lampooning those in charge—on the contrary, his crisp military regalia and upright bearing would fit into a Fourth of July parade. Even when the *Nutcracker* battle is imbued with comical, lighthearted moments, the soldiers are clearly meant to be heroes. Just how far the carved version of the Nutcracker has strayed from his subversive roots was evident in 1991, when the Gulf War inspired one German manufacturer to carve an "Operation Desert Storm" nutcracker, which was dressed in khakis and shipped in a container that looked like a munitions box. This was not in the spirit of the thing, an indignant fellow German manufacturer protested; nutcrackers aren't made to glorify military victory. But nutcrackers do tend to reflect the times, as could be seen in the wake of the September 11, 2001, terrorist attacks, when another U.S. soldier nutcracker emerged, this time called the "Champion of Freedom." There is also a model dressed as a member of the New York City Fire Department.[1]

In the ballet, the Nutcracker is usually a cartoonish military man, clean-cut, patriotic, and—to remove him from our everyday fears about war—attired in an old-fashioned dress uniform. Sometimes, he is transformed into the Nutcracker Prince (adult or child version) and remains Clara's consort, and he gets to retell their story in mime

Two Nutcracker recruits: The "Operation Desert Storm" nutcracker (left) was dismissed as tasteless by some in 1991, while the similarly designed 2001 "Champion of Freedom" might be assessed differently.

on arrival at the Land of the Sweets. Then they usually sit like bumps on a log through the rest of act two. Perhaps nondancer Macauley Culkin, the Hollywood addition to the movie version of Balanchine's *Nutcracker,* best exemplifies the bump-on-a-log kind of Nutcracker Prince, even though he attended the School of American Ballet before attaining movie stardom. With his wooden mime and clueless pretty face in the close-ups, he probably hasn't done a lot for the profile of boys in ballet.

The fact is, for all his putative centrality, the Nutcracker is really a figurehead, not a character who has a lot of impact on audiences. He's a team player, and if he were not fictional, he would no doubt be the first person to credit his fellow characters with much of his success. What are *they* really like, then? These are roles with which people get very familiar, whether they're aspiring to dance them or just looking forward to renewing an acquaintance from the audience—what kind of impressions do they leave?

There are several good male roles in *The Nutcracker,* but the traditional handsome prince is not among them. Even in versions that transform the Nutcracker into an adult dancer who partners the Sugar Plum Fairy, he rarely attracts attention for long. He's more of a "minuteman"—at under sixty seconds, his solo is probably the shortest male variation in the classical repertoire. He doesn't even get a name most of the time—he's just "Cavalier." There's a reason for this. In the original ballet, the Nutcracker Prince was a student dancer throughout both acts, and the adult who partnered the Sugar Plum Fairy was called Prince Coqueluche—French for Prince Whooping Cough. Because this prince is a mere consort—it's the Sugar Plum Fairy who rules and officially welcomes strangers to her realm—such a name seems to add insult to injury. To be fair, there's a French idiom that turns the word *coqueluche* into a term of endearment, and in the seventeenth century it could mean someone who was much loved or admired. Still, just the sound of that name perhaps led to the current preferred title of Cavalier, which is short for "the guy needed for the grand pas de deux."

A character who tends to attract at least as much attention as Cavalier is Drosselmeier, Clara's godfather (or uncle or family friend). Indeed, in some productions, this role has been beefed up to make him the orchestrator of events, edging the plot closer to the Hoffmann story. Musicologist Roland John Wiley, who has researched the first *Nutcracker* extensively, champions Drosselmeier as the savior of the ballet's original plot problems. Wiley served as a consultant for the Royal Ballet's version (seen on a 1985 videotape), and he keeps the old guy visible throughout the ballet, having him stop time, guide Clara, and wave his hands to set events in motion. Clara becomes a pawn in this game, basically following orders in order to break the spell that has turned Drosselmeier's nephew into a nutcracker. Played by adult dancer Lesley Collier in the 1985 video, this Clara looks like an overgrown teenager who falls for the Nutcracker Prince but is too young to get involved. At any rate, she's nowhere to be found at the end of the ballet; presumably the sled in which she and her Cavalier left the Land of the Sweets dropped her back home. The final, heartwarming image is that of Drosselmeier embracing his liberated nephew, while a portrait on the wall reminds us that he used to be a nutcracker. Clara never drops off to sleep in this version, so it's clear that the "dream" isn't hers—it's all Drosselmeier's doing.

Clara also loses sovereignty over her dream in reenvisionings like James Kudelka's for the National Ballet of Canada, in which Marie and Misha (Clara and Fritz) both travel to the fantasyland of the second act. Many Toronto audience members I spoke to thought this "equal opportunity" aspect was interesting, even progressive. "It's nice for the boys in the audience to see that the brother gets to go too," one of them told me. But the tone of approving comments like this one was often grudging, and a certain amount of nostalgia for Clara as a lone adventurer lingered. Kudelka also expanded other male roles while he was at it—the Cavalier suddenly has a back story, for instance. At the start of the ballet, he's Peter, a servant close to Marie; then he shows up in the fantasy world as a prince. It's hard not to imagine that when the young Kudelka came through the National Ballet School of Canada, he got tired of *The Nutcracker* being the "Clara and Sugar Plum Show," because he also turns Drosselmeier into the role of Nikolai, a young bearded magician who does virtuosic leaps and twirls. Usually Drosselmeier is a character dancer who is good for a few amusing tricks and some comic mime before using his magic to help Clara enter an altered state. He tends to disappear for the majority of the ballet, and the dream world usually has Clara's psyche written all over it—her fear of mice, her longing for adventure, and her toys and favorite candy coming to life.

There are other male roles in the ballet that may make as large an impression—or larger, depending on the version. The Mouse King is central to the plot, in that he provides a formidable adversary over which good must triumph (audiences sometimes get into ritualistic booing and cheering). After lunging, spinning, and slicing the air with his sword, the royal rodent is cut down dramatically and mourned to very sympathetic music. He also makes a dynamic evil action figure at the ballet boutiques. The Mouse King's motivation for waging war on the Nutcracker was lost in the ballet scenario (Hoffmann provides lots of revenge plot detail), and he is often a comical villain, but he nonetheless can remind audiences of serious conflict, probably because of Tchaikovsky's bracing battle music. In some versions, the king of the mice wears Middle Eastern–style pantaloons and vest, an Orientalist detail that seems to escape comment. I first noticed it the year after the Gulf War, when my eyes were attuned to stereotyped images often used to characterize factions in the Middle East. Putting the Mouse King in Arabian gear seems to be another of those historical traditions no one has thought to question (the children in blackface who imitate African dance in *La Bayadère* also come to mind). It probably escapes censure because ethnic stereotyping that would cause picketing elsewhere is seen only by those too far inside ballet's charmed circle to notice the implications. Of course, in many productions, the Mouse King has no ethnic markers; he's just an oversized rodent who has pretensions above his outcast status. Whatever the nature of his menace, the Mouse King is basically a cameo role, the villain with an embarrassing fatal flaw—forgetting to cover his rear flank because he underestimates the clever battle tactics of a girl with one loose shoe.

Who else cuts a memorable figure in most *Nutcrackers*? The macho soldier doll at the party is usually popular, as are the high-flying Chinese and Russian guys strutting their strenuous stuff in the Land of the Sweets. They have some of the flashiest parts, and their female counterparts often have eye-catching moments as well—the mechanical Columbine doll, the whirling snowflakes, the va-va-voom Arabian soloist. But are they the heartbeat of the ballet? The characters people like and remember because of who they are and what they represent? Probably not. For many, many *Nutcracker* aficionados, the major *Nutcracker* players are Clara and the Sugar Plum Fairy. After all, it's Clara's trip (usually), and in addition to representing childhood optimism, she provides viewers with a link to their Walter Mitty sides. The Sugar Plum Fairy has a more enigmatic identity; she's a seemingly mild-mannered sovereign who makes her impression in a less flashy fashion than other ballet heroines, but makes an big impression all the same.

Perhaps not surprisingly, given the ballet's focus on a child's dream and fantasy world, Clara has inspired a bit of armchair psychologizing over the years. This, of course, did not happen in the pre-Freudian era of the Maryinsky, before anyone knew they had an unconscious mind. Back then, Clara was hardly the subject of probing analysis; in the original *Nutcracker,* she was played by twelve-year-old Stanislava Belinskaya, whose party polka solo was deemed "quite unsuccessful both in composition and execution."[2] Poor Stanislava probably got the role of her little lifetime only to discover that the imperial ballet world wasn't yet ready for an underage ballerina. Whether it was choreography, nerves, or lack of skill that did her in, the first Clara is a footnote in *Nutcracker* history. But the role became increasingly important in the New World, as childhood itself became something to be treasured, understood, and, in some instances, survived.

Possibly the first critic to notice that Clara is a character who survives her social environment by balancing everyday life with fantasy—and is therefore of great interest—was Edwin Denby, who wrote about meaning in *The Nutcracker* during the 1940s and 1950s, using the Ballet Russe and New York City Ballet versions as examples. Denby places Clara at the sensitive center of the ballet's two different worlds—home and away—suggesting that she not only delights young audience members, but draws in adults by representing their "buried yearnings" for liberation from routine. What does Clara have to escape? Denby notes that she's burdened by the social pressures of her upper-class home—"the locus classicus of ambivalent anxiety," he calls it, a "gloomy and oppressed" place where the dancing is earthbound and confined. There are brutal overtones galore: when Fritz snatches and wounds the nutcracker doll, things get ugly, of course, but even earlier, Denby suggests, something's not quite right. When "an elderly bachelor with one eye gives a pre-adolescent girl a male nutcracker," couldn't that be a "cruel sexual symbol"? You get the feeling that Denby is having a little fun with the priapic preoccupations considered by many to be the heart and soul of psychoanalysis. By 1944, when Denby first analyzed *The Nutcracker*, psychoanalysis was "practically a household remedy," he declares with breezy authority. But he's also making a point, and doesn't let the *Nutcracker* characters linger on the couch for too long. Mainly, he uses the idea of repressed desire to emphasize the complex emotional undertones that can lie beneath the surface of any Christmas party. In other words, Denby says, although *The Nutcracker* may look like "nonsense" at first glance, Clara's world should be taken seriously.[9]

Writing about Balanchine's *Nutcracker* ten years later, Denby seems to recognize the friendlier place that Clara's home had become in the New World, noting that the party scene provided "amusing family bits" and "the pleasure of seeing children onstage who are not made to look saccharine or hysterical, who do what they do naturally and straight." Still, there was a need for the Clara/Marie character to escape the behavioral constraints of her childhood home. Audiences sense the tension, he notes, when they see bad manners expressed in musically accented ordinary gestures—a shove here, children fighting there. Denby shrewdly emphasizes the point that qualities in the dancing and mime help define Clara's world. Everyone is very grounded in the party scene, tied to everyday responsibilities, sometimes peevish, he says, but in her dream, Clara enters a world where everyone soars, everyone is polite and straightforward. Clara wants a safe, stable world and she finds it—and we can find it, too, Denby suggests—in her fantasyland, where clear, radiant classical dancing is not only a calming influence, it represents human nature at its best.[4]

In *Nutcrackers* today, what Denby called Clara's "odd imagination" and "wonderful premonitions" may still resonate within the unconscious desires of children and adults who want to escape and find ways of dealing with their worlds. I often heard *Nutcracker* participants say that Clara was the one who showed "your dreams can come true." One of the Leesburg dancers who played the Sugar Plum Fairy looked back on her days as Clara with an expanded idea of what her actions could symbolize. "I love the story of Clara—I think that's what we all want in life," she said, "to be able to be there and to make a difference, the way Clara makes a difference in the Nutcracker's life by breaking a spell." Others noted that Clara is brave, she believes in something, and she fights for what she believes in.

Poor Clara sometimes has to keep up a level of optimism that seems exhausting. It's no wonder she's been reenvisioned so often as a love-starved teenager—who else would act so rashly? Who else would get a stern-faced doll with oversized teeth for Christmas, immediately and unaccountably love him devoutly, feel his pain enough to risk her life for him, and enter into what must certainly be a relationship fraught with inter-realm obstacles? She can't possibly be just a fluffy little girl—one of the Clara stereotypes that has grown from the reality of the fluffy little girls who are sometimes cast in amateur productions. It's true that she may be choreographed as a slightly passive character when she's not given any bold moves to distract the Mouse King or hit him with her shoe. The Nutcracker is often given the job of running his distracted enemy through with his sword, and Clara's key role in the action is glossed over so quickly that it looks like she's just skittishly batting at a fly. Still, Clara does at least bat at her enemy; then she takes even more risks, setting out on an adventure into the unknown, weathering a barrage of snowflakes, and settling into an alternate universe of strange characters who crown her.

Clara, on a good day, is downright reckless, something that doesn't escape the notice of many *Nutcracker* viewers. "I think of her as feisty, independent, and courageous," a female balletomane in Toronto told me, countering the impression the Mattel people evidently had when they decided to produce *Barbie in The Nutcracker*. They thought they had to make Clara "more proactive, more the heroine of the story," a publicist told me, perhaps not understanding that to many girls, Clara was already a heroine. It's possible that Barbie's handlers didn't look beyond the surface-level impression one gets from Clara's costume and small stature, but not everyone interprets the traditional Clara as a lightweight. Not surprisingly, many *Nutcracker* dancers and aficionados I spoke to had noticed Clara's complexity. An amateur dancer who had played both Clara and Sugar Plum registered the two major facets she found in Clara's character: "I felt that she was a cross between a little girl and a woman, right on the edge. Parts of her were just very vulnerable and scared, and then she was very womanly and very in control. It's such a neat combination."

Parents of young dancers also seemed particularly primed to recognize the basic duality of Clara's character; the fact that she is a girl who also embodies aspects of adulthood was reflected by the changes they saw in their own children who were in the ballet. Watching a daughter or son master aspects of ballet technique and acting, they marveled at seeing the disorganized exuberance their children exhibited offstage turn into poise and control onstage. The role of Clara, the Loudoun Ballet artistic director told me, is tricky to cast because a young dancer has to be caught just at the moment when she can transmit two things—the power of controlled dancing combined with a certain optimistic spark that has not yet been tempered by too much experience with the world. "She can be sweet and caring," one of the small dancers who played Marie in Toronto told me, "but when someone gets in her way, she's not afraid to fight back."

Where does Clara get her courage, her poise, her willingness to take risks? It's always been clear to me that she gets all these qualities from studying ballet—and here I elaborate on what Denby already knew back in the 1940s, that classical dancing transmits messages that go beyond storytelling and the creation of sheer beauty. In other words, the narrative and grace of ballet aren't the only things that give Clara her character; otherwise, I probably wouldn't have heard a Toronto audience member saying one minute that Clara/Marie is "a typical wide-eyed child," then quickly adding, "It's probably a job with huge pressures." I found that many *Nutcracker* aficionados seemed to assess Clara by factoring in their knowledge of her dancing expertise. In both Leesburg and Toronto, the Claras did a considerable amount of technical dancing, and the young performers I saw in the role attracted a lot of attention with their powers of concentration, acting, and technical skill. But not all Claras are created equal, of course. While in Virginia, I also saw something I call a "recital *Nutcracker,*" in which a barely mobile Clara fumbled through two acts and proved that being the center of attention isn't always a good thing.

Many Clara wannabes find out that she's made of sterner stuff than they think, as I saw one afternoon between the matinee and evening performances of the Loudoun Ballet. In the hallway outside the high school cafeteria that served as a dressing room, I came upon a group of ten- and eleven-year-old dancers who had talked the affable adult playing Cavalier into lifting each of them above his head, the way he lifts Clara in a dramatic pas de deux. In their production, the Nutcracker Prince is a father figure (played by the same dancer who plays Mr. Stahlbaum), and their duet before the snowflake dance is full of exuberant twirls and cradling, as well as classical lines. The aspiring Claras were all of an age and size to audition for the part the next year, and they all wanted to try one particular moment of the pas de deux—

At the Loudoun Ballet, Clara (Sarah Terry) soars picturesquely above her Prince's head (Frank Shumaker), but only when she has the stomach muscles and correct ballet alignment to make it work.

when Clara stretches into a perfectly balanced arabesque and is lifted above her Prince's head as snow starts to fall. Their obliging Cavalier talked each of them through it, and each began by confidently taking an arabesque pose in front of him. The lift, of course, wasn't as easy as it looked, requiring strong stomach, leg, and back muscles that not everyone had developed. From the panicked expression on many faces, it seemed clear that there were a few would-be pilots who were thinking they should sign up for more flying lessons. But a few had another look, a determined, concentrated calmness. When they reached the top of the lift, they registered which body parts had to be adjusted, held their lines with authority, and let just a hint of a smile escape. These were the dancers who ended up filling Clara's pointe shoes the next season.

In the right choreography, with the right training, a young Clara can look like a very sturdy and talented person who has nerve and compassion beyond her years. Still, some artistic directors prefer casting an adult in the role. Then she either towers over the other kids or else they're all played by adults, too—never mind that it makes the Stahlbaums' living room look less like a Christmas gathering and more like a Halloween party full of people with Peter Pan complexes. The Russians started this tradition of casting an adult as Clara, making *The Nutcracker* less of an adventure story and more a coming-of-age tale. It's all about "the ripening soul of a little girl," Russian composer Boris Asafiev once said, because Clara goes from playing with dolls to "arriving at the dawn of love through dreams of love of a brave and virile hero."[5]

So much for any other plans Clara might have had in mind for her soul; she is destined for romance. With adult Claras, we're presumably supposed to focus on the moment when she teeters on the brink of something dewy called "womanhood"—in ballet, that's the moment when she finds a man and dances in a swooning pas de deux. One of the dewiest romantic Claras was Gelsey Kirkland, who, although now long retired, returns every year on television in the 1977 American Ballet Theatre *Nutcracker* staged by Mikhail Baryshnikov (with his own choreography and some of the Vainonen version he learned in Russia). Tiny, wide-eyed Kirkland, an adult at the time but looking frail in a slim chiffon nightgown (she struggled with eating disorders at the time), combines a believable innocence and wonder with stunningly beautiful dancing. Her journey ends sadly, when it turns out that Clara's foray into premature adulthood has all been a troubling dream. The last shot in the film version is a close-up of Kirkland looking out her bedroom window, prince-less, seemingly lost in troubled thoughts. In essence, her expression is not unlike the enigmatic looks on the faces of Dustin Hoffmann and Katherine Ross in the last scene of *The Graduate,* when they suddenly realize that life and love are more daunting than they ever imagined. But the narrative impact of this familiar *Nutcracker* was lost on more than one young dancer I talked to—why did Clara look confused, they wondered. Was she depressed? Hadn't she just had a great trip and done all that incredible dancing? Older viewers seemed to get the point— if the point was that finding your prince did not guarantee he'd stick around.

Rudolf Nureyev also followed the Russian custom of having an adult play Clara, except that his adult is dressed like a ten-year-old and becomes romantically involved with Drosselmeier. Nureyev first set his version on the Swedish Ballet in 1967, revising it several times afterward for various companies around the world (it was recorded by the Royal Ballet in 1968). Making an old man with an eye patch into the dream date of wee Clara, and also having the mice in the battle scene rip her skirt off, inspired a record number of critics to use the word "Freudian" in a ballet review. Clara's act-two dream encounter includes a horde of bats who turn out to be her relatives in disguise, perhaps a less controversial psychological twist. Everyone, after all, can imagine a time when relatives might show up in dreams looking like bats.

The idea that Clara has a fraught adolescence and dreams of meeting her prince one day doesn't seem an unreasonable theme for *The Nutcracker,* given that many adolescents are fraught and little girls invariably dream of growing up. But fortunately, Clara has a diverse life in many versions of the ballet, so she isn't always limited to fixating on finding her prince. She's often a younger character whose ruffled dress doesn't obscure the fact that she's a go-getter with nerves of steel and killer ballet technique for her age. For many of my respondents, both Clara and the Sugar Plum Fairy share an ability to have a foot in two camps—the glittery pink feminine one and the realm in which they dazzle onlookers with physical feats and determined personalities. In many ways, of course, most all ballet heroines inhabit both of these worlds, but there has been some debate over whether or not the qualities they embody are beneficial or detrimental in terms of their effect on contemporary women. This is a debate that involves interpretation—deciding what ballet characters represent and what messages they convey.

There has been a fair amount of theorizing about the way women in audiences and studios interpret ballet images and experiences, but not much response from the women themselves. Because *The Nutcracker* is so well known, and so many dancers and audience members see the same two quintessential ballet heroines every year, it seemed a good place to learn something about the way they relate to these images. One of the questions I asked was, "What can you tell about the Sugar Plum Fairy from her dancing?" Followed by: "What about her partner?" Poor Cavalier spurred little, if any reflection. One adult audience member, evidently unaware of how many male ballet stars have dominated the landscape, said about men in ballet, "They work hard, but it's a shame—nobody really notices them." Others enjoyed the men's performances at least as much as the women's, but there was always more discussion about Clara and the Sugar Plum Fairy.

In her lifetime, the Sugar Plum Fairy has witnessed many changes in attitude when it comes to her purpose in life and her effect on audiences. At first her existence was pretty straightforward—she emerged in Russia to provide ballerinas another way to conquer audiences with their pirouettes, pointe work, and personalities. In the New World, she became a prominent archetype of a classical ballerina, many times the only person in a tutu to be seen for miles around and something of an ambassador and recruiting officer for ballet. Her reputation has remained solid in many *Nutcracker* locations, but in the late twentieth century, feminist writers started to cast aspersions on her core values. In a word, "fairy-tale princess" as a job description suitable for contemporary women was passé.

Although the Sugar Plum wasn't by any means alone in being singled out as a regressive role model, critics have made some unflattering insinuations that she might reasonably take personally. Questions they ask go along these lines: Are women objectified by the display and manipulation of ballerina bodies? (In other words, is it all about sex and controlling males?) Does the Sugar Plum Fairy look passive? (Could she even stand up without a guy there supporting her?) Do stories about princesses and fairies send repressive messages about women's choices? (If she wore sturdier shoes, wouldn't she be able to get further?) Are women's self-images damaged by ballet's demands for ultrathin, hipless bodies? (Should anyone be living on lettuce?) Ballet has always been an arena in which women are encouraged to achieve, but astute dance analysts started posing key questions about how the profession treats them, and whether or not women are able to survive and thrive onstage or backstage in a profession dominated by male choreographers and artistic directors.[6]

I'd like to think the Sugar Plum Fairy, despite her abundance of decorative and impractical tulle, her delicate choreography, and her noncombative nature, might take on these questions with the determination of a woman who has, for over a century, been sole monarch of a burgeoning candy nation. But, alas, she is rarely heard from, and scholars haven't really taken up her cause, what with first attending to all the ballet heroines who get more stage time and more detailed plots. But the Sugar Plum has inspired at least a little bit of scholarly attention in the recent past. Dance historian Selma Jeanne Cohen discusses her while exploring various pathways to finding meaning in a ballet, and looks for clues in her appearance and solo variation. Does her name mean anything? Cohen guesses not: the Sugar Plum Fairy, after all, does not look like a plum. What about the narrative? Well, in the story, her only clear role is a "charming hostess [who] provides entertainment for her guests." But the choreography does offer hints: the Sugar Plum Fairy is neat and performs exacting symmetrical movements that match the delicate, staccato beats of the music. (Cohen's description of the her movement qualities is based on steps that often appear in traditional versions and are presumed to have

much in common with Ivanov's original choreography.) "Though requiring considerable strength and control, these movements look
soft but their yielding quality is balanced by a sharp clarity of focus,"
she says. "The dancer seems always aiming at a particular position in
space, which, once attained, is held just long enough for the viewer
to take it in and admire it. She does not force her way to the position;
her movements are unhurried. She seems poised and confident, yet
gracious."[7]

Cohen thinks that "we may look in vain for crises and complexity"
in the Sugar Plum Fairy's dance, but her description surely indicates
that there is more than one facet of the character's personality; she is
soft, yielding, and gracious, but at the same time sharply focused and
confident. Delving a bit further, Cohen hints at the number of contextual variables that may affect the way a viewer might interpret the
Sugar Plum. For instance, contemporary theatergoers who have seen
many dances containing "profound ideas" may expect some kind of
statement of ideas in a dance, while for others, it's enough to be di-
verted by a formally pleasing solo. Ballet in general could remind
viewers of "childhood lessons in manners and poise," Cohen says, or
a bygone age about which they have read. Or some may enjoy having
a glimpse of the "vanished virtues" of other eras—the seventeenth-
century French court or the imperial circles within which the *Nutcracker* premiered.[8]

Like Cohen, dance scholar Sally Banes turns to the *Nutcracker* narrative and the character's movement qualities to define the Sugar
Plum Fairy, calling her "magisterial, the supreme commander of her
realm." Then Banes emphasizes the character's delicate side, this
time referring to the quality of her music—the ethereal, tinkling
celesta—and the decor of her kingdom, which "is metaphorically
coded as feminine, even though many of her subjects are male."
Banes is interested in the way the Sugar Plum Fairy might be perceived, both in the nineteenth century and today. She tells us that
the Sugar Plum Fairy didn't break any ground when she was created

and didn't reflect the concerns of women at the time, when Russian feminists were struggling to achieve advances in education and employment. In its 1892 context, then, *The Nutcracker* endorsed "the dream—or the fantasy—that marriage will be sweet, smooth, and all-fulfilling for women." But she also suggests ways in which the Sugar Plum Fairy and other heroines of imperial ballets can be seen to represent power and authority, given that they are rulers, they make life-changing choices for themselves, and they display complex technical skills. Banes rejects, as I do, the "homogenizing and essentializing" view that women in classical ballet pas de deux are manipulated and dominated in ways that prevent them from exerting any independence.[9]

My respondents—mostly *Nutcracker* dancers and insiders, but also a few less-connected audience members—tended to confirm the idea that the Sugar Plum Fairy has a more complex image than her mild demeanor might at first indicate. "She's not some flighty fairy," said a member of the National Ballet's production staff. "She's definitely a fairy who has control over the people and the situation she's around. And she's definitely chosen her partner, as opposed to being won over in a very Jane Eyre-esque way. So she's actually quite a strong, strong female, even though she's—hate to say it, but—sugar-coated and very pretty and fluffy." Young dancers also talked about the by-now familiar ballerina dichotomies, not hesitating to combine what may seem like contradictory qualities. They called the Sugar Plum sweet, floaty, and "just the littlest thing," but also "peppy and very organized," and "the queen of the world." Perhaps my question "What can you tell about the Sugar Plum Fairy from her dancing?" encouraged them to talk about her technical skills, but they had no trouble switching between assessing her as fictional character and as a very real dancer. "I think the Sugar Plum Fairy is a happy sort of fairy-type person," a ten-year-old girl said, "but in real life, she has to be a very serious dancer." Another young dancer agreed that "she's got a lot of experience, and she's worked really hard, even just to do that turn right or get that leg high enough." She added that the Sugar Plum and her partner don't "just do the steps—they always perform for you. They, you know, almost talk to you by just showing off."

More than one young performer acknowledged a hint of romance in the Sugar Plum Fairy's stage life, often describing the pas de deux in familiar, fairy-tale terms. A thirteen-year-old former Clara, operating in the Venus-Mars mode, pronounced the Sugar Plum and her Cavalier "the perfect couple," because the Sugar Plum's steps were "small and detailed," making her look fragile, while her partner was "the opposite. He's a warrior. . . . a protector." But the "marriage made in ballet heaven" aspect didn't come up in many conversations. A very talented future Sugar Plum summed up the role as one needing a well-rounded and balanced dancer, noting that "the focus is usually on the female dancer 'cause she's usually the lead role, and her partner is usually overlooked." And an adult who frequented the ballet said that, although she loves the romantic aspect of many ballets, the Sugar Plum didn't appear to be dying for love like so many ballet heroines. "She's kind, she's safe, she's calm, you can have faith in her," she said. "She's going to make things right. And people respect her, look up to her, that sort of thing."

The Sugar Plum Fairy is not a ballerina role commonly associated with "power moves"—unlike, say, the Black Swan in *Swan Lake* or one of Balanchine's steely neoclassical roles—but she does perform impressive physical feats. Audience members I talked to admired her high extensions, her sharply delineated pauses on one toe and the way she "ate up space" with her circle of pirouettes at the end of her variation. While it's true that her style of dress is well within the fluffy range and her strength is cloaked in ease of movement—more so than that of her male counterpart, who has more obviously athletic steps—today's Sugar Plum Fairies have an extraordinary range of motion, and in the last few decades, they even tend to have lightly muscled upper bodies, due to a weight training trend among female dancers. Few *Nutcracker* audience members would be unaware of the strength required to hop on pointe or spin like a top.

But what of the Sugar Plum Fairy's old-fashioned manners, the way she allows herself to be supported, guided, and hovered over by her Prince? After all, he's the one who lifts her into orbits over his head, twirls her at the waist, and yanks her in all directions so he can display her in decorative poses. As dance scholar Ann Daly has pointed out, there are ways in which the male-female relationship in classical ballet echoes sociocultural patterns.[10] The male partner in ballet stands securely on flat feet, while the ballerina is unstable on pointe; she takes his hand when offered, and he literally manipulates her, looking like the kind of "take charge" guy whose initiative might be admired. These protocols are based on a conventional view of sexual difference and are not mandated by any biological imperative. Men *could* dance on pointe, for instance, and women could stand behind their partners and steady or spin them, as they often did during the age of the "travesty dancer" in the nineteenth century, when women replaced many men in leading roles.[11] The fact is, classical ballet enforces a division of labor that echoes the graceful manners of another age, one in which women and men were even more limited by templates of "appropriate" behavior. Do viewers of *The Nutcracker* today imagine that, in a duet like the grand pas de deux, the Cavalier has all the power and the Sugar Plum Fairy is window dressing?

I've explored this issue more often in classrooms than in the field, so I'll take a small detour here to talk about ballet relationships in general. Think of it as a kind of "*Nutcracker* couples therapy" to answer this question: "Can the Sugar Plum Fairy and her Cavalier *really* be happy in a world where she is the head of government but must wait for his extended hand before walking across the stage, and he gets all the big leaps but has no official title?" In many dance history and criticism classes, I've shown duets from different ballets and asked students to talk about the relationship between the man and the woman—who has the power, who seems most important or impressive? I offer some of their comments as a kind of Sugar Plum "consciousness raising session." It's by now a hackneyed term, but the "self-help for ballerina fairies" movement has historically been slow to get off the ground.

So who has the power in a ballet pas de deux? To both dance outsiders and insiders the word "power" seems appropriate to describe the bounding leaps and double turns in the air that a male dancer does in his variation and his part of the coda. But, like the many *Nutcracker* viewers who barely notice the Cavalier, students often can't erase the first impression they get of the male as the "silent partner," the guy who does all the heavy lifting and unobtrusive steadying. One look at the face of a male dancer smashed under a tutu as he struggles to keep a ballerina on his shoulder and cross the stage with composure convinces many viewers that it's a job with a big downside. Still, he gets to be very flashy for a few eventful moments. People argue from all sides about whether the man or the woman makes the biggest impression in a pas de deux, often betraying their own interests and agendas. I've seen this at work most clearly when I've asked a roomful of serious dancers (at a conservatory or among dance majors specializing in ballet). Then, the lines are drawn in iron-clad fashion: the female dancers say their role is obviously the more important, while men think the opposite. They laugh when they hear each other make these claims categorically, but don't budge in their assessments. In the end, there's usually affable agreement that, gee, each of them gets a turn in the spotlight, so it's a good combination of energies. But sometimes I suspect that their opinions aren't the least bit softened—they like their own roles best. In my experience interviewing audience members, their focus is often pulled toward women or men for any number of personal reasons, too.

Dancers are particularly good at coming up with physical "proof" to back up their impressions about which partner seems in control of a duet, and nonspecialists often come up with fresh assessments be-

Sugar Plum Fairy Kelly Lamoureux demonstrates the way to momentarily
obscure a Cavalier in the Inland Pacific Ballet's *Nutcracker*. It's her
prerogative as sole monarch of a burgeoning candy nation.

cause they come to dance analysis with fewer preconceptions. Occasionally, a college student's major area of study can influence his or
her point of view; those studying science or math have noticed a
dancer's height or the position of limbs, and what effect that physical impression can have. When a woman is on pointe, one of them
said, "she towers over her partner," and takes up space with her high,
stretched-out extensions. Another found that when a male partner,
in customary fashion, pursues a ballerina who takes flight across the

stage it looks like "she's leading him around wherever she wants to go." Just because a flashy male solo makes a dancer look like he can leap tall buildings in a single bound doesn't necessarily make him Superman, one student pointed out, because physical feats aren't always associated with superior beings anymore; in fact, the ballerina's emphasis on more detailed, contained movements may seem more thoughtful and worthy of the respect given to those who think for a living. Asked to analyze the movement qualities that might telegraph power in a pas de deux, a dance major pointed to the ballerina's authoritative, superior way of operating: she didn't even have to make eye contact with her partner to know where he would be—she just reached out a hand and expected him to be there. Surely that was power.

By quoting comments and summaries from my discussion groups about who has the power in a ballet pas de deux I don't mean to offer definitive answers; in fact, the relevance of power defined in conventional terms is limited when you consider the Sugar Plum Fairy. Yes, she's a head of state and looks impressively in control, but she also comes closest, of all classical heroines, to being a motherly figure. The moments when she tenderly welcomes and shepherds the young Clara and her Prince can impress some audience members as much as her "power moves" do. Questions about control and importance in a duet are often useful as a provocative way of uncovering attitudes and opinions, which in turn suggest the many ways people interpret ballet duets. And although some *Nutcracker* lovers may not notice the Cavalier much, I don't think male dancers are in danger of being devalued overall. In amateur versions, I've seen Cavaliers and Trepak dancers of indifferent quality barely make it out of a pirouette without toppling and still garner applause for their stab at stirring up some excitement.

As I casually polled *Nutcracker* audience members during intermissions and after performances, I often had enough time to ask only a single question: "What was your favorite part of the ballet?" Some

answers seemed related to gender preferences as they're stereotypically defined. Men and boys tended to like the battle scene—perhaps
it was the part they found easiest to remember or describe. Men admired the sexy Arabian dancer in Leesburg, sometimes sheepishly,
making sure to say she was, of course, a very talented dancer. Girls
liked the ballerinas who wore the fullest pastel costumes and danced
on pointe; kids liked the clownish parts; mothers talked about the
sweet relationships between parents and kids; and women in general admired the Sugar Plum Fairy and many of the "ballerina" roles.
But there were also less predictable choices: girls loved the bumbling,
athletic mice because they didn't have to use such "neat and proper"
dancing; fathers enjoyed the family feeling of the party scene; and a
guy in punk leather attire and skull-and-crossbones jewelry gushed
about a young woman who danced the candy cane solo because of
her bounding, complex jump combinations.

I realized that it would be impossible to understand exactly *why*
people singled out certain parts of the ballet as their favorites. If they
were anything like me, they were affected by a dozen overlapping,
complex concerns and experiences in their lives; and even within
their assessments of *The Nutcracker*, there were shifting attitudes and
perhaps contradictions—not to mention the fact that they each made
choices about what to tell me.[12] When I was able to have slightly
longer conversations with people, and when they became brave about
offering assessments, the responses were more detailed and revealing. After a Loudoun Ballet matinee one day, two men who had come
with their wives under some duress surprised me by saying their
favorite part was the dance called "Petit Fours" (danced to the Mirleton Flutes). This consisted of four young women, wearing their first
classical tutus, struggling to keep knees straight and arms soft in a
long series of classroom steps using a lot of pointe work. The men
admired their balance, wondering what kind of special shoes they
were wearing to perform this "trick." When told that pointe shoes
were just stiffened glue and canvas, and that female dancers depend

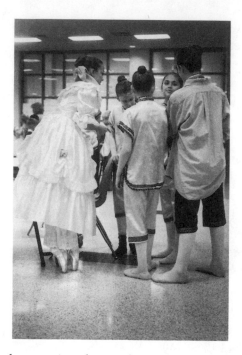

Girls with newly won pointe shoes at the Loudoun Ballet like to put them
into use at every opportunity. They talk about the towering feeling
they get from wearing them and from mastering movements
that require strength and skill.

on strength training and not trick shoes, they were even more impressed.

When I talked to young dancers, not surprisingly, a fascination
with pointe shoes often surfaced. At the Loudoun Ballet in Leesburg,
a group of ten- to twelve-year-olds girls were especially voluble during
discussions while we sat on the floor of their dressing room during
performances. Dancing on pointe made them feel strong, they told
me, like they were special and in control. I could see the number of
times young dancers offstage drew themselves up on pointe—ostensibly to test their shoes and warm up, but in fact, some of them didn't

dance on pointe in *The Nutcracker;* they just seemed to like the towering feeling of walking around on their toes backstage. They talked about the expertise required to dance on pointe; you had to be tough, they said, to build muscles that support altered weight and to deal with blisters and other foot ailments. And you had to keep developing your skills to be able to balance in the shoes and make steps look easy. "Boys think ballet is for sissies," said one eleven-year-old, rolling her eyes, "but they should just try wearing pointe shoes for a few minutes—it would *kill* them."

Because of my interest in the question of what women get out of ballet, I was particularly alert to the ways in which women operated backstage. So many people get their first taste of dancing in a *Nutcracker*—what impressions might a young performer get of how the ballet world works? At the National Ballet of Canada, there were almost equal numbers of male and female dancers, but the technical staff and stage crew were predominantly male, and the choreographer/artistic director and his associate director were both men. Although there are exceptions, this configuration is common in large professional companies: men tend to have the most authoritative, highest-paying jobs, while women often hold many of the teaching and coaching positions, as well as populating departments such as costumes and shoes. But at the Loudoun Ballet, as in many other amateur settings where *The Nutcracker* thrives, there were more women than men running things, including the artistic director, the ballet mistress, stage manager, producer, and most of the volunteers (although over the years, there have been some men in key positions, such as president of the ballet board).

In Leesburg I sat back on many occasions and surveyed rehearsals and backstage areas during performances, trying to discern what this world of women looked like in action. I approached the task almost as I would a dance analysis, noting what elements of the "choreography" might be interpreted in what ways. I saw that not only were there mostly women around, but their ways of operating were more authoritative than those of their male colleagues, their movements more definitive, their voices constantly heard making decisions. At rehearsals, I could see women in managerial positions, standing alone or at the head of a group, supervising men who hung lights, did carpentry, and moved sets. Some women pitched in on these tasks as well, or sometimes took over, but men did much of the heavy physical labor. Adolescent boys who had been drafted to play party guests in the first scene were always hanging around— usually somewhat awkwardly, like wallflowers at a dance—and were happy when they could be useful pushing a flat or steadying a ladder. Many fathers helped out in various ways, but more often, mothers provided performers with supervision and help. The overwhelming, unremarked-upon impression was that *The Nutcracker* was run by women. An interesting exception, when it came to backstage preparations, were the brief prayer circles that some participants formed before each show, which were led by male performers.

Among the dancers of the Loudoun Ballet, there weren't many males with much training or stage experience; consequently, the gaze and bodily focus of the men and boys tended to be scattered much of the time. They handled unfamiliar clothing awkwardly, submitted warily to makeup and hair spray, and shifted from one foot to the other before going onstage. Girls and women had the burden of responsibility onstage, and because of their dance training and performing experience, they remained focused, organizing their backstage spaces and making elaborate preparations before going onstage. These gender differences weren't absolute, but it was an overwhelming trend. Mothers would help younger girls, while older ones would set up their own base camp where rehearsal clothes, makeup, and costumes were kept. (Some volunteers weren't parents but almost all of them had had a child in the production at some point.) Dancers claimed a space to warm up, test out pointe shoes, and run through bits of a dance. They relaxed briefly after performing, but when they weren't onstage they were usually watching their comrades from the wings or listening carefully for their cues. And while there was some flirtation going on between adolescents who danced together in the party scene, it happened in an atmosphere unlike other social contexts in which they might interact. "They're not like regular girls at school," one of the young men told me. "I don't know, they're like . . . older."

That the *Nutcracker* world is often dominated by women perhaps isn't a surprise to the few men who do get involved. One single father in Leesburg complained that his involvement was curtailed by a general reluctance to have male volunteers backstage with so many girls and young women. And when it comes to performing, men face all kinds of societal pressures *not* to be part of the ballet world. In Toronto, the boys of the National Ballet School of Canada had received permission not to wear their uniforms on field trips because they were often harassed and threatened when their affiliation was recognized. In small towns, it can be even more difficult to break the taboo. Several boys who were enjoying their Leesburg *Nutcracker* experience told me they planned to take ballet in the new year, but I also heard tales of how this never works out. Boys who had tried it — or their parents — told me they quit because it was hard being the only boy in class. This, I guessed, was the easiest way to say that boys in ballet get teased or at least get the message that they're doing an odd thing. It's possible that some attitudes changed after the popularity of the film *Billy Elliott,* about a miner's plucky son who bravely enters the world of pink satin and survives, but the prejudice against men in ballet doesn't seem likely to disappear overnight.[13]

Although newspaper articles about men in ballet intermittently trumpet changes in the "real men don't dance" status quo, ballet has always been a suspect profession for men in North America (and, contrary to popular belief, in many other countries around the world). In the so-called dance boom of the 1960s and 1970s, there was some talk of high-profile dancers like Edward Villella, Jacques d'Amboise, and Rudolf Nureyev making ballet safe for boys, because these dancers had powerful, athletic physiques and were widely perceived as sex symbols for women (although Nureyev's homosexuality was well known to many). In the 1970s Villella even appeared on the popular television comedy *The Odd Couple,* in an episode that took pains to show off his athletic prowess and "regular guy" personality. But the strategy was evidently a drop in the bucket. In the 1990s, television's animated *The Simpsons* reflected all the old fears in an episode that has Bart taking ballet. At one point, he says to his instructor: "I fear the girls will laugh at me. I fear the boys will beat the living snot out of me." As a columnist in the *Washington Post* said, commenting on this episode and her own son's involvement with ballet, "There's something about a boy in leggings that makes people nervous."[14]

As enticingly "all-American" as Fritz and the Nutcracker can be in the New World, they definitely haven't conquered the prejudice about boys in ballet. In Leesburg, the word *ballet* is scrupulously avoided when male performers are recruited for *The Nutcracker.* No one says, "Would you like to be in a ballet?" to teenage boys who are needed for the party scene, but it works to say, "How would you like to dance with some girls from your high school?" (In fact, getting the young women to recruit young men they know usually gets results.) Emphasizing that warfare is involved helps entice young soldiers into rehearsals for the battle scene. At first the new recruits are excited to get their toy rifles and only then do they hear the bad news about having to dance with girls in the party scene. Talking to boys and their parents about attitudes toward male dancers, I found a reluctance to comment on the stereotypes and prejudices that dominate a lot of thinking about the subject. "Well, if he really wanted to take ballet, that would be okay," a parent would say, "but so far, it hasn't come up." I sensed that everyone was being polite or "politically correct," because I knew it was a community in which some parents held conservative views about gender-appropriate behavior. Finally, one Loudoun Ballet volunteer was frank about the subject. She and

During the act-one "adolescent party guest dance" at the Loudoun Ballet the boys tend to walk, the girls to dance. Many boys are lured into performing by girl dancers their age—and the promise that they won't have to wear tights.

her daughter had both performed in *The Nutcracker,* but she told me she didn't think her husband would let her young son participate. When I asked why, she answered immediately, "Oh, well, I think he's homophobic."

The prejudice against male ballet dancing must surely exist in many *Nutcracker* communities, but it's sometimes mitigated by elements that separate *The Nutcracker* from other classical ballets. I could tell by talking to people in the amateur context that *The Nutcracker* is often defined as "not *really* a ballet" by some participants. In other words, guys who ordinarily avoid ballet decide to perform in *The Nutcracker* because they think, "It's not exactly a ballet, it's more of a Christmas celebration," or, "I'm not really in a ballet, because all I do is walk around wearing a suit or a uniform, not tights." Reluctant parents might decide that it's not really a ballet, it's just a show in which their sons get to play toy soldier for a while. Audience members, too, may come to see *The Nutcracker* because it's defined more as a "Christmas thing" than a "ballet thing." Meanwhile, boys who are determined can slip under the radar into the ballet world, while the rest of the world takes its time to evolve.

Over the years, the Nutcracker himself has had a few gender identity crises—if I can return to the conceit of the Nutcracker as a character who tries his best to fit in everywhere. Mostly, he seems comfortable with traditional family values, happily surrounded by antiquated caricatures of sugar-and-spice ladies and puppy-dog-tail guys. But he's also been open-minded about who should play what role, as seen in the many conventional productions in which girls fill in as soldiers and the character of Mother Ginger is played by a man. But those are accepted theatrical traditions—a kind of "don't ask, don't tell" gender situation. On the other hand, Mark Morris's sincere satire, *The Hard Nut*, treads a more progressive path but doesn't lose the spirit of *The Nutcracker*. Morris's unisex snowflake scene is highly unconventional but so classically crafted and so musical and celebratory (dancers toss handfuls of artificial snow throughout), you forget to notice how many of the midriff-baring tutus are worn by men and how many by women. There's a kind of egalitarian camp in the identical hats that make them all look like Tastee-Freez cones. Morris also inserts drag roles in unexpected places—Clara's mother, for instance, is played by a man, as is the family maid, who teeters around on pointe.

In more traditional *Nutcrackers*, boys will be boys and only girls can be snowflakes or mothers. Having lived through a century of revolution when it comes to male-female behavioral customs, *The Nutcracker* still often reverts to easy stereotypes. In most party scenes, the little girls are all docile doll lovers while the boys stamp, run, and generally act as if unruly behavior is charming. Watching this dynamic time after time, I find myself thinking that, yes, it's an era gone by—

but weren't there ever any tomboy daughters who ripped their ruffles, or sensitive sons who refused to harass the girls? Would it hurt to suggest this? Choreographers have adjusted other aspects of the ballet to reflect changes in ballet technique, costumes, and hairstyles, and now no one quibbles over whether or not nineteenth-century women would have bared that much leg. Why not tweak the male and female stereotypes occasionally?

But in general, I don't expect traditional *Nutcracker*s to radically alter genteel ballet etiquette; I am hopeful that experiments along those lines are taking place on different fronts, reflecting the cornucopia of contemporary ways gender identity is evolving. But I do wonder how dancers and audiences are affected by ballet's ultrafeminine or ultragentlemanly portrayals. Do they believe that boys and girls should be like the ones they see in the party scene? Do they think there is some message in the way the Sugar Plum and her Cavalier treat each other? Do they think that women, just like dancing snowflakes and flowers, should all move gracefully and never carry a big stick (as, say, the soldiers or a master of ceremonies might)?

Not surprisingly, most people I talked to about *The Nutcracker* hadn't given much thought to the significance of the courtly characters and old fashioned boy-girl etiquette shown on stage. When I drew their attention to it, many of them seemed content to watch or embody the quaint grace and civility of a time when, they could imagine, everyone knew his or her place and loved it. Parents laughed as they told me they preferred the version of their children behaving as proper Victorians onstage to the kids who were sloppy and rude at home. Few people had thought about comparing their own relationships to that of the Sugar Plum and her Cavalier. The only time this was even suggested was in Leesburg, when I was having conversations with self-described "strong Christians," whom others would call part of the Christian right. A few women told me that the teachings of their church mandated the husband as head of household and women as supportive spouses, and I was referred to a book that compared "the Christian walk" to the process of learning ballet. It compared repeated barre exercises to prayer and suggested that learning choreography was like following God's will, because each requires "humility and discipline." A few of the Christian women I talked to found this part of the book interesting and inspirational, but there was some eye-rolling about the chapter that said women should obey their husbands, just like a female dancer matches her movement to her partner's, in exchange for being supported by him. I got the idea that you could lead a woman to a repressive ballet metaphor, but she'd still interpret choreography the way she wanted.

Another attitude toward ballet's extreme version of femininity arose more often—that it's something you master, perform, and then leave behind as you exit the studio or stage. Both amateur and professional dancers talked about learning the princesslike demeanor of the ballerina as one would master any task—sometimes it was a fun fantasy, sometimes they felt silly or hopeless at having to be dainty and regal. Mainly, they tried to get it right; it was one of ballet's tools, part of the art form, something to be mastered and performed.[15] I started to call the kind of persona women have to take on in order to dance ballet's traditional princess and fairy-tale heroines "femininity in context." As one dancer said as she reassured her artistic director she could make the matinee even if it snowed the next day, "Don't worry, I'm a Sugar Plum with four-wheel drive."

One of the ways I hoped to get dancers to talk about the impact of having to inhabit their ultrafeminine roles in *The Nutcracker* was to ask whether there was something about their characters that related to their everyday lives. Younger women said they experienced the same problems with their brothers that Clara has with Fritz, when he teases her and they fight. One or two said they daydreamed like Clara did. More often, they pointed out the differences between stage demeanor and "real life." One of the sweetest Claras I had seen, a young dancer with bright eyes and a brilliant line, was dressed in low-cut jeans and a small, torn tank top when she told me, "Well, I'm not really like Clara, not an innocent little girl, you know."

Professional female dancers I interviewed found the discussion about their relationship to ballet characters interesting, probably because they are sometimes bewildered by people who expect them to be princesslike offstage. "It's not like I wait for a guy to carry me over puddles or take my hand and lead me everywhere," one of them said to me, laughing, wondering how anyone could confuse her with the sylphs and fairies she plays in ballets. But she acknowledged that she'd met male fans who had done just that. These aren't the men ballet dancers usually end up getting to know, she told me, they're the starstruck ones who admire ballerinas from afar and find it hard to relate to them offstage. Back at the time *The Nutcracker* first emerged at the Maryinsky, ballerinas might have expected and fostered a worshipful air from fans; it was an age when women were judged differently and dancers craved respectability. Up until the social changes of the 1960s, North American ballet dancers also tended to be concerned with dressing and behaving in ways that were closer to their onstage image—early Sugar Plum Fairies like Alexandra Danilova and Marie Tallchief surely wouldn't have blinked an eye if they had been mistaken for royalty offstage. But today's female dancers live in a different world, and their audiences are familiar with the transformation process that goes on between sweaty studio and stage.

Profiling the characters in *The Nutcracker* and finding out how audiences relate to them is an assignment that has no end, especially because the ballet is a living thing and changes so much over time. But in North America, the Nutcracker and his gang have become archetypes to some degree. When changes take place in a local production, opinions fly—what's Drosselmeier without an eye patch? Clara should never be over twelve; the Sugar Plum Fairy would never wear that; and where are all the tiny angels who were here last year, and why did they change the flower costumes? In Toronto, people were

Where does the Sugar Plum Fairy come from? Karen Kain descends from above in the 1964 Celia Franca production at the National Ballet of Canada (top left); James Kudelka's 1995 version finds Sonia Rodriguez (bottom) living in a jeweled egg; and Lisa Johnson's Sugar Rum Cherry (above) looks like she comes from wherever she wants to in Donald Byrd's *Harlem Nutcracker.*

still getting used to the changes in the life of the Sugar Plum Fairy, and still speaking of her as a person they knew, even though she had changed so much in their new production. She used to make her entrance sitting in a balloon that dropped out of the sky, like a sugar-coated deus ex machina, but now, she evidently lived in a large jeweled egg, waiting for her Cavalier to let her out. Suddenly she looked passive, like a closeted rare jewel that her Prince discovers, and some people missed her more authoritative entrance from above—alone. But they hadn't forgotten who she "really was." They were still thinking of a more autonomous Sugar Plum when they described her to me, and they knew they could always find that image in another stage version, or in their favorite *Nutcracker* videos.

In some ways, the characters in *The Nutcracker* have a lot in common with the carved nutcracker dolls that inspired the ballet: to everyone, they represent something similar but variable. And you can dress them up and interpret them in different ways. Nutcrackers can be merely decorative, or—if the teeth are sturdy enough—they can crack the hard shell of nut and reveal its delicious interior.

When I first started contributing dance writing to the Los Angeles Times, in the mid-1990s, I was phoned by their full-time dance writer in November and asked tentatively if I would mind reviewing a few Nutcrackers. What he said was something like, "I know it can be terribly boring, but there are tons of them, as you know, and we just have to review some of the better ones." I was told to address issues that distinguished one production from another—did the plot make sense, were the dancers technically skilled, what was the quality of the orchestra or tape? His tone was apologetic, as if he were asking me to sweep up after horses in a parade. Clearly, among newspaper critics, The Nutcracker was seen as hardship duty. "Don't worry, I like Nutcrackers," I told him. "I've become fascinated with the idea that it's a seasonal ritual." There was a pause. "Yes, well, just remember this," he said briskly, "you're the dance critic, not the ritual critic."

Well, yes. Therein lies the downside of Nutcracker studies, a scholarly field that has only recently emerged (as I write, actually). Dance critics know the history of The Nutcracker best and are therefore most likely to grasp its many facets and subtleties, but they are used to viewing it only as an aesthetic product. The Nutcracker has not traditionally been part of discussions about ritual, and only recently has there been any significant consideration of ballet in an ethnographic light. For many Western scholars and performers, ancient cultures and rigorous classical dance forms elsewhere are something to be revered—something new and exciting to explore—while the West's oldest classical dance form, ballet, tends to be categorized as simply "old-garde," or at least too elitist to reflect anything but itself.

I recall a colleague once explaining to me the difference between ballet and bharata natyam, which has religious roots. "You see, for me, the way I move onstage, the way I watch bharata natyam, has everything to do with the way my grandmother wore her sari," she said, referring to the inextricable links between Indian classical dance and its cultural context. "Whereas, ballet is just everywhere." Her tone was assured and somewhat dismissive. "Ballet can't be as deeply important to you, because it has nothing to do with the way you live your life."

I thought of the way my grandmother wore her house dresses on the farm and changed into her best silks to come see me in The Nutcracker, and I was unwilling to concede the point. I thought about my mother, who had loved seeing me onstage, dressed as an angel, with my gold halo and long gauzy dress, or a snowflake in tulle, the epitome of her vision of femininity. And I remembered the respect I got for studying a "highbrow" art form as I was growing up in an upwardly mobile American suburb. Then there was my own relationship to ballet as a symbol of agency and achievement, and the feelings of transcendence I experienced as both a dancer and an audience member. I thought of the little-acknowledged fact that ballet is an ethnic dance form, developed largely in various European and North American locales and reflecting culturally specific ideals, themes, and aesthetics. The Nutcracker, of course, reflects and promotes the ideals of one of Christian North America's most important holidays, Christmas. But that wasn't what gave it its resonance in my life. I no longer found meaning in the static Presbyterian ceremonies of my youth, but I often felt great spiritual renewal after a really good ballet.

The Meaning of Life

The meaning of life for *The Nutcracker,* despite its many strong connections to people and the holidays, hasn't always been clear. Everything seemed fairly straightforward at birth—the ballet needed critical and popular acclaim to fulfill its destiny at the Maryinsky. But life on the imperial stage proved rocky, and the ballet's reason for living remained tenuous for a while. Once *The Nutcracker* went on the road, the copious renaming, twisting, and truncating resulted in a kind of identity theft—or at the least, a series of identity crises—so that a deeper meaning became even more elusive. Then came the new beginning. As an immigrant to North America, *The Nutcracker* expanded its horizons and, no matter how many different incarnations resulted, became more and more the solid citizen. Gathering folk wisdom through grassroots experience, Citizen *Nutcracker* became older, wiser, and more diverse. But who could have predicted the next step? Somewhere along the line, *The Nutcracker* was elevated to ritual status. Granted, this was conferred by various dance writers who were trying to find a snappy nickname for the annual *Nutcracker*—"a Christmas ritual," "a holiday tradition," "a rite of passage." They did everything but say that the ballet brought us good tidings of great joy. Still, the labels were more than ink-deep.

What dance writers usually mean by mentioning ritual in this context is that *The Nutcracker* comes back every year like clockwork and people embrace its familiar music, steps, and symbols. The rite of passage label fits in two ways: *The Nutcracker* is often the first ballet people see, providing a kind of threshold to the dance world; and, for performers, the "passage" through one role after another marks various status changes in a dancing life. But how seriously can we apply the title of "ritual" to a ballet? The philosopher Francis Sparshott suggests that if a ballet like *The Nutcracker* were really a ritual, it would include a ceremony in which "the spirit of Yule would be invoked or that of Petipa appeased."[1] As far as I know, this kind of thing has not caught on. Sparshott's assumption that ritual involves the explicit acknowledgment of divine beings or heavenly forces is not unusual—much of the ethnographic research on ritual, rites, and ceremonies has involved sacred societies and religious organizations, where a sharp distinction is made between sacred and secular activity. For dance, this categorical difference has meant that lines have been drawn between theatrical performances designed for aesthetic pleasure and entertainment, and religious-based rituals that contain movement-filled choreographic protocols. But these distinctions haven't always been absolute. What label is put on Mevlevi dervish spinning (meant to induce religious trance) when people buy tickets to watch it on a stage? Or on *The Dying Swan* if it is danced at a memorial service in church?[2]

People who talked to me about *The Nutcracker* took for granted the distinction between religious ritual and ballet, naturally enough. So when I asked them whether or not *The Nutcracker* had anything to do with religion, most of them answered quickly that it didn't, saying things like, "It's not Christian just because it has Christmas in it." But when I followed up by asking if there was anything spiritual about the ballet, people often became thoughtful and talked about spirituality and ballet in various ways. There were even times when they got around to linking organized religion to their *Nutcracker* involvement—this happened frequently with people who were self-described "strong Christians." When I learned the ways in which they thought their beliefs dovetailed with dancing or watching ballet, I could see that *The Nutcracker* presented few obstacles to that practice.

On the other hand, for nonreligious people and the few people I spoke to who mentioned being Jewish or Hindu, *The Nutcracker* provided a secular way to share in seasonal celebrations. Some of them saw its potential to forge community spirit, even if it was sometimes a temporary, tenuous thing. What bond is complete and permanent, anyway? one active Leesburg volunteer asked. She talked about the benefits of finding at least a little common ground with people who held very different opinions. She was also aware that it helped to avoid certain topics—for instance, the participation of several *Nutcracker* volunteers in marches on nearby Washington, in support of various causes. Instead, they focused on themes they shared at *Nutcracker* time, like the warmth of family togetherness, childlike enthusiasm and optimism, and the pursuit of excellence.

Ballet, which was at the center of most discussions about the Leesburg *Nutcracker,* was universally appreciated and often loved, but people came to it from different angles. One of the things some religious Christians in Leesburg talked about was whether or not ballet was a selfish pursuit. A few mothers had had initial fears about daughters who seemed obsessed with ballet—was it a frivolous activity that took too much of their time? Then they reassured themselves that you could dance "for the glory of God," and that the arts were a valuable contribution to society. One backstage volunteer told me she thought young religious women involved in ballet could serve as role models because of their devotion and hard work. In conversations and in the prayer circles that took place before performances, the message I heard was that God makes room in his kingdom for dancing and plot lines that echo family togetherness. Another *Nutcracker* volunteer said she'd been brought up in a conservative religious family where dancing was against the rules, but she had broken with this belief. "God uses dance in the Bible," she said. "It can be

Before a *Nutcracker* performance at the Loudoun Ballet, cast and
crew members often form small prayer circles.

used in a worshipful way, used correctly—not in an obscene way." It
wasn't hard to figure out what "an obscene way" of dancing was for
many of these *Nutcracker* aficionados; although no one was anxious to
describe it, I got the idea that mobilization of the pelvis was involved.

Ballet, on the other hand, was considered a "correct" use of the
body by conservative religionists in that an uplifted aesthetic gave
it a kind of dignity and propriety that could fit into their agendas. I
could see that what was aristocratic in one context became worshipful and heavenly in another. When a dancer's gaze and limbs floated
skyward, this could look like homage to heaven, and in many *Nutcracker*s Clara travels even further toward this illusion when she arrives in her dreamed-of land on a cloud of fog, with Tchaikovsky's
harp, celesta, and trilling flutes underlining the celestial mood. For
some participants, it seemed fortuitous that *The Nutcracker* includes
a family Christmas party in the first act, angels in the second, and
"right triumphing over might" in between.

For most everyone else, these events had meanings unrelated to religious ideology. I just happened to run into vocal Christians in one *Nutcracker* location, and they became an interesting example of an "interpretive community"—a group of people with shared values that they rely upon to interpret ballet.[3] In Leesburg, the Christian participants constituted a fairly close-knit group, but even within this group, I could see that there were differences of opinion. And there were many other potential interpretive communities, including people who shared a view of ballet and classical music as generally uplifting. Young women and men who experienced physical control and ambition as signs of independence or rebellion constituted another interpretive community; some of them felt like they were breaking the rules by dancing in *The Nutcracker*, some thought they were following the rules, depending on family and peer attitudes. There were also many dancers and audience members who seemed to let the aesthetic pleasures of the ballet wash over them, never pausing to untangle or explain inchoate reactions. Some people thought ballet was a great equalizer—given the proper physical talents and maybe a scholarship, anyone could succeed with hard work, and in the amateur context, almost anyone could participate. Others associated ballet with sophistication and upward mobility, although the reality of the "pitch-in" *Nutcracker* was often at odds with would-be elitists.

Many *Nutcracker* aficionados who had no involvement with organized religion still spoke about spiritual resonance in a general way. "It's not necessarily God or Jesus," a thirty-something man who had become a ballet fan said, "but ballet has lots of spirituality—emotions and inner feelings." A backstage worker in Toronto talked about the spiritual tone he saw in the National Ballet's new version of Coffee, saying that James Kudelka's coolly enigmatic quartet almost put him in a trance because the choreography was "smooth and conditioned, almost intellectual." This particular Arabian featured two couples who didn't employ the usual double-jointed slinking. Instead, there was an emphasis on formal patterns and synchronization, which re-

An alternate vision of Arabia: the cool, precise symmetry in the
National Ballet of Canada's Coffee avoids some of the Middle Eastern
stereotyping found in other versions. From left: Andrea Burridge,
Julius Bates, Jana Soon, and Kevin Law.

minded my respondent less of romantic attachment or sex than of the
thrill to be had when "everything looks so together, attuned." A few
audience members said the "intense beauty" and "the zeal, the pure
classicism" of ballet "enriches the soul." Sometimes a respondent returned to the word "religion" for emphasis. "Ballet *is* the religion,"
one twenty-something balletomane who took evening ballet classes
told me. "It's the pursuit of perfection—you suffer for it, work for it;
it's a constant struggle, complete and total selfless dedication. I think
it has a religious fervor to it."

Citizen Nutcracker—always searching for a deeper meaning beneath surface-level popularity and financial incentives—would be
glad to hear that, although not surprised. Ballet lore is full of religious metaphors when it comes to single-minded devotion to and

reverence for the profession, and these circulate freely in the world of *The Nutcracker*, sometimes conferring on it a consecrating power. Although many performers in amateur versions aren't deeply immersed in the pursuit of ballet perfection, they participate in the protocols that surround it and sometimes feel touched by its fervor. Audiences, too, may understand what's at stake, from their general knowledge of the profession. From *The Nutcracker*'s Russian homeland, biographies and memoirs of pre–Soviet era dancers are particularly rich in spiritual references. Maryinsky ballerina Tamara Karsavina said she started her training (at the end of the nineteenth century) with "the exhilaration of a votary," and that being on the Maryinsky stage was for her "what Mecca is to a good [Muslim]." Anna Pavlova, another imperial luminary, who began her career in St. Petersburg during the early twentieth century, wrote that to enter the theater school was "to enter a convent whence frivolity is banned, and where merciless discipline reigns." These attitudes stayed alive in the New World, where "disciples" of Balanchine took them on. "In the theater we felt we were on hallowed ground," said New York City dancer Merrill Ashley in the 1980s. "In fact, we often heard Balanchine say that we should think and act as if the theater were a church."[4]

To speak of devotion to ballet in religious terms is perhaps less common today, but religious references still crop up in offhand comments. "I might as well be a nun for all the social life I have time for," one professional told me. Contemporary dance biographies often include more humor than their forbears, and less high-flown talk about the sacrifices that are made—as well as containing some clear-eyed critiques of draconian practices—but religious metaphors still surface. In Toronto, as I researched in the mid-1990s, many ballet fans were reading the autobiography of Karen Kain, a dancer with the highest of profiles in Canada. Kain describes ballet as "almost a form of religion: you took the veil and put every part of your life on hold," and she calls her training at the National Ballet School of Canada "concentrated, even cloistered," and ballet class "the dancer's most sacred ritual." She invokes Michelangelo's view of the human body as "an instrument of the soul, the noble means by which we reach God," and describes moments of performing when she felt "touched and elevated by something that far transcends the merely human," and sensed that she might be "the privileged instrument of higher truths."[5]

Kain puts into words feelings I often encountered while talking to people about *The Nutcracker*. It's not the only ballet to stir deep feelings—far from it, given the preferences of aficionados for any number of different works. But it is the ballet closest to the largest number of people, and the only one that benefits from a relationship with such an evocative time of the year. This surely accounts for the number of people who described to me their attachment to the ballet in ways that hover around the territory of ritual. Some of their comments were lighthearted but had a deeper side as well. "We go *religiously*," one fan told me emphatically, laughing at the idea of being so serious about *Nutcracker* attendance. But in the same breath, she became earnest again and reiterated, "I mean it, we're really religious about it." Her comment seemed to be less about liturgy and more about the fact that people are often compelled to experience *The Nutcracker* at the prescribed time, every December, every year.

This calendrical aspect, which is so crucial to many rituals, occasionally occurs with other theatrical performances, especially those tied to Christmas. Handel's *Messiah*, for instance, and versions of *A Christmas Carol* have become ensconced in the season. The *Messiah*, of course, is a bit more directly associated with the religious aspect of the holiday, whereas *A Christmas Carol* and *The Nutcracker* fit more snugly in a category called "secular ritual." That term was coined by anthropologists who studied events like graduation ceremonies, birthday parties, and political meetings, noting the way various elements of "ritual-like formality" can make a ceremony or gathering "a traditionalizing instrument." Many ballets and other concert performances contain these ritual-like elements, in that they feature a stylized way of moving, an orderly progression from beginning to middle to end, and an array of symbols that resonate in particular ways for the participants.[6]

One useful way of thinking about *The Nutcracker* as a kind of ritual is to compare it to a traditional "white wedding," which occurs in many different settings but has core elements that frequently recur. Wedding formal wear has a lot in common with ballet costumes, with its emphasis on flowing white or pastel fabrics for women, contrasting tailored outfits for men, and miniature versions of both for children. And the stately processions of wedding parties provide a choreographed sense of occasion, as do the symbolic joining of hands and kneeling that traditionally precede the consecrating final kiss. Onlookers are familiar with the symbols—the parents' "giving away" of the bride, marking her change of status and residence; rings and lighted candles suggesting eternal love. As with *The Nutcracker,* the details of the formal wedding vary and each "performance" differs in terms of its meaning to those present.

The events that surround *Nutcracker*-going occasionally mimic church rituals closely, especially those events formulated by individuals who have embraced the annual tradition. One family of veteran *Nutcracker* participants in Southern California makes a ceremony out of bringing its extensive nutcracker doll collection down from the attic each December. To the strains of the Tchaikovsky score, each family member holds a favorite carved figurine and marches in a processional downstairs to the living room, solemnly putting each nutcracker in its place on the mantle. On the opposite coast, the Loudoun Ballet's artistic director and her husband close the *Nutcracker* season by burning a nutcracker-shaped candle down to the wick and perhaps saying a few personal incantations over the flame. They fully enjoy the irony of mixing a devotional candle tradition with the destruction of a symbol of a stressful *Nutcracker* season.

At performances of the Loudoun Ballet in Leesburg, rituals of the theater are another way formalized ceremonial events bolster *The Nutcracker* as an annual tradition. Some of them were instituted by the artistic director in hopes of passing on the traditions of ballet, and some grew from the community's sense of occasion. Giving flowers to the dancers at the end of a performance gained popularity when a "flower boutique" joined the souvenir table in the lobby. To make the giving process orderly, volunteers covered a number of boxes with Christmas wrapping, labeled them, and lined them up on the floor under the lip of the stage, where bouquets for each principal dancer were kept until the stage manager handed them out during individual curtain calls. It was a process done with military precision. Nearly as organized, the end-of-run cast party was moderated by a master of ceremonies (usually the actor who played Drosselmeier). Special awards were given to people who had volunteered more than usual, or performers who had survived difficult situations—one was called the "There's no business like shoe business award," given to someone who finished a variation brilliantly after losing a shoe. Volunteer groups spent weeks making or buying gifts appropriate for each member of the cast and the leaders of the backstage crews (about two hundred people at the time). Some of the gifts were trinkets that related to a given role (a snowflake Christmas ornament), some were handcrafted and customized, like the time party children received small felt Christmas stockings with their names embroidered on them.

Less formal traditions spring up around various *Nutcracker* productions; dancers receive a different carved doll or *Nutcracker*-related gift every year, and couples, families, and friends organize yearly get-togethers and meals around performances. In my family, after I retired from my local *Nutcracker,* my mother and her friend started a mother-daughter lunch and matinee event that gradually attracted other members of both families. It still includes dressing up, catching up, and a postperformance rehash of which parts of our local *Nutcracker* are working well and which parts they should never have tampered with. This event is the official start of the holiday season, says my friend, an old ballet class compatriot who became a psychologist. In late December each year, she drives back to our hometown in a stressed state of mind after a crowded work schedule and rushed gift-buying; but as soon as the sprightly *Nutcracker* overture starts, she says, it's a signal that all everyday concerns can drift away until after Christmas.

In addition to its ritual-like aspects, *The Nutcracker* often drifts into the realm of festival when ballet companies create related events to expand the *Nutcracker* season. Some companies organize a "*Nutcracker* tea," a "Sugar Plum Fair," or a "Nutty *Nut*" charity benefit performance featuring high jinx and nondancing guest stars. Topical additions to year-round ballet boutique items add to an almost carnivallike atmosphere; in the New York State Theatre lobby alone, you can find all manner of *Nutcracker* talismans, from T-shirts, sweatshirts, socks, paper dolls, and finger puppets to jewelry, tote bags, and designer scarves. At one end of the lobby, for a moderate fee, you can have your photograph taken with a dancer dressed as a snowflake, standing in front of a blowup of the snow-scene backdrop. Most everyone I saw there was attired expensively and the atmosphere was fairly subdued, but the scene was otherwise not unlike a "pose with a cowboy" booth at a state fair. In the lobby of my local *Nutcracker*, performed by the Inland Pacific Ballet, you can buy a matching tutu, crown, and wand—the latter prop having been added to the production specifically to attract budding Sugar Plum Fairies.

It's this carnival-like, commercial aspect of *The Nutcracker* that worries ballet purists. Those who would dismiss the ballet as mere spectacle can point to advertising campaigns that lean on the "bigger is better" strategy. Countless press materials and program notes cite statistics more typical of descriptions of parades or half-time shows—how many feet the tree grows, how many pounds of artificial snow fall, how many dollars were spent on costumes and sets. Some *Nutcracker* ads count on selling tickets with just a few words—"beautiful

During *Nutcracker* season, ticket holders can have a photo taken with a snowflake in the lobby of the State Theater at Lincoln Center. The dancer is usually a student at the School of American Ballet, standing in front of a blown-up photograph of the New York City Ballet snowflake corps.

scenery and costumes . . . a delight to the eyes!"—but when a new or newly refurbished production arrives, so do lists of specific details. In the Toronto of the 1990s, ballet officials worried that they needed to pump up *The Nutcracker*'s glitz quotient to compete with the non-stop, eye-catching action of megashows like *Phantom of the Opera* and *Les Misérables*. Choreographer James Kudelka and designer Santo Loquasto rose to the challenge, and National Ballet of Canada press releases immediately started touting the new high-tech scenery and the lavish sets and costumes. There was a remote-controlled mouse, seven hundred feet of computer-controlled motorized track for moving scenery, and a Sugar Plum tutu that took two hundred hours to make and cost four thousand dollars (Canadian dollars, but still). Audiences could be forgiven for confusing the new National *Nutcracker* with the latest Disney movie when they read it would include "an army and cavalry of 17 cats and dogs, six baby mice, eight Cossack mice and the Mouse Tsar, a rat, nine lambs, a fox, a sheep, a bee, six unicorns, a ram, a rooster, a dancing horse and a bear on roller blades who dances with another bear en pointe!" Many of my respondents thought the ballerina bear was a little too whimsical, but it was generally agreed that *The Nutcracker* could survive a lot of whimsy.

Not every ballet company can afford to load a *Nutcracker* with extravagant costumes and special effects, but gestures in that direction are made all the same. The tiny budget of the Loudoun Ballet meant that the cloth Christmas tree didn't expand all that much when it grew, the battle-scene cannon fired its confetti load every *other* time, and the transition to the snow scene consisted of a black curtain being drawn to reveal a painted forest backdrop. Still, audience members often raved about "all the special effects," making me think that, once everyone agrees that spectacular visions will take place, the mere suggestion of them sets off the imagination. Despite the differences of scale in Leesburg, people seemed automatically to think that *The Nutcracker* was about action-packed visual pleasure. They loved it, but elsewhere, attempts at three-ring-circus moments tend to make critics more skeptical than ever. Contemporary dance writers often keep faith with the ballet's first St. Petersburg critics when they worry about popular elements contaminating the higher purposes of serious ballet. In the New World, the added element of constant repetition also makes *The Nutcracker* suspect. How can one take seriously the idea that deeply felt beliefs and resonant moments are involved when a ballet twinkles so forcefully and returns so frequently in so many glittering guises?

The answer requires a reconsideration of the categories that *The Nutcracker* has encountered since birth—is it "high" art, popular spectacle, festival-like fun, hackneyed tripe, just a way to earn money, or a resonant experience? From the first, the plot leaps and abundance of childlike pleasures didn't fit into the imperial ballet formula, and the New World emphasis on gigantism and festive tie-ins only weakened *The Nutcracker*'s reputation in that realm. When it comes to ritual, the parallels aren't quite right either; the category of ritual has never been easy to define, but a theatrical performance has obvious differences from rites and ceremonies that take place in cohesive societies with strongly defined core values. Participation in many rituals, for instance, is mandatory—every member of a group is required to attend and the penalties for failure can be severe—whereas *Nutcracker*s are voluntary activities, no matter what some cash-strapped artistic directors may think. Theater also makes a formal distinction between the roles of performer and audience, and, unlike ritual, there is an emphasis on individual creativity and achievement. Some *Nutcracker*s take place in tightly knit communities of amateurs and professionals, but on both sides of the curtain, a spirited multiculturalism often reigns and no single cohesive interpretation or purpose necessarily arises. No ticket buyer or performer expects that a *Nutcracker* "enactment" will appease the gods, improve a harvest, or ensure planetary alignment; yet in the rehearsals, the performances, and the communal gatherings that go on throughout *Nutcracker* season, spiritual concerns may arise.

What *The Nutcracker* needs is a new category, one in which "spectacle" isn't "mere" and multiple-personality syndrome is a positive attribute. Can all of the ballet's various elements somehow gain recognition as aspects of a new kind of ritual? Anthropologist John J. MacAloon provides a model that aids in this reassessment, especially in terms of evaluating the phenomenon of overlapping genres and spectacle. MacAloon has written extensively about the modern Olympic Games—not the first kind of "performance" you might think to compare to a classical ballet. But the games share with *The Nutcracker* a disconnect between original noble goals and current categorization as spectacle. The parallels are not exact, but there are productive similarities to be explored. Both events, in their separate ways, are imbued with the lofty rhetoric of aspiration, dedication, achievement, sacrifice, and dreams coming true. Olympic purists may believe that the "true spirit" of amateur athletics is destroyed by sensational press coverage, factionalism, doping, and commercialism; ballet purists may see the annual *Nutcracker* as a debased classical genre more concerned with giggling children, special effects, and raising money than lofty aesthetic values. With both events, critics and viewers argue about whether or not the goals are even partly achieved or if it isn't all empty spectacle.[7]

MacAloon's revelation is that spectacle isn't always empty, but in fact may be full of possibilities. Instead of saddling the Olympic Games with one previously existing genre label, MacAloon points out that its many aspects—ritual, festival, play, and spectacle—are "nested" within one overarching framework. In other words, it isn't one genre we're talking about, but many; he says we could call it a "metagenre" or "megagenre." What this means is that participants can find many entry points to an event, experience different moments in different ways, and fashion individual interpretations. At the Olympic opening ceremonies, for instance, you might feel a sense of spirited patriotic competition as the athletes march in under a nation's flag, then a moment of unifying consecration when the Olympic flame is lighted, then a festival-like cheer at the end, when impromptu dancing breaks out.[8] Similar shifts could occur for *Nutcracker* participants, who laugh at kids and clowns one moment and are immersed in spiritual and aesthetic exhilaration the next, when Tchaikovsky's music and the dancers soar. They may be focused on family loyalties (remembering their own, or preferring the stage family to reality), or artistic achievement; they may just have an affection for Christmas and fantasies; and they may experience any or all of these at different times.

Dance writers are more used to viewing a ballet as a unified whole —or at least as a discrete aesthetic experience—but a few have taken creative approaches that do not seem at odds with MacAloon's discussion of spectacular metagenres and the idea that the viewer "makes sense of" a performance. Back in the 1940s and 1950s, for instance, the tinseled flights of fancy and seemingly fractured plot of *The Nutcracker* weren't at all upsetting to that most sensitive of dance critics, Edwin Denby. In retrospect, his commentary adds yet another genre to the list already explored—*The Nutcracker* as a fantastic, satisfying dream that can create its own logic. Denby defends the second act, for instance, which has often been criticized for stopping the plot dead and being merely an excuse for one divertissement after another. Instead of lamenting this string of dances, Denby praises the "suite form," which "does not try so hard to get somewhere." Released from the demands of a narrative that marches steadily onward, the viewer's "imagination dwells on one [dance] at a time and then proceeds satisfied to the next." Denby loosens the requirement of logical plot progression and looks for what "graceful and clear" classical dancing can do for the psyche—mainly, in this case, to transform everyday trials (the fraught first act) into "lovely invention and social harmony."[9]

The dreamlike aspects of *The Nutcracker* are also noted by Roland John Wiley, which may seem ironic, because Wiley has been a primary detractor of the ballet's original plot and has campaigned for making it more conventionally cohesive. But in one essay, Wiley suggests that the *Nutcracker*'s magical events can be likened to a *duma,* the Russian word for a meditative, dreamlike state of mind. For logic's sake, Wiley attributes the dream to the character of Drosselmeier, whereas for Denby, the *Nutcracker*'s journey and effects are the province of each audience member. Critic Arlene Croce picked up on the concept of *The Nutcracker* as duma and declared that each of

Tchaikovsky's ballets has a transcendent power. "Duma means something between daydream and meditation: it allows fantasy to penetrate reality; it dissolves rational distinctions between what is real and what the imagination feels is true," she said in a 1986 *New Yorker* review. "Listening, we see, we touch, until we hardly know whether it is the timpani we hear or the hammering of our own hearts."[10]

Denby and Croce's emphasis on the ability of classical ballet and Tchaikovsky to transport audiences, along with my own observations, led me to think about the experience of "flow," which is the name psychologists have given to a heightened state of active involvement.[11] At *Nutcracker* time, it seemed to me that flow was all around. It's an almost trancelike state that individuals enter when an activity is complex, challenging, pleasurable, and rewarding—dancing, for instance, or mountain climbing, sculpting, chess, or gardening. Losing track of time is a side effect of flow, as is a kind of merging with the environment, and, afterward, a feeling of being refreshed and worthwhile. In the ballet world, the concept is best recognized when applied to dancers, designers, craftspeople, and choreographers—they become immersed in their creative worlds, in getting every detail right and "performing" their duties. But there is also something called "the flow of thought," or "mental flow," which can be experienced by audience members who know enough about ballet to become deeply involved in viewing. Mihaly Csikszentmihalyi, a primary investigator of flow, believes that mental flow is enhanced by a person's knowledge about a particular activity, and his or her powers of concentration and memories. In other words (or in my words, that is), the more you know about *The Nutcracker* and the ballet world, the more likely you are to "go with the flow" of a performance. The importance of memory is that it enables a person to "find meaning in the contents of [one's] mind," something that seems to relate to Denby's approach to interpreting *The Nutcracker*.[12]

Memory, familiarity, involvement, holiday mood—these are ingredients that help the annual *Nutcracker* form close relationships with both dancers and audiences. Each year, the ballet is back in our midst, and the fact that a wide assortment of people perform in it, or know someone who does, contributes to feelings of membership in a club that seems pleasantly open to many. During rehearsals and performances, the experience of "shared flow" can lead to feelings of increased human interconnectness, or *communitas,* which arises for so many at *Nutcracker* time.[13] From my observations, I think both personal and communal thoughts and feelings can exist at *Nutcracker* time, alternating or overlapping, folding into and flowing through various groups and locations.

During one particular matinee by the Loudoun Ballet, I experienced what I would call a peak moment of *Nutcracker* communitas, or shared flow. It was the last weekend of the run, Christmas was imminent, sold-out houses were responding enthusiastically, and, for once, major and minor mishaps seemed to be taking a holiday of their own. I stood at the back of the house, flanked by several volunteers and the artistic director, who was calling light cues through a headset. At the moment when the Nutcracker had just come to life and Clara's living room turned into a snow scene, Tchaikovsky's swelling and crashing music swirled around the two dancers. Clara was played by a luminous young dancer who looked ecstatic as she ran and leapt and was twirled by her Nutcracker Prince. Then, as the music reached its spine-shivering peak, he lifted her up high in one sweeping gesture, and she stretched into a wide arabesque in her billowing white nightdress. As she reached out to catch the first falling flake of artificial snow, it landed directly in her upturned palm and the music fell into a reverent hush. Suddenly, all audience rustling ceased; children stopped shifting in their seats or tugging at their parents' sleeves, and I thought I could hear something like a collective sigh.

Afterward, I found more than one audience member who described being swept into the flow of that moment—everything felt "just so perfect," "so touching," and the snowflake falling into Clara's palm was "like a sign." They had all been similarly touched but had

At the Loudoun Ballet, the dancer playing Clara's father
(Frank Shumaker, with Sarah Terry) reappears as her Prince in the dream
sequence. During some of Tchaikovsky's most radiantly ecstatic music,
they leap and spin after the battle scene and sometimes succeed in
producing a collective audience sigh as the first snowflake falls.

different pathways into the feeling of community and celebration. For a few, the progress of the young dancer, her glowing face and beautiful arabesque, reminded them of their own children's struggle to grow up and get things right, or, more generally, the fact that so much beauty could come of dedication. One ballet mother was struck by the serendipity of the double casting that led this Clara to dance with a Cavalier who looked like her father (the same dancer played Mr. Stahlbaum and the Nutcracker Prince). Their pas de deux was choreographed to look like a girl playing with her father in the snow, celebrating the fact that he had made it through the battle and could now lead her to new frontiers. The ballet mother appreciated the sweetness of "a girl who was still young enough to dream that her father is her prince." At intermission another volunteer was feeling a flush of enthusiasm when she told me about what she felt at such peak moments. "You have a bond, a kinship with these people that you've done *The Nutcracker* with. It's really one of the happiest times in my year. There's a kind of camaraderie that carries forward into the new year, and it keeps carrying on and on and on. I think it's the community spirit that you experience while you're doing it. . . . it's just fun to be part of a group."

Not everyone, however, goes with the communal flow. On the same day of this peak moment of togetherness a volunteer who was serving in a key organizational position backstage was having a bad day—too much noise in the cafeteria dressing room, too many people coming late or not doing what they were supposed to do. An altercation later led to all kinds of heated accusations being thrown at the artistic director (chief among them the claim that her casting decisions "ruined the lives" of young dancers).[14] It seemed that there was no such thing as a stable harmonious mood; it ebbed and flowed like a stream that gave hope to the parched one moment and drenched them unpleasantly the next. Moments of communitas in new rituals and ceremonies can be precariously short-lived, I thought. Yet in this amateur *Nutcracker* community, then working toward professional status, the spirit of the event seemed to survive the conflicts that arose from time to time. When I returned a year after this incident and some organizational conflicts had again arisen and again been ironed out, I was told by more than one participant that now "the spirit of *The Nutcracker* was really back." The artistic director assured me that the spirit came and went regularly, but the fervor of *Nutcracker* togetherness was what everyone wanted to remember—and succeeded in remembering, judging by their reenlistment rate.

Skepticism and cynicism regarding *The Nutcracker* seem inevitable, given its New World ties to a series of vulnerable ideals—the warmth of family togetherness, the innocence of children, dreams coming true, multicultural sharing, and safe returns from utopian adventures. As with the Olympic Games, *The Nutcracker* is always in danger of falling short of its intended goals. There has never been peace on earth as doves were released at Olympic opening ceremonies, just as there are undoubtedly any number of nasty family or professional squabbles behind so many *Nutcracker* scenes of domestic bliss. But if it doesn't work perfectly, there is always next year. For *The Nutcracker*, the goals are ennobled by the pursuit of ballet excellence, an embodied theme that thrives at the core of its spectacle-like exterior. Ballet is the dedicated, rigorous, aesthetically uplifting force that pervades most *Nutcrackers*, when classicism is pursued with enough enthusiasm and skill. Tchaikovsky's excellence provides moral support, and Christmas festivity keeps underpinning the mood, whether it's linked to religion, spirituality, general celebration, or just time off.

For me, *The Nutcracker* on a good day is like any other ritual that aspires to great heights of personal meaningfulness and communal togetherness. It's as difficult to assess the ballet's success as it is to decide whether or not church services renew faith, or the Olympics provide inspiration, or a wedding succeeds in launching a good marriage. Many of us are reluctant to commit wholeheartedly to the well-worn rituals and ceremonies of church, state, or theater; yet there is still a longing to commemorate, to celebrate together, to dig deeper, to believe in something true. MacAloon thinks that spectacle-like events can provide options that are liberating; people aren't required to attend, so they feel they are exercising choice, then they become more available, in a way, to being caught up in the mood unawares.[15] The Nutcracker can be a site of unexpected pleasure and meaning; there's no heavy-handed "high" art mandate—"this is serious so you should understand it"—to intimidate people or build up their expectations. After all, it's "just" *The Nutcracker*. "People enjoy their skepticism, doubt and sense of illusion," MacAloon writes, "when they know that underneath they really believe." He offers a description that I think matches the mood of many *Nutcracker*-goers, proposing that "modern men and women" are not passive in terms of the way they watch an event but "are active agents in the creation of events and performances that, however much they deepen the quandary, stand also as public forms of condensing, displaying, and thinking it out."[16]

You might think from reading critics' complaints and hearing groans about the inevitability of *Nutcracker* season that in professional circles, *The Nutcracker* has become the guest who has outstayed his welcome. Fitting in is one thing and earning enough money for ballet companies to survive is always appreciated—but the gregarious *Nutcracker* is sometimes seen as the affluent partier who never goes home and bores everyone by telling the same stories over and over. Still, would anyone want to throw him out permanently? One of the most revealing questions I asked Toronto professionals was, "If you could eliminate *The Nutcracker* from the repertoire, would you?" The first answer was always, "No way, it makes money, there's no sense thinking about that." It was hard to get professionals to think beyond the financial considerations, which are always looming on the horizon. But eventually I got them to start separating the weight of the *Nutcracker* tradition—in effect, its importance—from the monetary aspect. I persevered: "What if, magically, your company had all the money in the world and no need to raise more, would you *then* eliminate *The Nutcracker?*" This posed a serious challenge, and there was inevitably a pause and a furrowed brow. Life without *Nutcracker?* Enticing, but only for a moment. Almost none of the dancers I talked to wanted to see the ballet disappear, sometimes surprising even themselves with that decision.

There were complaints about the ballet's inevitability and its long run, to be sure; they never stop, and *Nut*-bashing becomes a habit. But it doesn't go very deep. In general, corps members who danced the same thing every night were more restless than those who were moving through the ranks, or the principals, who got some nights off. If costumes were cumbersome or old, or choreography too simple or awkward, carping increased. But an affection for the ballet inevitably surfaced. It turns out that many complaints about *The Nutcracker* are rooted in a love-hate relationship with its popularity and concomitant overcommodification. A longtime principal dancer of the National Ballet of Canada told me why he can't stand hearing the Tchaikovsky score in a restaurant and sometimes even asks that the music be stopped—not because he's sick of it, but because it's too important to be trivialized. "You hear certain passages, and you get so irritated and agitated," he said, "because it gets too . . . you know, it pulls, it does pull. It does have an effect, you know, it's not just pretty. It means something. It's like if you're playing around with someone's language—trying to speak German in Germany and you're treading on words that mean something to them, but you're not fluent, it doesn't flow with you. It's the same sort of thing, that these things mean something to the people who are so involved in them. That music comes on, and no one understands. No one understands that it's affecting you."

His comparison of the meaningfulness of *The Nutcracker* to the importance of language and communication is one indication of how much at home the ballet has become. Returning to the idea of the Nutcracker as a character in his own story, he has come a long way, having been an artistic aspirant and itinerant adventurer, an immigrant and citizen, and finally, a kind of spiritual mentor—incognito, of course. And, due to multiple personality syndrome, he is all of these things at once, a citizen of more than one sphere, although particularly attached to North America, where the most creative phases of his life have taken place. He is loved because he crosses the proscenium in so many ways—a regular guy who is flexible and likes learning different languages and new customs—yet he has a set of core values that are admirable and somewhat stable. His inheritance has given him enough cachet and character to get through hard times. From Vsevolozshky, he was given vision; from Ivanov, some lyrical moves; from Tchaikovsky, his backbone and his heart. Provided with a newly respectable image by Balanchine, *The Nutcracker* still takes much abuse—and doesn't always laugh all the way to the bank these days. There are rumblings in a few quarters that the annual *Nutcracker* doesn't always pay off the way it used to. But it has lived through depressions before. Perhaps the protean *Nutcracker* will require even more ways of inventively adapting to thrive in the future.

The ballet world can be forgiven for not immediately recognizing the potential of *The Nutcracker* to serve as a new kind of ritual in a fast-changing world groping for just this kind of thing. But it ignores the phenomenon at its peril, looking down on one of its most precious assets. Willam Christensen, who mounted the first full production in the United States, eventually called the annual *Nutcracker* trend more of a plague than a tradition. Never mind; *The Nutcracker* can endure name-calling—it always has. Like birthdays and weddings, the annual ballet is both dreaded and celebrated because it marks the passage of time. Once you surrender to that inevitability, you can shift gears and enjoy the endless possibilities. *The Nutcracker* isn't just another aesthetic performance, although it certainly can be that. It's also a wonderfully flexible, ritual-like, resonant phenomenon. And with rituals, repetition doesn't equal boredom—it equals power.

Notes

ONE
The Early Years

1. I am indebted to musicologist and dance historian Roland John Wiley for the meticulous primary research he has done on Tchaikovsky ballets, especially *The Nutcracker,* which he chronicles in both *Tchaikovsky's Ballets: Swan Lake, Sleeping Beauty, Nutcracker* (Wiley 1985) and in *The Life and Ballets of Lev Ivanov, Choreographer of The Nutcracker and Swan Lake* (Wiley 1997). In terms of providing context for that era, he briefly describes ballet audiences, as well as giving a glimpse into the institutional workings of the imperial theaters (1985, 1–23). Tim Scholl also provides excellent contextual information about the imperial ballet of the late nineteenth century in *From Petipa to Balanchine: Classical Revival and the Modernization of Ballet* (Scholl 1994; especially pp. 1–20). For a perspective on the prejudices of critics of the era from a Soviet-era Russian dance writer, see Slonimsky.

2. Wiley points out that the libretto is generally accredited to both Vsevolozhsky and Petipa, and that it differs slightly from the instructions to Tchaikovsky (1985, 197). Roslavleva notes that Petipa (who was a French speaker) adapted the Dumas version of the original Hoffmann story (Roslavleva, 130). A translation of *The Nutcracker* scenario (from the French) can be found in Wiley 1997, 240–46; Petipa's instructions to Tchaikovsky, in English and in French, are in Wiley 1985, 371–82. They differ in some details (and the performed version must have differed further), but these documents have often been used by choreographers looking for original *Nutcracker* elements. By the time the story became a libretto, the heroine,

whom Hoffmann called Marie, had become Clara, originally the name of one of Marie's dolls. (In the Hoffmann, Clara saves the Nutcracker, so it seems that these two characters from the original story were combined along the way.) Other features of early written plans for the ballet may be of interest to *Nutcracker* aficionados. The following details are taken from both the libretto and Petipa's instructions to Tchaikovsky. Clara's father is called President Silverhaus; Drosselmeier (also spelled Drosselmeyer) is Clara's godfather. The mechanical dancing figures Drosselmeier brings to the party are a sutler (a civilian purveyor of goods to the military), a recruit, a Colombine and a Harlequin. The nutcracker doll is said to be a gift for everyone, not just Clara. Fritz breaks it by cracking too large a nut, while today he usually drops it or pulls at it. Drosselmeier appears as the owl in the clock at midnight. In addition to the mice and soldiers commonly seen today in the battle scene, there are toy rabbits and gingerbread soldiers. Clara throws her shoe at the Mouse King when she sees the Nutcracker in danger. He's distracted, allowing the Nutcracker to wound him. When the Mouse King retreats, the Nutcracker is transformed into a prince. The original snow scene did not feature a pas de deux (some of Ivanov's notation for the choreography can be found in the Harvard Theatre Collection). The second act description for decor lists elements often used today—like different types of candy and cakes—although few productions include all the rivers and fountains of sweet liquids Petipa requests. The Land of the Sweets is called "Confitürembourg." Clara and the Prince, who is coming home, receive a welcome from silver-coated soldiers, pages, a master-of-ceremonies character, the Prince's sisters, and the Sugar Plum Fairy and Prince Coqueluche. The Prince tells about Clara saving his life. Petipa's words for the various dances are as follows: Chocolate, or Spanish; Coffee, or Arabian; Tea, which is "in the Chinese taste"; Trepak (now often called "Russian"); a "dance with little fifes"; "Dance of the 32 Buffoons and Mother Gigogne and her children"; "Waltz of flowers and large garlands" (Wiley 1985, 375–76). There follows the grand pas de deux for the Sugar Plum Fairy and Prince Coqueluche; then a coda for everyone. The last dance is described as an apotheosis with illuminated fountains, and it was presumably with this image the ballet is meant to end. There is no final scene to show that Clara wakes up in her own home.

3. Lesser known elements of the Hoffmann story are also found in the Pacific Northwest Ballet's *Nutcracker*, as well the current Royal Ballet version. A Soviet production by Igor Belsky at St. Petersburg's Maly Theatre in 1969 also incorporated the Princess Pirlipat story (Souritz, 82). Many other versions have returned to elements of Hoffmann, but overwhelmingly, the Dumas revision of Hoffmann's story, as adapted by Vsevolozhsky and Petipa, is the basis for most *Nutcrackers*.

4. Wiley 1985, 373.

5. Wiley 1985, 194–97.

6. Tchaikovsky, 629, 663–64.

7. This analysis is found in Wiley's 1984 article "On Meaning in *Nutcracker*" (20–21), which also examines further connections between the composer, the ballet's main characters, and the musical score.

8. Tchaikovsky, 678.

9. How much of the choreography for the original *Nutcracker* can be attributed to Petipa and how much to Ivanov has been much debated. As Ivanov's superior, Petipa had a great influence on Ivanov. In the case of *The Nutcracker*, initial concepts and a detailed scenario were the work of Petipa, and Wiley points out that Petipa might have attended rehearsals to stage parts of act one before he fell ill (1997, 137). In his memoirs, Petipa himself says: "Lev Ivanov, following my scenario, staged alone and created all the dances for the ballet *The Nutcracker*" (Petipa, 85) Further comments about the collaboration between Petipa and Ivanov can be found in Wiley 1985, especially pp. 202–3; and note 22 on pp. 308–9. Further details about Ivanov's life and work can be found in Wiley 1997; see also Soviet-era dance historians M. Borisoglebsky and Yuri Slonimsky's writing about Ivanov's life and contributions to the history of ballet in *Dance Perspectives* 2, 1959.

10. In Wiley 1997, Shiryaev is quoted on the differences in work techniques between Petipa and Ivanov (52). Shiryaev was the original Trepak dancer in the 1892 *Nutcracker*, and he also sometimes served as an assistant to both Petipa and Ivanov (51). His account of the way he ended up choreographing his own *Nutcracker* variation is found on p. 138 in Wiley 1997.

11. Wiley points out that the ballet-opera double bill may have been designed in imitation of a Paris Opera tradition (1997, 132). He believes that

an analysis of *The Nutcracker* should take into account the composer's intentions, which he assumes were affected by consideration of the way the two works would affect each other on the same evening. Wiley proposes that the deficiencies of the ballet were highlighted once it was separated from the opera. As potential support for this view, he quotes a letter Tchaikovsky wrote to a friend which states that "the ballet would not suit" if it were given alone (1985, 310, n. 46). This opinion from the composer, however, was written months before the choreography was completed, and therefore refers to the score and scenario only. Wiley also quotes turn-of-the-century music writer Herman Laroche, who proposes that *Iolanthe* and *The Nutcracker* should be performed together (in their "proper place") in order to provide the "unity of impression . . . based on contrast" that Tchaikovsky had in mind for the two works (1985, 205). These are interesting speculations, but I do not consider the composer's intentions, insofar as they can be surmised, to be significant factors in exploring the meaningfulness of the ballet as it has evolved over time.

12. A translation of Domino's comments can be found in Wiley 1997, 141. For more information about the ballet audiences at the time, see Wiley 1985, 10–17.

13. Several critical assessments containing these views can be found in Wiley 1997, 139–46.

14. Wiley 1997, 142.

15. Assessments of Dell'Era's performance can be found in Wiley 1997, 144; her suitability for the role and popularity is discussed in Wiley 1985, 204. Preobrajenskaya's performance in the first *Nutcracker* is assessed in Wiley 1997, 139, 142.

16. Descriptions of the first battle scene are found in Wiley 1997, 140, 142; and in Benois, 137.

17. Various of the original *Nutcracker* critics, as well as Wiley himself, outline complaints about the libretto in Chapter 6 of Wiley 1985, and Chapter 7 of Wiley 1997.

18. These descriptions are found in Wiley 1997, 144–46. Mention of the opening night dinner is made in Wiley 1985, 220.

19. Tchaikovsky's words are quoted in Tchaikovsky, 697; the account of the Odessa engagement appears on p. 700. The critic's quote can be found in Wiley 1997, 146.

20. Wiley 1997, 146–49, contains some details about the ballet's fate in St. Petersburg after the opening night. Russian dance historian Elizabeth Souritz offers an informative overview and discussion of the history of *The Nutcracker* during Soviet times (Souritz 1992). A less academic discussion of twentieth-century Russian productions and many photographs of the Bolshoi Grigorovich version are found in Grigorovich and Demidov. J. Anderson 1979, 77–89, also offers an overview and some photographs of *The Nutcracker* in Russia.

21. Souritz, 77.

22. Mention of Fokine's use of *Nutcracker* music in *Le Festin* is found in Garafola, 348. Pavlova's *Snowflakes* is described in Money, 137–38, 225, 281; and Kerensky, 87–90. Richard Buckle describes the various ways *Nutcracker* music was used in the Ballets Russes (388).

23. This partial *Nutcracker*, staged on May 27, 1931, at the Vancouver Theatre in Vancouver, British Columbia, was staged by the Russian Ballet of Boris Novikoff, using local ballet students. A photo of the students survives in the Dance Collection Danse archives in Toronto. I am indebted to Amy Bowring for bringing this production to my attention.

24. For an overview of early Western European productions, see J. Anderson 1979, 90–103. Sergeyev's contribution is noted on pp. 92–93.

25. Some filmed excerpts of North American Ballet Russe tours can be found in the Jerome Robbins Dance Collection of the New York Public Library. On p. 108 of J. Anderson 1979, the touring life and changes made in the Ballet Russe production are noted, as is the fact that contests with children's roles as a prize were sometimes held in cities where the ballet played—an early example of good publicity for a ballet that would eventually become rooted in various communities. Denby's affection for the Ballet Russe *Nutcracker* is found in Denby, 272–75.

26. Christensen had actually inaugurated a "Christmas ballet festival" in 1943, largely because San Francisco's War Memorial Opera House was available then. *The Nutcracker* wasn't his first choice; he had done *Hansel and Gretel* the year before (Steinberg, 63). The 1944 *Nutcracker* wasn't revived until 1949, and has been done every year since then. Accounts of the genesis of the 1944 Christensen *Nutcracker* is found in Steinberg, 63–64. Balanchine writes a bit about his choice to do *The Nutcracker* in Balanchine and Mason, vol. 2, 17.

27. The fact that North Americans might not be as startled as Russians by the combining of seemingly disparate qualities relates to the idea of "embracing the conflict," one of the principles of Africanist aesthetics discussed in Brenda Dixon Gottschild's analysis of West African aesthetics and their relationship to Western concert dance (Dixon Gottschild, 13–14). She points out that the pairing of opposites in music and dance (for instance, awkward and smooth, detached and intense) is a valued principle of Africanist aesthetics, one that influenced Balanchine's neoclassicism in various significant ways. I'm further suggesting that North Americans embraced many kinds of dualities when it came to *The Nutcracker,* such as its rapid transitions from reality to fantasy and its status as both a fun holiday celebration and a ballet with more serious concerns.

28. Clara and Marie are both popular names for the ballet's heroine (see note 2, above). Although Balanchine chose to use Marie, the name Clara was used in the television broadcasts, possibly because the Ballet Russe had made it so well known in North America.

29. Quoted in Volkov, 193, 184.

30. Tallchief, 187.

31. Volkov, 192.

32. Balanchine said he went back to the original Hoffmann story (Balanchine and Mason, 17), but his version actually seems closer to the original ballet libretto. There are a few details that hark back to Hoffmann — the character of Drosselmeier's nephew and the fact that Balanchine used character names from the Hoffmann, not the ballet (Marie, not Clara; Stahlbaum, not Silberhaus). The battle scene was staged by Jerome Robbins (Buckle, 201).

33. A number of *Nutcracker*-related magazine articles are found in the clippings files of the Dance Collection at the New York Public Library. I am indebted to Lynn Garafola, who shared with me many more from her personal collection.

34. In a 1976 *Newsweek* article noting the rising popularity of the annual *Nutcracker,* Hubert Saal likened the ballet's leading character to an immigrant who made good in America, calling him "a funny little fellow" no one "liked the look of" back in Europe, but "like many others, he came to America where he became a fabulous success." (Saal, 40)

TWO
Making Friends at Christmastime

1. Volkov, 179–83.

2. Details of the development of modern Christmas celebrations can be found in the work of several historians, including Gillis, Goldby and Purdue, Nissenbaum, Restad, and Waits.

3. Nissenbaum, 7–8.

4. Nissenbaum, 106.

5. Nissenbaum, 107.

6. Appropriate Christmas beverages were suggested by a Victorian writer quoted in Golby and Purdue, 57. This book offers many illustrations of the way Christmas themes were disseminated in nineteenth-century articles and advertisements in the popular press. Mistletoe cartoons are found on pp. 64–65.

7. Nissenbaum, 131.

8. Golby and Purdue, 45. The authors eloquently link Dickens's writing to the way modern Christmas evolved. I found in their analysis many parallels to *The Nutcracker,* in terms of the way Dickens's writing "stands as a metaphor for human sympathy and, because its appeal is associated with childhood, family and tenderness, it harnesses sentiment and imagination with consummate effectiveness" (45–46).

9. Gillis, 101; Golby and Purdue, 61.

10. Restad, 57, 61–62.

11. Golby and Purdue, 51.

12. Nissenbaum, 62–63.

13. The term "invented tradition" was coined by historians in *The Invention of Tradition,* edited by Hobsbawm and Ranger, who define the term in their introduction (Hobsbawm and Ranger, 2).

14. Sparshott, 72.

15. Alderson 1984.

16. Bourdieu 1987, 203. Bourdieu also states: "A work of art has meaning and interest only for someone who possesses the cultural competence, that is, the code, into which it is encoded" (1984, 2).

17. Ortner, 169–70.

18. Cynthia Jean Cohen Bull (a.k.a. Novack) reinforced ideas about ballet that were common as she grew up in the 1950s and 1960s in the American Midwest, where ballet was considered "a bit rarefied." (36–37).

19. Berger, 93–94.

20. Kirstein, 32.

21. McRobbie, 201.

22. McRobbie, 217.

23. This appeared in an article by Barbara Guilford in a special section of the December 1984 *Dance Magazine,* (HC-20).

24. Flett, 74.

THREE
Fitting In

1. In 1961, Jacqueline Kennedy started the tradition of having a theme for the White House Christmas tree and announced it would be "Nutcracker Suite" that year. But a photograph of that tree shows very little evidence of the ballet (using "Suite" in the title might have pointed to the music as the theme). There are hanging snowflake ornaments, candy canes, an angel, and a mouse visible in a photograph. There appears to be at least one figurine that could be a nutcracker, but no dancers visible. My thanks to Jim Hill of the Audiovisual Archives at the John Fitzgerald Kennedy Library for providing an image of that tree.

2. J. Anderson 1979, 134, 136. I first read about the localizing of the Cincinnati Ballet's *Nutcracker* in Jack Anderson's invaluable 1979 book, *The Nutcracker Ballet.* My thanks to Cincinnati Ballet publicist Susan Eiswerth for providing me with information about funding and with names of additional sources. Anderson was one of the first dance historians to chronicle the phenomenon of the ballet in North America, calling his 1966 *Dance Magazine* article about *The Nutcracker* "A New American Tradition." His book provides photographs of many productions around the world.

3. *Dance Magazine,* December 1997, 68–71. As a popular dance periodical, many of whose readers undoubtedly dance in *Nutcrackers* at Christmastime, *Dance Magazine* has been invaluable in terms of chronicling *Nutcracker* trends and version alterations. Many of the details about regional *Nutcrackers* in this chapter were reported in December *Dance Magazines;*

other mentions came from local advertising, posters, and newspaper reviews.

4. The choreographer of *The American Nutcracker*, Kirk Peterson, was the Hartford Ballet artistic director at the time of its 1997 premiere. When Peterson departed in 1999, his choreography was replaced. The current production, by artistic director Adam Miller, replaces Drosselmeier with a strong female character named Madame Noisette, played by Peggy Lyman, a former Graham dancer.

5. Kirk Peterson's choreography had already been dropped for the 1999 Hollywood Bowl excerpt, but the concepts and costumes remained the same.

6. Gary Smith in the *Hamilton Spectator*, Dec. 17, 1997.

7. Bob Pennington in the *Toronto Sun*, Dec. 21, 1989.

8. The original *Nutcracker* also had an apotheosis, not an unusual device for a nineteenth-century ballet. Its description in Petipa's libretto reads: "The apotheosis represents a large beehive with flying bees closely guarding their riches" (Wiley 1997, 246).

9. In a conversation I had with Byrd in October 2001, he said presenters didn't seem to have much faith in *The Harlem Nutcracker,* and it hadn't been mounted for two years. Previous attendance records had been good in general, but a slight fall-off seemed to have discouraged his most enthusiastic supporters. Byrd believes one problem in attracting black audiences to *The Harlem Nutcracker* has been inappropriate advertising. In his experience, arts presenters fail to recognize the fact that African Americans make decisions about what to attend based more on popular radio advertisements and interviews rather than offerings in upscale newspapers or on NPR, both traditional spots for arts features and advertising.

10. My analysis of Prakash's *Nutcracker* is made from a videotape of highlights of the production, Prakash's description of the rest, and her comments concerning the tone of her version, her ambitions, and her afterthoughts about the experience.

11. Slonimsky discusses the "Chinese" dance very briefly in "Writings on Lev Ivanov," 19. The definition of chinoiserie is from Impey, 9.

12. I thank Lynn Garafola for spotting this image in Cyril W. Beaumont, *Ballet Design Past and Present* (London: Hazell, Watson and Viney, 1946), 19.

13. My questions about potentially offensive second act *Nutcracker*

dances didn't receive too much serious attention from respondents in Lees-burg and Toronto. Often, a defensive tone was taken—"Nobody means any harm," and, "It's just a fun kind of thing." I believed that few ballet people dancing or watching Tea meant any harm, but I also thought they were un-able to grasp the issues unless they were familiar with prejudice, stereotyp-ing, essentializing, and orientalizing, either through experience or reading. In Toronto, choreographer James Kudelka chose not to include a "Chinese" dance in his new *Nutcracker;* some of his dancers and a few audience mem-bers guessed that he wanted to avoid any controversy over issues of repre-sentation. The previous Tea, in Celia Franca's version, had received negative comments and accusations of racism over the years.

14. A body of scholarly literature on dance of the Middle East is grow-ing and can illuminate issues relating to the history, representation, and stereotypes of belly dance (often called *danse orientale*) and other dance forms of the area. Prominent among this literature are Karin van Nieuw-kerk's *A Trade Like any Other: Female Dancers and Singers in Egypt* (Austin: University of Texas Press, 1995) and the work of dance scholar Anthony Shay, which includes his books *Choreophobia: Solo Improvised Dance in the Iranian World* (Costa Mesa, Calif.: Mazda, 1999) and *Choreographic Politics: State Folk Dance Ensembles, Representation and Power* (Middletown, Conn.: Wesleyan University Press, 2002).

15. Ross, 18.

16. This production came to my attention through newspaper and maga-zine articles in 1998 and 1999. Only parts of the Tchaikovsky score were used; caroling and staged events using music from other ballets and musi-cals were also part of the show. A flyer I saw in New York City in Decem-ber 1997 announced another dance-along *Nutcracker* by the New Dance Group Arts Center. That event seemed geared toward dance education, in-viting children to bring their dancing shoes and promising that "profes-sional dancers and children from the audience" would "explore the magical world of ballet together."

17. My major research periods occurred from 1995 to 1997; after this point, I kept in touch with each company by mail and phone. In Lees-burg, Va., I spent four weeks in November and December 1995 explor-ing the Loudoun Ballet "Nutcracker," choreographed by Sheila Hoffmann-Robertson (after Ivanov), and continued this research for six weeks the next

year at "Nutcracker" time. In Toronto, where I had begun my research during a week in the summer of 1996, I spent three weeks in January of 1997 (catching the tail end of their *Nutcracker* season), and then three months the following summer (June 1 to September 1). During that time I spent weeks backstage with the National Ballet, conducting many interviews and watching company classes and rehearsals at their headquarters. During the July 1997 summer session of the National Ballet School, I spent some or all of nearly every day watching classes and talking to students, teachers, and support staff. During that time a repertory class for prospective *Nutcracker* student principal dancers met. My interview subjects in both locations also included regular *Nutcracker* supporters (some of whom I class as "balletomanes") and both casual and devoted audience members. I used traditional participant-observation methods, with emphasis on interviews. In addition to face-to-face interviews, I experimented with a method I call "introspective interviewing," which involved respondents talking into tape recorders at home and creating monologues, spurred by a list of questions I provided. This method (inspired by anthropologist John L. Caughey) turned out to be very productive, giving the respondent time and a certain comfort level not usually available during conventional interviews.

18. My thanks to Ginny Harris in the National Ballet offices for sharing a file of subscriber letters received during the first year of the National Ballet's *Nutcracker* changeover.

19. B. Anderson, 6 (imagined community definition); 145 (unisonance).

20. As historian Stephen Nissenbaum points out, the fact that a tradition is invented should in no way mark it as "not really authentic" (Nissenbaum, 315). This conclusion would assume "that before there were 'invented' traditions, there were 'real' ones that were *not* invented," Nissenbaum says, whereas it is much more realistic to understand traditions and rituals as constantly evolving entities (315–16).

FOUR

Experiences and Relationships

1. Protests about the questionable taste of the "Operation Desert Storm" nutcracker were reported by Timothy Aeppel in "Wooden Soldiers Called Out of Step with the Holidays," *Wall Street Journal*, Dec. 24, 1991. Made

briefly by Holz und Drechslerwaren, these nutcrackers were marketed in shops that catered to U.S. military personnel stationed in West Germany. The "Champion of Freedom" nutcracker, made by the German manufacturer Steinbach, went on sale in 2002. Alexander Taron Importer featured the following text in their brochure: "We are all lucky to live in a country that is protected by the finest military force in the world. No matter what your political view, there is no doubt we all owe our freedom and security to our men and women in the military forces." A portion of revenues was donated to the National Military Family Association.

2. St. Petersburg critique quoted in Wiley 1997, 139.

3. Denby's thoughtful 1944 essay "Meaning in *Nutcracker*" appears in Denby, 272–75.

4. Denby, 445–50.

5. Quoted in Kisselgoff, 15. Asafiev worked on the 1934 Vainonen *Nutcracker* for the Kirov Ballet.

6. Notable interpretations that lean toward a negative assessment of the ballerina (often depending on psychoanalytic and semiotic theoretical tenets and theories of the so-called "male gaze") include Daly, both 1987 and 1987/88; Alderson 1987; Goldberg; English; Foster; Lansley; and Innes. Those that tend toward the rereading of the ballerina in a positive light include McMahon, Savage-King, and (pertaining to portrayals in literature) McRobbie. Most recently, dance historian Sally Banes, in her book *Women Dancing: Female Bodies on Stage*, has gone beyond some of the narrow-casting approaches of previous feminist ballet critics, and given contextual depth to the idea of ballerina agency in her interpretation of ballet heroines such as the Sugar Plum Fairy in *The Nutcracker*, Swanilda in *Coppélia*, and Aurora in *The Sleeping Beauty*. For a thoughtful preliminary ethnographic consideration of both positive and negative aspects of the ballerina, see Bull (a.k.a. Novack).

7. Cohen, 83–84.

8. Cohen, 85, 98, 101.

9. Banes's reflections on the Sugar Plum Fairy are found in Banes, chap. 2, especially pp. 60–61. Her comments about Aurora in *The Sleeping Beauty* and Odette in *Swan Lake*, also found in this chapter, help build her argument.

10. Daly 1987 and Daly 1987/88.

11. See Lynn Garafola's "The Travesty Dancer in Nineteenth-Century Ballet." *Dance Research Journal* 17 (2) and 18 (1) (1985–86).

12. This statement reflects some aspects of my theoretical approach to this study. When it comes to exploring the place of the annual *Nutcracker* in the lives of people who are around it, I call my approach "participant-oriented." It focuses on the way people argue for meanings and interpretations (an approach called "rhetorical hermeneutics," see Mailloux, 52), and owes much to formative influences from recent ethnographic practices in anthropology (especially those of feminist ethnographers), media studies, and literary criticism, especially various incarnations of reception theory and reader-response criticism. Ethnographers who were of significant interest in terms of analyzing the importance of subject position and recognizing shifts of identities were Dorinne Kondo, Kamala Visweswaran, and Cynthia Jean Cohen Bull (a.k.a. Novack). Literary theorists Louise Rosenblatt and Stephen Mailloux were formative influences for me in terms of understanding the way people make meaning of texts. In brief, Rosenblatt, Mailloux, and others (see also Ang, Bennett, Cruz and Lewis, Culler, and Radway) shift focus from previous theories that the text (in my case *The Nutcracker*) is the dictator of meaning, to an acknowledgment that the reader (or dancer or viewer) is an active partner in the transaction that results in meanings within specific contexts. A more detailed discussion and explanation of these influences and the way I draw from various theoretical concepts can be found in my larger *Nutcracker* study, a Ph.D. dissertation completed at the University of California, Riverside, and called "The Annual *Nutcracker*: A Participant-Oriented, Contextualized Study of *The Nutcracker* Ballet as It Has Evolved into a Christmas Ritual in the United States and Canada."

13. An increased interest in ballet among boys was called "the Billy Elliott effect" by the *London Telegraph* on April 14, 2002. For the first time in history, it was reported, more boys than girls had been accepted to train at White Lodge, the junior school associated with the Royal Ballet. Ballet insiders quoted were optimistic that the film had changed attitudes.

14. From Diana V. Morgan, "Unlikely Pas de Deux: My Son's Ballet with Bart Simpson," *Washington Post*, Dec. 7, 1997.

15. The idea that femininity is a "performance," learned as part of socialization, is put forth in the work of many feminists, from Simone de Beauvoir to Judith Butler. In relation to the physicality of the ballerina and possible ways to "read" her performance, I found particularly informative Mary Russo's approach to styles of performed feminine strength in her book *The Female Grotesque*. In her discussion of nineteenth-century actresses, Russo notes that these performers "used their bodies in public in extravagant ways that could only have provoked wonder and ambivalence in the female viewer, as such latitude of movement and attitude was not permitted most women without negative consequences" (68). About female circus fliers and acrobats of the same era, Russo says: "The representation of femininity as an effortless mobility implies enormous control, changeability and strength" (44). I suggest that today's ballerinas may still have something of the "extravagant" about them for most audience members—and for the dancers themselves.

F I V E

The Meaning of Life

1. One assumes that Sparshott (306) was thinking of Petipa because of the balletmaster's meticulous planning of the project, before he fell ill and turned the choreography over to Ivanov.

2. My exploration of ritual/theater crossover territory has been greatly influenced by the work of anthropologist Victor Turner, who defined ritual as "prescribed formal behavior for occasions not given over to technological routine, having reference to beliefs in invisible beings or powers regarded as the first and final causes of all effects" (1982, 79). But Turner recognized similarities between ritual in small-scale societies and what he called "industrial genres of leisure," a category that includes drama, art, dance, and poetry. His writing and that of theater director Richard Schechner, with whom he collaborated on occasion, offer many concepts and examples that illuminate ritual/theater relationships.

3. Literary critic Stanley Fish coined the term "interpretive community," which refers to shared interpretive strategies among people who share a common history or taste (Fish, 14). By applying this term to various fac-

tions of *Nutcracker*-goers, I mean to suggest that one's freedom to interpret a ballet idiosyncratically is affected by societal norms and conventions, which are combined with personal perspectives and experience.

4. Karsavina, 40; Pavlova quoted in Magriel, 5; Ashley, 22.

5. Kain, with Godfrey and Doob, 269, 10, 28, 273.

6. My brief summation of elements that characterize a secular ritual is taken from Moore and Myerhoff's excellent list (Moore and Myerhoff, 7–8). The category of secular ritual is a useful one in terms of recognizing the variety of rituals and ceremonies that aren't designated "religious." On the other hand, I want to add a dimension to the category of secular ritual by suggesting that an ostensibly secular ritual like *The Nutcracker* can also be the performative site to which some individuals bring their deeply held beliefs. In this regard, I understand why anthropologist Stanley Tambiah prefers not to "carve out a category of 'secular ritual'" while elaborating his notion of ritual as a performative "medium of communication" (Tambiah, 12). For Tambiah, there is no reason to emphasize the separation between the sacred and the secular by inventing a new category. Because *The Nutcracker* is more often identified as secular than religious, I do not object to the category of secular ritual, as long as it is not characterized as the opposite of sacred ritual. Instead, I want to enlarge the category by showing where overlapping territory lies in regard to ballet. Tambiah emphasizes the fact that the distinctions we make in a society between ritual and nonritual activity are relative, not absolute, and that differences can usually be determined by noting "the way words and acts are implicated and 'verification' procedures invoked, and results interpreted" (116). His emphasis on the way results are interpreted is relevant to my method of inquiry regarding *The Nutcracker*. By using interviews combined with participant observation, I explore the experiences, attitudes, and interpretations of my respondents.

7. I am deeply indebted to MacAloon for his astute reevaluation of the potential of spectacle and his description of various performance genres present the Olympic Games. The concepts I borrow and adapt are found in his article "Olympic Games and the Theory of Spectacle in Modern Societies," in *Rite, Drama, Festival, Spectacle*, a volume he edited. He provides a useful definition of spectacle (243–44) and other genres that contribute to a "ramified performance type," as well as suggesting ways in which a

"neoliminal" kind of ritual might serve various populations in the modern world (268–75).

8. "Nesting" genres are explained throughout MacAloon; megagenres or metagenres are defined on p. 250; a few ways in which individuals were caught up in the spirit of various moments of Olympic events are recounted on pp. 268–69.

9. Denby, 272–75.

10. Wiley discusses the concept of duma in his 1984 article *Meaning in The Nutcracker* (16–17); Croce picks up the theme in an article discussing Wiley's book, *Tchaikovsky's Ballets* (Croce, 79).

11. My summation of the phenomenon of flow is taken from the many writings of Csikszentmihalyi (see Csikszentmihalyi 1990 and 1993, for instance).

12. Csikszentmihalyi 1990, 123–24. The flow of thought in general is discussed in this chapter.

13. Anthropologist Victor Turner's discourse on communitas is key to the concepts I have discussed. For Turner, communitas is "an unmediated relationship between historical, idiosyncratic, concrete individuals" (Turner 1982, 45); or as he put it in private correspondence, it is "a quality of human interrelatedness that can 'emerge' from or 'descend' upon two or more human beings (though its expression is fullest in the small group)" (Alexander, 35). When this mode of human interconnectedness is experienced in its ideal form, what Turner calls "spontaneous communitas," a person experiences a "'gut' understanding of synchronicity" and becomes "totally absorbed into a single synchronized, fluid event" (Turner 1982, 48). Turner acknowledged Csikszentmihalyi's influence and said communitas is "shared flow" (Turner 1987, 133). For Turner, this ideal mood is characterized by honesty, openness, and a lack of pretentiousness, resulting in an atmosphere "free from the culturally defined encumbrances of . . . role, status, reputation, class, caste, sex or other structured niche" (133). Turner is careful to point out that communitas is not an experience in which the "I" is lost in a communal entity, nor is it a fantasy; instead, he says: "communitas preserves individual distinctiveness—it is neither regression to infancy, nor is it emotional, nor is it 'merging' in fantasy" (Turner 1982, 45–46). By implication, communitas is "real" for the person or people experiencing it:

"When even two people believe that they experience unity, all people are felt by those two, even if only for a flash, to be one" (47). Importantly, although much of Turner's work regarding communitas was based on his research on ritual in small-scale societies, he became increasingly interested in communal moments of theatrical performances in large-scale, industrial societies. "In industrial societies," he wrote, "it is within leisure, and sometimes aided by the projections of art that this way of experiencing one's fellows can be portrayed, grasped, and sometimes realized" (46).

14. From my observation at close range, the Loudoun Ballet officials in charge of casting were particularly fair in their dealings with dancers and sensitive to both parents and children when it came to casting, constantly meeting with them to discuss their decisions and trying to explain the ineluctable reality of the theater—that not everyone can dance every role he or she covets. The fact that some parents have a hard time accepting *Nutcracker* casting choices and hence accuse ballet officials of ruining a child's life arose in conversations with more than one artistic director.

15. MacAloon, 268.

16. MacAloon, 271.

Bibliography

Abu-Lughod, Lila. "Writing Against Culture." In *Recapturing Anthropology: Working in the Present,* Richard G. Fox, ed. Santa Fe, N.M.: School of American Research Press, 1991.

Abu-Lughod, Lila. *Writing Women's Worlds: Bedouin Stories.* Berkeley: University of California Press, 1993.

Alderson, Evan. "Decoding the Ballet Body." Presented at Dance in Canada Conference, Toronto, Ontario, June 4, 1984.

Alderson, Evan. "Ballet as Ideology: *Giselle,* Act II." *Dance Chronicle* 10 (3), 1987: 290–304.

Anderson, Benedict. *Imagined Communities: Reflections on the Origin and Spread of Nationalism.* London: Verso, 1991 (rev. ed., first published 1983).

Anderson, Jack. *The Nutcracker Ballet.* New York: Gallery, 1979.

Anderson, Jack. "A New Tradition." *Dance Magazine,* December 1966: 46–55, 68.

Ang, Ien. *Living Room Wars: Rethinking Media Audiences for a Postmodern World.* London: Routledge, 1996.

Ashley, Merrill. *Dancing for Balanchine.* New York: Dutton, 1984.

Bakhtin, Mikhail. *Rabelais and His World.* Bloomington: Indiana University Press, 1984.

Balanchine and The Nutcracker, tape one: "The Cradle: Balanchine's Childhood and *The Nutcracker.*" Video recording of a panel at an oral history seminar. Jerome Robbins Archive of the Recorded Moving Image, Dance Collection, New York Public Library for the Performing Arts, 1992.

Balanchine, George, and Francis Mason. *Balanchine's Festival of Ballet,* vol. 2. London: W. H. Allen, 1984 (first published 1954).

Banes, Sally. *Dancing Women: Female Bodies on Stage*. New York: Routledge, 1998.

Bennett, Tony. "Text and Social Process: The Case of James Bond." *Screen Education* 41, Winter/Spring 1982: 3–14.

Benois, Alexandre. *Reminiscences of the Russian Ballet*. London: Putnam, 1941.

Bentley, Toni. *Winter Season: A Dancer's Journal*. New York: Vintage, 1982.

Berger, Bennett M. *An Essay on Culture: Symbolic Structure and Social Structure*. Berkeley: University of California Press, 1995.

Borisoglebsky, M. "Lev Ivanov" (excerpts from *Materials for the History of Russian Ballet*, vol. 1, Leningrad, 1938). *Dance Perspectives* 2, Spring 1959.

Bourdieu, Pierre. "The Historical Genesis of a Pure Aesthetic." *The Journal of Aesthetics and Art Criticism* 46, 1987: 201–10.

Bourdieu, Pierre. *Distinction: A Social Critique of the Judgement of Taste*. Cambridge: Harvard University Press, 1984.

Brady, Joan. *The Unmaking of a Dancer: An Unconventional Life*. New York: Harper and Row, 1982.

Briginshaw, Valerie. "Dancing Dicks: A Case in Point(e)." Unpublished paper. Chichester Institute of Higher Education, University of Southampton, Chichester, West Sussex, U.K, 1996.

Buckle, Richard. *Diaghilev*. New York: Atheneum, 1979.

Bull, Cynthia Jean Cohen (Novack) "Ballet, Gender and Cultural Power." In *Dance, Gender and Culture*, Helen Thomas, ed. London: Macmillan, 1993: 34–48.

Castor, Harriet, ed. *Ballet Stories*. New York: Kingfisher, 1997.

Caughey, John L. "Ethnography, Introspection, and Reflexive Culture Studies." In *Prospects: The Annual of American Cultural Studies*, J. Saltzman, ed. New York: Bert Franklin, 1982: 115–39.

Cohen, Selma Jeanne. *Next Week, Swan Lake: Reflections on Dance and Dances*. Middletown, Conn.: Wesleyan University Press, 1982.

Cristaldi, Kathryn. *Baseball Ballerina*. New York: Random House, 1992.

Croce, Arlene. "The Dreamer of the Dream." *New Yorker*, Feb. 24, 1986: 76–79.

Cruz, Jon, and Justin Lewis, eds. *Viewing, Reading, Listening: Audiences and Cultural Reception*. Boulder: Westview, 1994.

Csikszentmihalyi, Mihaly. *Flow: The Psychology of Optimal Experience: Steps Toward Enhancing the Quality of Life.* New York: Harper and Row, 1990.

Csikszentmihalyi, Mihaly, and Rick E. Robinson. *The Art of Seeing: An Interpretation of the Aesthetic Encounter.* Malibu, Calif.: J. Paul Getty Museum and Getty Center for Education in the Arts, 1990.

Csikszentmihalyi, Mihaly. *The Evolving Self: A Psychology for the Third Millennium.* New York: Harper Collins, 1993.

Culler, Jonathan. "Prolegomena to a Theory of Reading." In *The Reader in the Text,* Susan Suleiman and Inge Crosman, eds. Princeton: Princeton University Press, 1980: 46–66.

Daly, Ann. "The Balanchine Woman: Of Hummingbirds and Channel Swimmers." *Drama Review* 31 (1), 1987: 8–21.

Daly, Ann. "Classical Ballet: A Discourse of Difference." *Women and Performance* 3 (2), 1987/88: 57–66.

Denby, Edwin. *Dance Writings,* Robert Cornfield and William MacKay, eds. New York: Knopf, 1986.

Dixon Gottschild, Brenda. *Digging the Africanist Presence in American Performance: Dance and Other Contexts.* Westport, Conn.: Greenwood, 1996.

Eagleton, Terry. *Literary Theory: An Introduction.* Minneapolis: University of Minnesota Press, 1983.

English, Rose. "Alas, Alack the Representation of the Ballerina." *New Dance* 15, 1980.

Fish, Stanley. *Is There a Text in This Class? The Authority of Interpretive Communities.* Cambridge: Harvard University Press, 1980.

Flett, Una. *Falling from Grace: My Early Years in Ballet.* Edinburgh: Canongate, 1981.

Foster, Susan Leigh. "The Ballerina's Phallic Pointe." In *Corporealities: Dancing, Knowledge, Culture and Power,* Susan Leigh Foster, ed. London: Routledge, 1996: 1–24.

Garafola, Lynn. *Diaghilev's Ballets Russes.* New York: Oxford University Press, 1989.

Gillis, John R. *A World of Their Own Making: Myth, Ritual, and the Quest for Family Values.* New York: Basic, 1996.

Golby, J. M., and A. W. Purdue. *The Making of the Modern Christmas.* London: Batsford, 1986.

Goldberg, Marianne. "Ballerinas and Ball Passing." *Women and Performance* 3 (2), 1987–88: 7–31.

Gordon, Susan. *Off Balance: The Real World of Ballet*. New York: Pantheon, 1983.

Grigorovich, Yuri, and Alexander Demidov. *The Official Bolshoi Ballet Book of The Nutcracker*. Neptune, N.J.: T.F.H. Publications, 1986.

Guilford, Barbara. "Nutcracker Scrapbook: The Magic of Clara." *Dance Magazine*, December 1984.

Hobsbawm, Eric, and Terence Ranger. *The Invention of Tradition*. Cambridge: Cambridge University Press, 1983.

Impey, Oliver. *Chinoiserie: The Impact of Oriental Styles on Western Art and Decoration*. London: Oxford University Press, 1977.

Innes, Shona. "The Teaching of Ballet." *Writings on Dance 3: Of Bodies and Power*, 1988: 37–47.

Kain, Karen, with Stephen Godfrey and Penelope Reed Doob. *Movement Never Lies*. Toronto: McClelland and Stewart, 1994.

Karsavina, Tamara. *Theatre Street: The Reminiscences of Tamara Karsavina*. London: Readers Union, 1950.

Kealiinohomoku, Joann. "An Anthropologist Looks at Ballet as a Form of Ethnic Dance." In *What is Dance?* Roger Copeland and Marshall Cohen, eds. Oxford: Oxford University Press, 1983: 533–49.

Kerensky, Oleg. *Anna Pavlova*. New York: Dutton, 1973.

Kirstein, Lincoln. "What Ballet Is About: An American Glossary." *Dance Perspectives* 1, 1959.

Kisselgoff, Anna. "And They Said *The Nutcracker* Wouldn't Last." *New York Times*, Dec. 18, 1977.

Kondo, Dorinne K. *Crafting Selves: Power, Gender, and Discourses of Identity in a Japanese Workplace*. Chicago: University of Chicago Press, 1990.

Krementz, Jill. *A Very Young Dancer*. New York: Knopf, 1977.

Lansley, Jacky. "Off Our Toes." *Spare Rib* 64, 1977: 5–8.

MacAloon, John, "Olympic Games and the Theory of Spectacle in Modern Societies." In *Rite, Drama, Festival, Spectacle*, John MacAloon, ed. Philadelphia: Philadelphia Institute for the Study of Human Issues, 1984: 241–80.

Magriel, Paul, ed. *Nijinsky, Pavlova, Duncan: Three Lives in Dance*. New York: Da Capo, 1977.

Mailloux, Steven. "The Turns of Reader-Response Criticism." In *Conversations: Contemporary Critical Theory and the Teaching of Literature*, Charles Moran and Elizabeth F. Penfield, eds. Urbana, Ill.: National Council of Teachers of English, 1990: 38–54.

McMahon, Deirdre, "The Feminist Mystique." *Dance Theatre Journal* 3 (4), 1985: 8–10.

McRobbie, Angela. "Dance Narratives and Fantasies of Achievement." In *Feminism and Youth Culture*. Boston: Unwin Hyman, 1991: 189–219.

Money, Keith. *Anna Pavlova: Her Life and Art*. New York: Knopf, 1982.

Moore, Sally F., and Barbara G. Myerhoff, eds. *Secular Ritual*. Amsterdam: Van Gorcum, 1977.

Neufeld, James. *Power to Rise: The Story of the National Ballet of Canada*. Toronto: University of Toronto Press, 1996.

Nissenbaum, Stephen. *The Battle for Christmas*. New York: Knopf, 1996.

Novack, Cynthia. *See* Bull, Cynthia Jean Cohen

Ortner, Sherry B. "Reading America: Preliminary Notes on Class and Culture." In *Recapturing Anthropology: Working in the Present*, Richard G. Fox, ed. Sante Fe, N.M.: School of American Research Press, 1991: 163–89.

Petipa, Marius. *Russian Ballet Master: The Memoirs of Marius Petipa*. Lilian Moore, ed., trans. Helen Whittaker. New York: MacMillan, 1958.

Radway, Janice A. *Reading the Romance: Women, Patriarchy, and Popular Literature*. Chapel Hill: University of North Carolina Press, 1984.

Restad, Penne L. *Christmas in America: A History*. New York: Oxford University Press, 1995.

Rosenblatt, Louise M. *The Reader, the Text, the Poem: The Transactional Theory of the Literary Work*. Carbondale: Southern Illinois University Press, 1994 (first published 1978).

Roslavleva, Natalia. *Era of the Russian Ballet*. New York: Dutton, 1966.

Ross, Janice. "The Dance Brigade Offers a *Nutcracker* with a Difference for Christmas." *Dance Magazine*, December 1989: 18.

Russo, Mary. *The Female Grotesque: Risk, Excess and Modernity*. New York: Routledge, 1994.

Saal, Hubert. "*The Nutcracker:* Visions of Sugar Plums." *Newsweek*, Dec. 27, 1976: 40–46.

Said, Edward. *Orientalism*. London: Routledge and Kegan Paul, 1978.

Savage-King, Chris. "Classical Muscle." *Women's Review* 2, 1985: 2–9.

Schechner, Richard. *Between Theatre and Anthropology.* Philadelphia: University of Pennsylvania Press, 1985.

Scholl, Tim. *From Petipa to Balanchine: Classical Revival and the Modernization of Ballet.* London: Routledge, 1994.

Siegel, Marcia. "Decomposing Sugar Plums and Robot Mice." *Ballet Review* 19 (1), Spring 1991: 58–62.

Siegel, Marcia. "Kingdom of the Sweet." *Hudson Review* 50 (2), Summer 1997: 255–67.

Slonimsky, Yury. "Writings on Lev Ivanov," trans. and ed. Anatole Chujoy. *Dance Perspectives* 2, Spring 1959.

Souritz, Elizabeth. "One Hundred Years of *The Nutcracker* in Russia." *Ballet Review,* Fall 1992: 77–84.

Sparshott, Francis. *Off the Ground: First Steps to a Philosophical Consideration of the Dance.* Princeton: Princeton University Press, 1988.

Steinberg, Cobbett. *San Francisco Ballet: The First Fifty Years.* San Francisco: The San Francisco Ballet Association, 1983.

Streatfeild, Noel. *Ballet Shoes.* New York: Random House, 1937.

Streatfeild, Noel. *Dancing Shoes.* New York: Random House, 1994 (first published in 1957).

Tallchief, Maria, with Larry Kaplan. *Maria Tallchief: America's Prima Ballerina.* New York: Henry Holt, 1997.

Tambiah, Stanley. "A Performative Approach to Ritual," *Proceedings of the British Academy* 65, 1979: 113–69. New York: Routledge, 1997: 1–7.

Tchaikovsky, Modeste. *The Life and Letters of Peter Ilich Tchaikovsky,* Rosa Newmarch, ed. London: John Lane, 1906.

Turner, Victor. *The Anthropology of Performance.* New York: PAJ, 1987.

Turner, Victor. *From Ritual to Theatre: The Human Seriousness of Play.* New York: PAJ, 1982.

Turner, Victor. "Variations on a Theme of Liminality." In *Secular Ritual,* Sally F. Moore and Barbara Myerhoff, eds. Amsterdam: Van Gorcum, 1977: 36–52.

Visweswaran, Kamala. *Fictions of Feminist Ethnography.* Minneapolis: University of Minnesota Press, 1994.

Volkov, Solomon. *Balanchine's Tchaikovsky: Interviews with George Balanchine.* New York: Simon and Schuster, 1985.

Waits, William B. *The Modern Christmas in America: A Cultural History of Gift Giving.* New York: New York University Press, 1993.

Weyn, Suzanne. *No Way Ballet* series (nos. 1 to 6). Mahwah, N.J.: Troll Associates, 1990.

Wiley, Roland John. *The Life and Ballets of Lev Ivanov: Choreographer of The Nutcracker and Swan Lake.* Oxford: Clarendon, 1997.

Wiley, Roland John. "On Meaning in *Nutcracker.*" *Dance Research* 3 (1), Autumn 1984: 3–28.

Wiley, Roland John. "Reflections on Tchaikovsky." *Dancing Times* 80 (956), May 1990: 801–03.

Wiley, Roland John. *Tchaikovsky's Ballets: Swan Lake, Sleeping Beauty, The Nutcracker.* Oxford: Clarendon, 1985.

Wiley, Roland John. "Three Historians of the Russian Imperial Ballet." *Dance Research Journal* 13 (1), 1980: 3–16.

Videography

American Ballet Theatre and Mikhail Baryshnikov. *The Nutcracker.* MGM/ UA Home Video, 1977.

Australian Ballet. *Nutcracker.* Kultur, 1994.

Barbie in The Nutcracker. Mattel Entertainment, 2001.

Bolshoi Ballet. *The Nutcracker.* Kultur, 1978.

Kiev Ballet. *The Nutcracker.* Video Treasures, 1992.

Kirov Ballet. *The Nutcracker.* 1984.

Mark Morris's *The Hard Nut.* Elektra Nonesuch, 1992.

New York City Ballet. *George Balanchine's The Nutcracker.* Warner Bros. Family Entertainment, 1994.

Pacific Northwest Ballet. *Nutcracker: The Motion Picture.* Atlantic Releasing Corporation, 1986.

Royal Ballet Covent Garden. *The Nutcracker.* Kultur, 1985.

Rudolf Nureyev in *The Nutcracker.* Royal Ballet, Kultur, 1968.

Index

Photo Credits

107	Jane Philomen Cleland for the San Francisco Lesbian/Gay Freedom Band
109	Victor Avila
113	Alan Ulbricht
115, 116	Author's collection
134	Leavenworth Nutcracker Museum (left); Taron Collection (right)
143	Philip Storm Ulanowsky
153	Inland Pacific Ballet
156, 161	Philip Storm Ulanowsky
166	Andrew Oxenham, National Ballet of Canada Archives (top); Lydia Pawelak, National Ballet of Canada Archives (bottom)
167	Susan Kuklin
174	Author's collection
176	Cylla von Tiedemann, National Ballet of Canada Archives
182	Jennifer Coletta for the New York City Ballet
189	Philip Storm Ulanowsky